STORNOWAY

HARRIS

BENBECULA

N-UIST

ASKERNISH

WESTERN ISLES

SOUTH

Hell's Golfer

Other books by Tom Morton:

Going Home: The Runrig Story
Spirit of Adventure: A Journey Beyond the Whisky Trails
Red Guitars in Heaven

HELL'S GOLFER

A
GOOD
WALK
SPOILED

TOM MORTON

MAINSTREAM
PUBLISHING

First published in Great Britain in 1994 by
MAINSTREAM PUBLISHING COMPANY (EDINBURGH) LTD
7 Albany Street
Edinburgh EH1 3UG

ISBN 1 85158 656 3

A catalogue record for this book is available from the British Library

Typeset in Sabon by Saxon Graphics Ltd, Derby
Printed in Great Britain by Butler and Tanner Ltd, Frome, Somerset

To Martha Jane Euphemia

Tom Morton lives in the Shetland Islands, where he devotes himself to motorcycle maintenance, sanitary engineering, roofing repairs, seeking a cure for baldness and hitting golf balls into the sea. He was formerly *The Scotsman*'s Highlands and Islands reporter, and still writes a weekly column for that newspaper. In 1994 he received the Columnist of the Year prize in the Bank of Scotland Press Awards.

Of this diversion the Scots are so fond, that when the weather will permit, you may see a multitude of all ranks, from the senator of justice to the lowest tradesman, mingled together in their shirts, and following the balls with the utmost eagerness. Among others, I was shown one particular set of golfers, the youngest of whom was turned of fourscore; they were all gentlemen of independent fortunes, who had amused themselves with this pastime for the best part of a century, without ever having felt the least alarm from sickness or disgust; and they never went to bed without having each the best part of a gallon of claret in his belly.

Tobias Smollett, *Humphrey Clinker*, 1770

And then there's golf, its shrunken ball and chivalrous conventions
A kind of secular – God help us – global new religion.
The stretched glove flipping from back pocket like a rabbit's tail
And vaguely vulgar splay-legged stance to hit the ball
May be the stuff of inadvertent comedy, but these Sky heroes
Live to tell unavian tales of birdies, eagles; mesmerising
Couch potatoes not with violence, or the hope of it,
But sheer monotony of green . . .

Lesley Duncan, *Sporting Men*

Acknowledgments

I would like to thank: Caledonian Macbrayne for generosity and practical advice; John McNaught and Gillian Jones for the Marks and Spencer beetroot; the late Ruby Downie of Cathkin Golf Club, Glasgow, for the clubs; Audrey for unstinting help and drying out my boots; Susan, John Magnus, James Patrick and Martha Jane for being next door; Peter Frances and Val Rose at Mainstream for ball-retrieval; also all those golf partners past, present and future for agreeing to play with someone as unbelievably inept as myself.

Excerpts from the radio series *A Good Walk Spoiled* are reproduced by kind permission of that splendid entity BBC Radio Scotland. Special thanks to Gordon Adam, Carol Haining and Maggie Cunningham for bringing rebel golf to the wireless. *Love, Hatred, Rock'n'Roll, Golf* was originally commissioned by *The Scotsman* and published as part of the paper's 1994 Open Championship coverage.

Contents

Love, Hatred, Rock'n'Roll, Golf

An Introduction

GOLF is an Emerson Lake and Palmer triple concept album, a Rick Wakeman mock-rock-opera, an interminable 25-minute instrumental by Yes. It is fat, self-satisfied, drunk on its own bourgeois snobbishness, racist, sexist, caught in some 1970s fashion timewarp of Pringle sweaters and hideous tartan trousers made of Crimplene, a substance long abandoned in every other sphere of human existence. Golf is acknowledged for the breeding of truly hellish haircuts, bleary gin-and-tonic politics, obsessive collectors of monogrammed tees, and an entire range of supremely boring Volkswagen cars.

So why do I love it so?

Why am I waiting in hope, praying for the arrival on the international circuit of a niblick-armed cross between John McEnroe and Johnny Rotten, someone who will rampage across Muirfield dressed in leather jeans and a Blur tee-shirt, ritually punching out Royal and Ancient dodderers, swearing at the crowd, spitting before he putts and knocking the likes of Montgomerie and Els into the nearest whin bush? Why do I cling to the notion that golf, beneath its money-eyed, glossy, jowly public face, is still the rough-and-tumble, open-to-everyone sport which was once played in any open space, which can still quicken the spirit and set the heart racing in pure pleasure?

Well, because I've played the game, off and on, since I was seven years old, since I first sneaked through our back hedge on to Troon's Fullarton course, armed with an old wooden-shafted mashie my father had cut down for me. And I have known That Moment, that explosion of bliss when the body somehow finds the ideal geometry of movement necessary to swing a golf club; when the skylarks are singing above a deserted, dew-powdered course, and you're on the first tee, with 18 holes of potential in front of you. At That Moment, you are John Daly, Nick Faldo, Sevvy. You can do anything, score birdies, eagles, albatrosses, skuas, ostriches, budgies . . . whatever. You unwrap a new Maxfli, ram it into the cool ground on a fresh wooden tee, take out that driver, and empty your mind of mortgages, work, family and car-loan schemes. Begin that slow swing back and . . . .

Maybe once or twice in a round, it's perfection. The rest of the time, you, me, all of the great mass of struggling, hopelessly enslaved hackers, fail the perfection test. We are not Daly, Faldo or Ballesteros. We are unpractised, debt-ridden, psychological wrecks who, shot by shot, inflict on ourselves a growing sense of failure. For lo and forsooth, we are truly, on the whole, pure dead garbage at the gowff.

And yet we love it. We love it despite ourselves and despite its unignorable faults. Fortunately, and uniquely in Scotland, it is possible to play golf cheaply at courses where men and women, rich or poor, bad or good, be-Pringled or be-jeaned are made welcome. At Kyle of Lochalsh, the beautiful little nine-hole costs just £1.50 a round, which would be the cheapest game in Scotland were Ruchill in Glasgow not, at the time of writing, on free play, due to the clubhouse having been burned down and all the pins stolen. The pins are stolen nearly every time they're put out, by the way, except during tournaments, when they're guarded against the local flag-thieves.

We love it despite the inadequacy we feel when presented, as we often are in Scotland when the world's top Pringleers arrive to compete on one of our great, classic links, with the sight of a great golf course being casually humiliated by men whose gigantic driving abilities will, we comfort ourselves, undoubtedly lead to crippling back problems in later life. In fact, the deep, dark truth is that as we flock to the Ailsa, Royal Troon, Turnberry or Muirfield or settle back to watch the action on telly, we do not want these wondrous creatures who play professional golf to succeed. Oh no. They have caused us too much pain for that, made us feel foolish too often. True, they inspire us with hope, for that split-second of golfing nirvana we have all known: that birdie we got that Palmer didn't manage; that freak drive longer than Big John's. But their sickening consistency makes us long for their failure. Like a motor-racing crowd, we are really there for the crashes, and, let's face it, these pro-golfers owe us some ignominy of their very own. I want to see Faldo twisted in anger at a slew of double bogeys. I especially want to see Colin Montgomerie lose a ball or two, preferably at the same hole. I long, I positively yearn, for John Daly to top his drive, Greg

Norman to hit a tree and see his ball bounce behind him. Schadenfreude isn't in it.

Of course, there are the characters, inevitably the bruised, tormented and wildly unpredictable players; the ones you want to succeed, and who never do. These days, Sevvy can't turn hacking into an art form any more; Sam Torrance's roll-up droops soggily; best-dressed golfer Gary Player – admittedly the epitome of cool consistency – and his all-black French existentialist look has virtually vanished from the fairways; and the enigma that was Ken Brown now commentates for radio.

Ken could have been, indeed briefly was, an unlikely *enfant terrible* of the linksland. When he was playing as a pro, he was continually punished for slow play, for having an attitude which was as close to rock'n'roll, to punk at its most solipsistic, or maybe even jazz, in fact, as I've ever seen. He just didn't seem to care what the authorities, the crowd, what anybody thought of him. His game was a tortured interface between his own inner demons and that little white pellet down on the grass. It was rivetting to watch, at least I thought it was. But that sort of play, that Coltrane or Wire riff among the portentous warblings of golf's great Barclay James Harvest LP, was fresh and inspiring in its own way.

Now money talks, shouts, sings and screams and whispers all over the Open, and shuts many men and most women out of clubs which these days employ security guards to exclude the riff-raff; how long before golf is played behind razor wire and electrified chain-link fences? Meanwhile nice, ugly men in their horrible clothes rule the pro-golf roost, with their psychologists and advisors, their trainers and chaplains and hypnotists. Oh, that they fail. Oh, that some young, bright, sneering punk jazzateer, a McEnroe, Agassi, an Eric Cantona, a Charlie George-meets-Pat Nevin-and Joe Strummer, will come along soon and blast golf out of its middle-aged, middle-class, suburban pomp-rock torpor. Because, unfortunately, I love this game.

I love it enough to actually want to play, but I'm not interested in taking out a second mortgage to do it. I live, thank goodness, in a place where golf is accessible, cheap, classless and plentiful, even if those blasted Pringle sweaters still abound. This book tells the story of Arnold Evelyn MacLachlan Palmer's search for various things – consistency of swing, true love, good sex, cheap golf, solitude on the first tee – and of mine for similar, but not identical things. It's a curious hybrid, I know, but all true, nevertheless.

Tom Morton
Shetland, July 1994

CHAPTER ONE

Disputes, Decisions and Doubt as to Rights

HEAD still, gaze exact, link-grip firm, little finger of right hand hooked round first finger of left on the cool, serrated rubber coating the upper 18 inches of my ancient Slazenger Peter Oosterhuis nine iron. Relaxed, slow backswing, up, up, keeping that left arm as straight as possible, then don't force it, let the weight of the club generate its own power; hear that whooping hiss as it falls past the right ear, eyes set, mind clear, empty, consumed and cauterised in the act.

The green Denby eggcup shattered into a thousand pieces, some bouncing off the Ray-Ban Wayfarer sunglasses I was wearing for protection. The Casio digital alarm clock I'd balanced precariously atop the hen-shaped eggcup – the last of four matching hollow china chickens which were now peeking from the uneven pile of the cheap, foam-backed carpet in jagged lumps – looped airborne in four component parts, bleeping its unforgiving wake-up tone defiantly. The largest section, the almost-complete outer casing, hit the far wall of the lounge with a satisfying crack. Its innards continued to give off electronic burblings until I crunched through the wreckage-strewn rough of my carpet and let my Doc Marten Commando soles put it out of its inhuman misery. My boots were hardly *de rigueur* for golfing, but they seemed somehow apt, given the circumstances.

'Satisfied, bitch?' I shouted at the top of a voice already hoarsened by the past two hours of high-volume indoor golf. 'That was your head, my dear. That was your expensively educated brain which just bleeped its last. A perfect nine-iron shot, on to the green, over the bunker, and trickling inexorably towards the hole. Not that you care, you evil, conniving, manipulative. . . ' I hiccupped suddenly, inhaling a shower of excited spittle, and felt for a microsecond the onset of death by drowning. Spluttering and coughing and retching, I sank to my knees by the tiled, 1950s fireplace, scrabbling for the bottle of Wild Turkey bourbon I'd left there, having early on played some blinding approach shots into the kitchen with its top. That was before I decided to move on to heavier and more breakable objects. The damage didn't matter; I was not going to replace my divots, be they carpet, wood, china or flesh.

There was hardly anything left in the bottle, but sufficient burnt-caramel liquid made its way down my raw throat to anaesthetise the nerves which were screaming for oxygen. They got whisky instead, and stopped hassling me. Breathe whisky, that's the answer. I gulped down some air to get them off my back, the bastards. How dare they spoil my game, those pesky nerves? Here I was, having the round of my life, after all. I went into the kitchen, where I'd filled the sink and had already played two very tricky water shots towards the open fridge, using a pitching wedge and hard-boiled eggs. Surprisingly, the eggs didn't shatter easily, although the water did tend to be fairly widely distributed. The idea was to drop the eggs from mouth into the water, a pitching stance already assumed above the sink. Fortunately, the flat, in a red-sandstone Wilton Street tenement, near the BBC and in the middle of what those with sufficient cash to live there considered a Glaswegian bohemia, had high ceilings, and with a truncated backswing I just about had time to catch the eggs as they settled into the gently lapping water of the sink. There were no dishes. Most were already broken, including a stunningly successful drive out in the hall using an expensive art-deco china teapot.

I opened the wall units, reached in an arm and carelessly scraped everything within out on to the floor. I poked a half-hearted shot at a tin of baked beans, but the shock of hitting it ran up the club shaft uncomfortably. There was a knocking coming from somewhere. The door? No, the ceiling. A dull, thumping noise. 'Want to make up a foursome?' I yelled. 'Come on down, then!' But the old lady upstairs, Mrs Braithwaite, was no golfer. I couldn't understand what she wanted. 'Get off the fairway, you old bat!' I raked among the debris for something else to play. A small bottle of Granny's Caribbean Hot Sauce swam into my vision, and I addressed myself to it. After four attempts, I finally hit the small brown bottle, which broke into several sticky, spicy sections but refused to shatter spectacularly. I stamped on it petulantly and moved off towards the bedroom, where the golf bag was, intent on playing some real balls around the flat, and maybe, it struck me with brilliance and clarity, out through the windows on to the street, or away, up beyond and over the rooftops . . .

My arms were getting tired, though, and I was beginning to feel slightly sick. Also, it was becoming more and more difficult to focus on the object of my swing's attack. Everything was moving, including the floor. It was tilting. I smiled. 'Shipboard golf! I love it, I love it. Splice the mainbrace, captain! Fore! Get those passengers out of my way . . .' But just then a tidal wave of nausea swept under the tenement and over me; everything moved crazily, sickeningly upwards and over, including my stomach. There was a splintering, grinding noise, as the ship, building, body, golf course capsized and sank beneath a black, evil-smelling sea. I was drowning. There was no doubt about it.

I awoke with a mouth like a bunker on the downtown Baghdad nine-hole. My head hurt in a variety of different ways. There was the massive internal pounding, the sensation of having shrunk the brain so much that the Dunlop 65-sized intelligence-producing object remaining was battering away at the skull's soft, whisky-ravaged internals in a vain, dying attempt to have its presence, its importance recognised. There was also something warm, red and apparently gritty on my temple and cheek. I lay still, afraid to move. Gingerly rocking my head a millimetre at a time from side to side, I could hear scraping and grinding noises. Oh God, it's finally happened! Everything inside has come loose, been freed from its binding by the dissolving effects of drink! I must have lain there for 15 minutes, sure, too, that if I tried to sit up, I would be sick again. Again, because in front of my nose was the sure and certain aroma of Wild Turkey vomit. I would have recognised it anywhere. It had, over the past weeks, become a regular acquaintance.

But I had to move. Had to find out at least where I was. Memory was still not functioning; it was marshalling itself, readying itself to reveal the full horror of my behaviour, my situation, my guilt. I tinkled and crackled upright, eyes shut. There was a roller-coaster sensation, but not quite as bad as I might have expected. Then I opened my eyes, and was sick again.

I'd trashed the flat, stopping just short of breaking up the furniture and smashing the windows. If oblivion hadn't descended, I would probably have shot out every pane of glass, and it was a miracle that only moveable items had suffered my attacks. Golf clubs lay scattered among the broken china, overturned chairs (some dim recollection almost surfaced of attempts at reconstructing famous holes using the sofa as a bunker substitute) and dismembered food. The blood on my head and face came from dozens of cuts and abrasions caused by the glass and pottery shards adhering to me. I tried to stand up. A mistake.

There was a noise, like some demented bird screeching in a jungle; tinnily. It took 30 seconds for me to recognise the sound as that of a telephone. I crawled towards the source of the screaming, flailing through an overturned bookcase until the phone was revealed. I picked up the receiver; grunted.

'Arnold? Arnold, is that you?' I racked my brain. Was I this Arnold? I decided I probably was.

'Yes . . . who's that?'

'Arnold, it's Bob at the factory. Are you coming in today? I mean, we've got the technical guys from Itsuoko Industries coming off the shuttle from London to talk about component quality control, and listen to the new amps, and . . .'

Bob. The factory. Connections were being made inside my abused head. I knew this Bob. I had something to do with a factory. What did it make? A surge of nausea washed through me. I lay down on the riddled, raddled floor, clutching the receiver to my ear like a drowning man a lifebelt. If I could only hang on, everything would be all right.

'Bob . . .'

'Yes, Arnold. Arnold, are you OK?'

'Bob . . . I'm . . . I'm not . . . not OK.' It was no use. I let the

18

phone fall away from my head, and turned my head sideways on to the snap-crackle-and-pop carpet. The black wave was coming for me again. I could sense it in the distance, in the grey blurring and darkening of my vision. I let it wash over me, through me, as a tiny, tinny voice yelped somewhere, then vanished.

When light broke through again, it was dark, and the sustained banging couldn't be mistaken for anything but the sound of some-one hammering on the front door. It had a sort of flimsy, glassy rattle and when my eyes ungummed themselves, my brain had rest-ed, rid itself of at least a little poison and expanded, maybe, to the proportions of a cricket ball. I knew where I was. I knew the broken stuff on the floor had made me bleed, although there was no warm red liquid left, just a hard caking of something and a little pain. There was still a dull throb, a birdcage filth to my mouth, a ragged ache in my throat. The nausea returned when I stood up, shedding all kinds of smashed, golf-garbaged material around me. I made my way to the door, leaning groggily against the wall as I undid the Yale and opened it. It was Bob.

'Jesus, Arnold . . .'

'Don't say it, Bob.' I shook my head carefully. Nothing crucial seemed to be coming loose. 'Come in, if you must.'

Robert Applegate, partner in the manufacturing company of Pitch Electronics Ltd, stepped into my somewhat more than messy hallway, and stopped dead. 'Arnold, what the hell happened here? Christ, this is unbelievable. Was it a burglary or something? Listen, are you all right?' His anxious, well-meaning face, long and thin and topped with thinning sandy hair, made me grin despite myself. I thought I could feel the skin on my face splitting. He had on a suit, too, something from Marks and Spencer, too baggy for his elon-gated frame. It was a mistake.

'Yeah . . . yeah. I'm fine. No burglary. No fights. Just a bit of a crisis. I decided to cheer myself up by playing some golf, indoors. Using Belinda's head as a ball. Only she wasn't here, so various other things, bits of . . . this and that came to hand. I suppose I got a bit carried away. And I had a few drinks.' Bob gaped slowly around, then focused on me in a sort of resigned, worried disbelief. He shut his eyes; opened them again.

'Well . . .' he coughed. 'Well, the Itsuoko people came and looked round, and I think we managed to convince them that you were ill. They seemed to like the sound of the amp, but then they would do, or they would say that . . . I mean, they think their com-ponents are gifts from bloody God, and that's why the thing sounds good . . .'

19

'Well, I was ill, in a manner of speaking. In fact, I still am.'
Amps. Amplifiers. Something was stirring amid the frazzled synapses
. . . But Bob's look of concern was turning to a mixture of annoy-
ance and disgust.

'Yes, well . . . anyway, Peter hit them with all his research and
development bullshit, and we had the specs for the new circuits,
which they seemed not to have any problem with. They're over at
the Pot Still, having a try at some of the malts there, prior to dinner
at the Chip. There's haggis on tonight, but then you were the one
who booked the whole thing, so you should know that.' Oh yeah.
Haggis. I gazed down at the imported Iranian, supposedly bankrupt-
stock rug on the hall floor. 'They're staying at the Hilton, by the
way, on the Japanese floor, as you insisted. And seeing as you're
supposed to be a partner in this firm, and you arranged their accommodation and this bloody dinner, I think you should come and say
hello to them. Or maybe not. I don't know any more . . . Aw, God,
is that blood?' He was looking at the caked scab on the side of my
head.

'Ah well, listen, Bob, this is component stuff, and you know
that's not my scene . . .'

'Nothing very much is your scene these days, you arsehole.
God almighty, how long is it? A year? Divorces happen a lot,
Arnold. Jesus, you can't let it suck you down completely. We've
been carrying you for months now.' I breathed in deeply. Maybe I
could stage a rapid recovery, help Bob out with his Japanese sup-
pliers. Mine. There was still pain and vagueness, but blood was zap-
ping through my brain cells now; memory had returned. Some of it.

Pitch had been my idea, my notion: a hi-fi-amplifier company
producing really high-quality, utterly simple units which could make
music sound warm and real and involving, not cold and sterile and
annoying, like most so-called hi-fi. The problem with compact-disc
players is that grating edge they all seem to have. I thought there
had to be a way of getting rid of it, and Bob, electronics whizzkid
and pal, had set to work, using my ears to tell him if he'd found the
solution. He had. Now we were expanding, producing a second
model of amplifier to follow the wildly successful Pitch Fork. This
one, reflecting the sense of humour I once had enjoyed exercising,
was to be called the Pitch Black. It would be finished in red only.
The Fork had been available solely in green.

'Bob, listen . . . Belinda's not going to allow me to see the children. Not at all. Apparently I'm a destabilising influence, whatever
that means . . .' Bob, silent, looked at me. He shut the rattly door.
My voice was thick, but the words came landsliding out, the broken

banks of a flooded stream bringing the dirt and detritus washing, tumbling. 'We went to the pictures last . . . two nights ago. Saturday? Yeah, Saturday. When I took Paul and Patti back home, to . . . to her home I suppose it is now, she shooed them upstairs and then hit me with it. No more access. Cards and letters, OK, but the bitch'll probably read them all first and never pass them on . . . Now she's got this arsehole Victor staying with her, she wants rid of me. Wants to play happy families . . . know what he is? An undertaker. A bloody corpse-collector. God, I can just imagine what he's like. I've never met the bastard but he drives a bloody Ford Escort, one of those Cosworth small-penis heaps . . .'

'Come on, Arnold. You've got access to lawyers who can sort that kind of thing out.'

'She knows that. And maybe there's just about enough money to do it, too. Maybe not, though, given . . . you know, the factory, the new factory and all that. But she says she'll fight it all the way, court after court after court, social workers, the lot. And if I try and contest the whole thing, she'll go to the Child Support Agency, get them to screw me for everything they can. That's what she says, anyway. She even hinted at getting her hands on my piece of Pitch, too. I mean, financially, you know that things are OK but not OK, depending on what happens, depending on expansion, the Itsuoko components . . . but if she gets her hands . . . och, to hell, anyway leaving that, leaving that, the court stuff, that means a seven-year-old boy and an 11-year-old girl standing up, day after day, giving evidence. Do you like your father? Do you love him? Does he ever drink any beer or wine or whisky when you're with him? And all the time she'd be pumping them full of propaganda, that I left, walked out on them. Fell over a few times, was sick in the lounge. Unfit. That I really hate them, that I'm worthless . . . And OK, I did leave, I did walk out but I didn't kill the thing, it wasn't just my fault, was it? I mean what do you think they're going to say or do? What kind of effect would that have on them, if I had to make them go through the whole thing in public? And with no guarantee of even getting access at the end of the day? They're upset enough even now, the two kids. Christ, one of them's had this sore throat for two months, and Belinda says they scream for hours after I've gone . . . anyway, it's a deal she's offering. I get lost and she'll leave me and the business alone. Christ, that sounds pathetic, doesn't it? That there's even a choice. As if I don't care about the kids, but it's not . . . it's not . . .'

'She's just bluffing. She knows you're a soft-hearted old dick-head who crumbles at the idea of those kids being harmed. That's why you put up with her for so long.' Bob was shaking his large, sorrowing head, which perched atop the thin, gangly body, out of proportion, slightly horse-like. A bachelor of the confirmed variety, he was not, so far as I or anyone else knew, gay, so much as sexless. A kind of Cliff Richard of the circuit board. I was shaking. I could feel the tears starting. They would probably smell of Wild Turkey, too.

'It doesn't matter, Bob. Don't you realise. It doesn't bloody matter. She's got them. She has them all week, I have them one evening. I can see them changing. They won't talk to me. She tells them to tell me I have to ask her about things like presents, holidays, coming away with me to Crieff Hydro or something . . . Christ, Crieff Hydro, as if it was a den of bloody iniquity . . .' But Bob was looking at his watch. 'I have to go, Arnold . . .' He reached out, embarrassed, awkward, and touched my arm. 'Look, if you can get cleaned up, shaved, showered, put some Gold Spot on your breath and come down to the Chip. At least put in an appearance. If you're fit, that is. I think you could be. Come on, you're the image man. You're the face of Pitch. We need, your . . . bullshit.' And he backed out of the door, embarrassed, smiling, nodding.

Arnold Evelyn MacLachlan Palmer. Imagine, being called Arnold Palmer and not even because of a golf-obsessed father. By accident. Literally by accident of birth. Two names had alternated in the male Palmer line, raised in the shipyard territory of Govan since God or the management knew when. Arnold, Jonathan, Arnold, Jonathan. So I had been Arnold, Arnold Evelyn, in fact, because my mother had read *Brideshead Revisited,* for some bizarre reason, and thus landed me with an unusable middle name to add to my indelibly golf-linked moniker. MacLachlan, my mother's maiden name, was at least identifiably normal.

My lack of golfing prowess, the family's complete indifference to mashies and niblicks and spoons or birdies, eagles and albatrosses, brought endless chiding and joking down like a mishit drive on my innocent head from the age of five upwards. Until at 14, in self-defence, I'd taken it up, learning the game on Glasgow's seven municipal courses, the largest number of public courses of any city in the world, rattling by bus and subway from King's Park to Lethamhill, or sometimes crossing the border into Renfrewshire to play Deaconsbank at Rouken Glen Park, which has now been privatised, unbelievably. Or believably, given the politics of this country. I'd never got good, not really. Playing off 12 as a junior, then losing interest, selling the clubs when I was a student to buy my first proper hi-fi system: an old Thorens turntable, a Rogers valve amplifier, which looked like some kind of medical appliance, and then-revolutionary Mission loudspeakers. Music and sound had taken me over, until last year, emptily, throbbingly separated, when some secondhand clubs caught my eye, glinting in the window of a junk shop in Dumbarton Road. Slazenger Oosterhuis irons, a 3, 5, 7, 9, wedge and two Ben Sayers Trophy woods, a driver and a four. An old leather bag, and inside the score-cards of many an average round at Lethamhill and Littlehill, the public 18-hole courses in the north of Glasgow. I was, after all, Arnold Palmer.

'Arnold Palmer's finally got an outside interest,' Bob had announced one day to our small, chummy workforce. No labour problems at the factory over in Dalmuir, the anonymous Scottish Enterprise unit with its brick facings and leaky roof. We all mucked in together, or used to, before I began drifting, 'feeling my grip on the tiller loosen', as my sofa-stranded, would-be skipper father would have said, he of the Queen Park Pond paddle-boats and other such nautical adventures. 'Yes, Arnold Evelyn, your employer and pal, has found something other than music.' Bob was in one of his occasional manic modes. 'And guess what it is? Arnold Palmer's taken up golf!' Everyone laughed. I laughed. Day by day I took myself off to the Dalmuir course, again public, although outside Glasgow's city boundaries, actually controlled by Clydebank District Council, and embarrassed myself horribly in front of the queuing punters.

The 14th at Dalmuir is infamous. Some players, some professionals, reckon it among the most difficult holes in the world. Called 'Gully', its name only hints at the horror in store for the unsuspecting and the untalented. It's a par-three, 240-yard monstrosity which led me to score an ignominious and ludicrous 15 on my first comeback round, very early on Wednesday morning, before a late start at work. But then, I part-owned the company. To hell. Good psychological preparation for the cut-throat world of modern marketing. There's a 30-foot-deep gorge between tee and tiny green, running almost the whole way up what should be a fairway, but isn't. This hole is full of trees, bushes and a burn, not to mention dogs and small boys from the nearby Drumchapel housing scheme, both sets of creatures lying in wait for balls to appear so they can be stolen and held to ransom. Or sometimes, in the case of the dogs, swallowed. If you go left you risk coming thundering down towards the third tee, and can end up some 80 yards from the green, but miles below it. Going right brings woods into play. As I said, I scored 15, including two lost balls and some nauseating, spiritually debilitating hacking in the undergrowth, moving the ball a few feet at a time. As I finally holed out, I heard the distant sound of applause from the three sets of players waiting at the tee for me to finish. Ha bloody ha. Gully is an evil, mean, son-of-a-bitch hole, but the weirdest thing was what happened while I was waiting to play at the next tee, in a queue of old-age pensioners engaged in some kind of massive competition for geriatrics. Some could hardly walk, let alone hit the ball any distance. Wheelchair golf. Anyway, one doddering old gent in front of me smiled as I sweatily slammed my clubs down.

'Bit of trouble at the Gully, then, son?' I nodded, once, fiercely, sullen.

'Do you know whose favourite hole that is? Favourite hole, mind, the one he likes best? Eh?' I shook my head, once, fiercely.

'No less than Arnold Palmer, son. The great Palmer has played Dalmuir, see, and that hole just inspired him. Amazing, isn't it, that Arnie himself should have played here? Stood where you're standing right now, maybe. Anyway,' and I should have seen it coming, 'what's your name son? Whereabouts you from? The Drum?' Drumchapel. It must have been the clothes. I hated all that golfing cashmere and had on jeans and a sweatshirt with the single word Pitch on the front. Apt, I had thought. I looked solemnly at him and said that my name was Arnold Palmer. He returned my gaze, then just turned his back on me, and proceeded to wait in silence for his turn to play. I think he thought I was kidding.

I went into the bathroom, which had been left almost intact during my onslaught. My memory was working overtime now. I'd come back from Belinda's, driving my Ford Sierra over the Kingston Bridge in a daze. Saturday night. I'd gone drinking along Byres Road, solo, determinedly resisting even the most warm of Glaswegian overtures, from males, females, gay and straight, sober and puggled. Friendship, contact I didn't want, didn't need. I drank half pints of heavy and large Grouses, pumping them down, and finishing off by slumping over the bar until 3.00 a.m. in a horrible, semi-illegal disco off Maryhill Road called Heaney's. The next day, Sunday, I'd gone golfing with my lawyer, Michael Harris, a long-standing arrangement which had the advantage of allowing me to pour out my woes to a professional ear. Cheaply. As I stripped off my clothes, I found a score-card for the nine-hole Knightswood course in my pocket. The details of the dismal game started coming back.

It was always going to be busy, Knightswood on a Sunday afternoon. The course, in the middle of an upmarket council housing scheme, much of it now sold off to tenants for peanuts under Tory vote-grabbing policies, is flat, but not by any means an effortless walkover. The problem is that because the cost is only £2.10 for nine holes, every would-be Nick Faldo or Big John Daly who can beg, borrow or steal three or four clubs goes out, hacking and bashing their way around the course, mostly four at a time. It means waiting around both for a tee-off time and at many of the shorter holes while grave damage is done to the course, the game of golf, the art of swearing, various balls and your patience. Then you set up for your own shot and make just as big a hash of it, and realise you're just a hacker as well.

Michael is at about the same appalling golfing standard as me, but Knightswood really brought out the worst in both of us. Turning up at 2.00 p.m., my hangover had receded to working proportions. Michael stepped out of his restored MG Midget, immaculate in white slacks and ludicrously expensive Pringle sweater, his Dunlop Max 357 Special Edition clubs, all carbon fibre and beryllium and bullshit, neatly taking up the second seat in the little convertible. He could afford such indulgences. Tall, married to an Anglo-Argentinian ex-air-hostess and with a large, old house in Milngavie, Michael ('Don't call me Mike. I'm not some implement for amplifying the voice') had always been suave, nicely turned out, confident and, to cap it all, thoroughly pleasant. Sickening. Ever since I'd met him at university, he'd had success written all over his open, humorously crinkled face. Having a lawyer like that, I'd always felt, was a good omen. Even if he was a Tory of the deepest, most impenetrable blue.

'How come we couldn't go to Dougalston, Arnie?' Michael has never had any qualms about shortening my name to silly proportions. 'I'm a member there, good, testing course, book your tee-off time, have a drink at the bar, bit to eat. Though God knows, you look as though you tied one on last night.'

'Oh come on, Mikey.' The excessively familiar nomenclature was calculated to annoy him. 'You know I've got this allergy to private golf courses, the bourgeois fat of the land at play, that sort of thing. Bloody Pringle sweaters. Bank managers. Gin bellies. Lawyers . . . you know.' He had the grace to laugh, as he slipped off his immaculate LL Bean loafers, sitting with his feet dangling on to the pavement through the tiny open car door, and began putting on his Adidas Bernhard Langer shoes. All I had were my Doc Marten Commandos. For Knightswood, I felt they would do.

'But you are the bourgeois fat of the land, Arnold. Partner in your own burgeoning firm, prospects good, expensive divorce notwithstanding. Time you washed that bloody pretend socialism out of your hair, jumped onboard the winning wagon, so to speak. Besides, there are tax breaks for golf membership now, if you play your cards right. Corporate membership for the firm, take clients out for a day's conference *à la* fairway, that sort of thing. Have a word with your accountant.'

'No thanks, Michael. But I will pay your £2.10 for you, if that'll shut you up.' There would be a two-hour wait before we could tee-off, the gum-chewing girl at the ticket office told me. So we wedged ourselves into the ridiculous Midget and headed along Great Western Road for the cavernous pseudo-Mexican delights of Chimmy Chunga's, a kind of themed café-bar restaurant on the site of an old supermarket. There I had a Budweiser to Michael's fresh orange and lemonade, and immediately felt the heaviness of the previous night's drinking jerk, lighten a little. Maybe the golf would lift it entirely. 'Listen, Michael, I saw Belinda and the kids last night . . .' He leaned back in his bentwood chair, smiled resignedly, sipped from the chinking ice of his drink.

'So tell me about it. What now? Hasn't the bitch had enough from you? House, cash, car, sufficient to support new hanger-on boyfriend?'

I told him the tale. When I'd finished, there was a brief silence, and then he shook his head.

'Oh yeah. The CSA threat is being used quite a lot now. Get out of my hair and I won't leave you destitute. If you'd listened to me right at the start, this could have been avoided. But you were so determined to get the thing settled, and so sure that the Bride of Frankenstein – eh, no offence Arnold, just a little joke – was going to co-operate in an amicable, informal set of access arrangements . . . it was just guilt, Arnold. OK, so you left her, but these things happen. You have to make the correct arrangements, or all hell will break loose, given time.'

I ordered another Bud. Irretrievable breakdown, we'd called it. Ten years of marriage, the last four a gradually-speeding-up slide into the morass of lies and argument and shouting and hatred. Until the final deadening, parched argument, and the feared absence of feeling, and the children's tears. And me with that wretched Randy Newman song anthemic in my mind for months, that astonishing portrait of sickening fatherly selfishness and stunted, incoherent grief: 'I Just Want You to Hurt Like I do . . .' No I don't. Truly, I don't.

How can you end up hating someone you once loved? Finding that everything they do, from failing to squeeze the toothpaste tube properly to making the bed in a certain way, buying the wrong air freshener to making up amusing little lies about her past for the sake of dinner guests . . . everything begins not just to annoy you, but make you wish the person was dead. At first I couldn't handle the horror of those thoughts; then I wished I was dead. Finally, I realised it was time to go.

'Fine, Michael, but what do you think? Is it worth fighting the whole thing out, tearing myself apart, maybe damaging those kids badly in the process? Losing in the end? Losing the business? Who knows?' Michael toyed with the plastic cocktail stick in his glass, which was empty apart from melting ice-cubes.

'I don't know, Arnold. I just don't know. There are some fathers who will literally move heaven and earth, who will all but destroy themselves to get equal access to their kids in a separation or a divorce. But you're right, it can damage everyone. And at the end of the day, when they're older, they're going to know they've got a father, aren't they? Then you can get to know each other as equals, as adults . . . I don't know.'

I looked at him. I'd finished my beer, and there seemed nothing else to say. He stood up. 'Let's go and play some golf.'

It was a dry spring Sunday, and the ravaged Knightswood tees were devoid of grass, were just dusty pits of Glasgow dirt. We both fluffed our tee shots at the first, me comprehensively with a driver, Michael with a two iron. Things got worse and worse on this long, ostensibly straightforward par four, and ended with me scoring an appalling ten to Michael's nine. We blamed it on the delays caused by the foursome ahead of us.

'Bloody bears,' swore Michael under his breath, as we watched each of them top their balls unnervingly on the second tee. 'They're even worse than we are. All our psychological preparation is going to naught.' Certainly, I was a long way from having the right mental attitude for the game. Thoughts of children, ex-wife, revenge and loss coursed through every shot, down the shaft into the ball, slicing and hooking and making miserable what might have been a chance to escape. It was a bad walk ruined. Huge tower blocks soared above the course, and in the distance, the craggy Kilpatrick Hills held out the hope of another, more spacious, more rugged country. At the eighth hole both of us played rather good long-iron approach shots to the green, but saw our balls bounce through the wrecked chicken-wire behind into a stinking, jaundiced burn. Neither of us felt like putting our hands into the foetid water to retrieve them. They'd probably have dissolved.

'You know, I was once playing here when I was a kid,' I told Michael, as we walked through clouds of brick dust from the ash football pitches adjoining the 18th fairway. 'I think it must have been on the sixth, in the woods. I'd hit a ball into the undergrowth, and what should I come across but this couple, giving it the old beast with two backs in the deep rough. It wasn't even that nice a day. Cloudy.'

'Did you play the shot?'

'Emm, well I did, actually. I mean, I clocked what they were up to, but in those days I had this purist notion of golf, play it as it lies no matter what kind of thing, and in fact they didn't notice me until I actually hit quite a good five iron out of the rough. They were muttering and moaning like blazes, giving it *Basic Instinct* all over the place, this white bum bumping up and down and underpants round the ankles, and then they just sort of froze. The guy rolled off her and they both kind of looked at me, breathing heavily. Genitals on display, full frontal. Not a pleasant sight. I just sort of scampered off.'

'Getting a good score at Knightswood,' said Michael, grinning. 'Not like us, eh?' And truth to tell, we had played some hideous golf. At the 18th, though, I had for the first time in the whole scrappy match played a truly power-packed shot, driving the ball perfectly off the worn tee, and it was, significantly, the only swing in the game which hadn't been deliberated upon, rehearsed, performed tensely by leaden muscles as my mind raced over the personal trauma of family dissolution. It was a magical hit, mindless, blank and perfect, complete in itself. Unfortunately, my second at the par-five hole, a hard, hooking but low and long three iron, went into some totally deceptive, green and greasy rough, and I lost the ball. When I tried to repeat my thundering, hammering style on a five iron to the green, the ball simply disappeared. Vanished. I took my eye right off it, and it could have gone into orbit as far as I was concerned. Another lost ball, so the final pitch on to the green was seven. And then, inevitably, I three-putted. Michael, meanwhile, plodded home in seven, but his total for the nine holes was 52 to my execrable 61. I felt leaden and tired, too tired to be angry. Instead I set my mind on that one superb, satisfying drive, shook his hand and muttered something about needing some practice.

'We all need that,' he replied. He looked thoughtful. 'Why don't you take some time out, play some golf, get a game together, think things through? I doubt you're being much help at Pitch just at the moment, are you?' I nodded reluctantly.

Michael followed me back to the flat, where I dropped off the clubs, got washed and dressed in something less greasy and grimy than my golfing gear, and let Michael drive me out to Milngavie, where we went out for an Indian meal with his wife, Lisa. I drank so much lager I thought I was going to explode, behaving reasonably well in the restaurant as far as I could remember, kissed the Harrises goodbye, Lisa looking tearful and sympathetic – we'd once more gone hopelessly and helplessly over my looming lack of family – then got a taxi down Maryhill Road, ending up in the same horrible disco-cum-drinking club I'd been in the night before. Heaney's was full of dodgy men in shiny suits and heavy, gold jewellery, coupled mostly with glittering diamante women who'd stepped straight out of catalogue hell, Argos and Freeman's. But the heavy-duty, no-neck door staff let me in, and I was able to consume enough Grouse to penetrate the lager and bhuna lamb, leaving me able to stagger home in the early hours of Monday morning, more and more viciously angry as taxi after taxi passed my flailing, unco-ordinated but somehow still perambulating body by. So when I got inside the flat, the golf had begun again.

Now I was clean, relatively recovered, if slightly shaky from lack of food. Two small strips of sticking plaster decorated my temple and face. But hey, I'd always been ruggedly built, until the last few months had kept in shape by doing nightly press-ups and, after I'd moved from the family house in leafy Newlands to bachelordom in Wilton Street, occasionally braved the jeers of wee boys and hassles from cruising gays by jogging down into Kelvingrove Park, dressed as inconspicuously as possible in jeans and a sweatshirt. So that people might, at a stretch, think maybe I was running for a bus or something. Nevertheless, I noticed my hands were shaking, so, dressed in a Boss suit, Muji shirt and a silk tie scranned out of the Next seconds shop, I downed a tin of Coke and one of Irn Bru, the Glaswegian drunkard's pal, that I'd found lurking in the fridge. And on the way to the car, I bought a Mars Bar from Vazz's all-day, most-of-the-night, just-about-everything emporium. Maybe my appetite would be spoiled, but I might appear less obviously wrecked. I de-alarmed, then opened the Sierra, a Sapphire turbo with all go-faster badges removed, not a Cosworth because they last about five minutes before being nicked to order in Glasgow. Sitting in the leather Recaro seat, I wondered if I was still over the limit from the night before, then started the engine and headed for the Chip. Despite the Mars Bar, I was hungry. And thirsty.

The occupants of the Pitch Electronics table were clearly in a fairly good emotional state by the time I arrived. They'd been given one of the large tables out in the huge, indoor courtyard area of the restaurant, where the leafy wall-growth now almost totally obscures the murals painted by novelist and artist Alasdair Gray in exchange for food, many years ago now. Bob looked happy, his tie askew, his sallow Clydesdale's face flushed pink. Four Japanese men, three fairly young, one with iron-grey hair and an air of solidity, sat smiling and talking and smoking very heavily indeed. Four empty wine bottles adorned the table, and by the looks of things, they'd finished their main course, and had enjoyed themselves extensively beforehand at the Pot Still. I bowed to the grey-haired man. 'Mr Fuyaki, I presume?' He stood up, rather too hastily, and bowed unsteadily towards me. We shook hands. 'I apologise for my late arrival, I have been struck down by a Scottish sickness which is, unfortunately, a particular problem at his time of year and one I am unhappily susceptible to.' The other, younger Japanese men were rising now, bowing and shaking my hand. There was an empty chair, opposite Bob's, so I sat down.

'Arnold, Arnold,' cooed Bob. 'Look, we've probably eaten enough, I think, everybody here. We were just going to order up some malts, to cap the meal off. Join us? Or maybe you need to eat something?' Bob's innate sobriety was returning as he remembered my condition earlier. I ordered some haggis and turnip, and a bottle of 16-year-old Lagavulin with two bottles of peat-tinged Islay mineral water.

'Please,' I said. 'We must all drink. To co-operation, Bob?'

'Ah, yes, to co-operation. And prices suitably agreed. Not to mention quality, that hallmark of the Itsuoko operation.' Bob had been boning up on his negotiating skills, I could see. Mr Fuyaki bowed to Bob, then to me. The whisky arrived, and I poured it with all due ceremony.

Later, things eased, then began to blur. Fuyaki spoke perfect, if slightly mannered English, and after we had moved from the Lagavulin on to a 1974 Clynelish at truly vast expense, and we had talked hi-fi into extinction, he began to ask me about golf. No, the name Pitch Electronics had not come from a golfing stroke, but from music, the term perfect pitch. But was I not a golfer? Indeed I was, a very bad one. So a perfect pitch was also a golf shot of unsurpassed brilliance? It was, I agreed. Fuyaki smiled.

'In Tokyo, I have this year become a member of the Togaki Golf Country Club. I have been on the waiting-list for ten years, and the joining fee was, I think, £75,000. Plus I must pay £100 per round, £200 for guests. You must come and play, when you visit our factory, you and Mr Braithwaite.' I smiled, laughed.

'Here,' I said, 'here in this city there are many, many golf courses, but there are seven golf courses, seven, the perfect number, seven. They are open to anyone, at any time to play, no matter who they are, or how bad they are.' I could hear my words slurring, see Fuyaki's face moving in and out of focus. 'How bad they are at golf, I should say. They are owned by the city, and none is more expensive than £4.50 per round. No joining fee, no annual membership. If you want that, there are also plenty of private clubs in the city and just outside. Glasgow has more golf courses than any other city in the world. More public courses too, and the cheapest . . .' I was conscious suddenly that I was standing up, banging the table, and fell silent. Fuyaki and the other Japanese rose to their feet and began to applaud, smiling broadly. I waved a self-deprecating hand, and reached for the Clynelish.

Dawn was breaking over Barlinnie Prison. The grim stone walls of the giant human cage glowed as a lemon-yellow sun rose over the city, glinting off the soaring Legoland of the Red Road flats, revealing the shadowy outlines of the Cathkin Braes, and over there, far away, the crags of the Kilpatricks, and the Campsies, and out towards Loch Lomond, where Belinda and I had done our early courting, was that Ben Lomond? Maybe. In the smokeless atmosphere of post-industrial Glasgow, you could see for miles. At least Pitch made things, even if we had to import components from the Land of the Rising Sun. In one hand I had a tin of Tennent's Lager, and in the other a bottle of Grouse. My standards had deteriorated. Stumbling beside me was Fuyaki, while behind us staggered Bob and one of the young Itsuoko assistants, somewhat disjointed in his movements. The other two were asleep in the Renault Espace I had booked for the evening, back when I had planned it out, semi-soberly, before Belinda had hit me with her threats and promises; before the game of destruction golf in the flat; before things began to slip, and I was still a competent executive of Pitch Electronics Ltd. It was the kind of thing I did well. The Renault was being driven by James, a regular driver of ours, a long-standing employee of the taxi firm we used, the Maryhill-based Armour Cabs. I always asked for him because I liked saying 'home, James' at the end of an evening. And he never complained. Now he was sitting in the deserted carpark of Lethamhill Golf Course, one of Glasgow District Council's three 18-hole courses, out near Stepps. We were on the hill which contains a leaky reservoir, and which affords spectacular views over the city.

'Only five pounds,' muttered Fuyaki. 'To play this magnificent course. In Japan . . .'

'I know.' A lifetime's waiting, saving and putting your soul in hock just to set foot on the thing. I took a swig from the Grouse, offered the bottle to Fuyaki. 'Less than a fiver, actually. Four pounds and fifty pence. Less if you're unemployed or old. Less in the winter, too. And over in your country, for those not rich enough, not bloody millionaires, nothing but driving-ranges, 30 balls at a time, an hour here, an hour there, with some never playing on a real course in their lives. Isn't that true?'

Fuyaki nodded as the light spread over Glasgow, yellow to blue. He put the bottle of whisky to his lips.

'Ah, but Mr Palmer, it must be very busy, no? Surely many, many people want to play, and I see that your tees here are not so grassy. Worn, perhaps? By too much cheapness?' And he laughed, loudly but politely.

'Four pitch-and-putt courses,' I shouted. 'I bloody counted them, years ago, and they're all still here. Three 18-hole courses, Lethamhill, Littlehill and Linn Park, all pretty damn good, if yes, OK, a bit worn in places. Four nine-holers, Ruchill, Alexandra Park, Knightswood and King's Park. Innumerable putting-greens. And maybe sometimes you get your balls stolen by runaway dogs or wee bastard boys. Or your clubs, if you're really stupid or careless. And maybe you find used syringes in the bunkers, or paper bags smelling of Evo-Stik. But it's accessible, it's the people's . . . besides, you get all the same hassles at the private courses, too, unless you've got hundreds of security men and great big Alsatian dogs patrolling . . .'

'Arnold?' It was Bob, a great deal less inebriated than the rest of us. Certainly less than me.

'OK, Bob, we'll go back. I just want to . . . one more course after this, just one . . . just a minute, then we'll take them back to the Hilton. Listen, Mr Fuyaki, over at Littlehill, we haven't got the time to go there, and besides it's flat, sort of flat. But I, listen, the names of the holes, they're something. I learned them when I was 14. Listen: Glasgow golf is right there. Right *there*! In the words, in the names. Listen to this, see if I can get them all: Aff Ye Go, No Hooky, Mind the Houses, Stolen Baas, Get O'er, Chip or Run, Watering Hole, Slope, emm, wait a minute, no, *slopy*! Slopy Lefty, Get O'er Again, Nae Problem, Mind the Cars, Never a Four . . . ach . . . Ach, that's it. Ach Wrang Side, Better Short, Aff the Waa, Nearly Hame, Ruined Medal, Aff Furra Pint. Off for a pint. Of beer. Isn't that brilliant?' But even the eternally smiling Fuyaki was regarding me with confusion written all over his dawn-lit face. Face of the Rising Sun.

We slumped into the Espace as the light grew stronger, and James took us west, threaded us through the hard and grimy streets of unkempt Glasgow, then up beside Ruchill Park, until we stopped at a gap in the railings. James switched off the engine. 'Here you are then, Mr Palmer.' I slid open the door and looked out.

'This can't be right, James. There's no clubhouse.'

'Aye, well. They burned down the clubhouse, Mr Palmer.'

'They what? Who did?'

'Local lads, Mr Palmer. Local boys, some of the boys, from around and about. You know how it is. High spirits. Petrol. That kind of thing.' I'd forgotten that James lived in Summerston, the massive half-council, half-private housing scheme nearby. 'I'm actually in the Ruchill Club, and we play every Friday and Sunday.' God, James was a golfer. He'd never vouchsafed this information before. 'We have to put out our own flags, know what I mean? The weans just nick them if they're left. Council's got the place on free play at the moment, because of the fact that there's no clubhouse. No way of collecting money. They keep it up, though. Mow the greens. Need to play in foursomes, though, with an extra guard if you can get someone. It's no just balls that go missing up here. This is golf on the edge, Mr Palmer. Golf on the edge.'

There was silence in the Espace. Day was almost fully with us, now and we were looking out west, to the dim shapes of the early Highlands, out beyond the city, beyond the hump of Wilton Street, where my smashed and littered flat awaited me. Suddenly, all the drunkenness and adrenalin lifted like fog, and in a second's brilliant clarity, I saw the debris-ridden carpet, the strewn golf clubs and food. And I saw myself throwing fortunes away on this wooing of businessmen to benefit some pathetic little hi-fi company, a firm which sold auditory tricks to people with more money than ears. This was what I was good at. This, crappy, pimping, selling, scamming . . . The fog descended again. I took a slug of the Grouse, and without being asked, James started the engine and drove us to the Hilton.

I Know a Dog Who Can Play Football

Derek Park, Assistant Golfing and Ancillary Recreations Manager of the Parks and Recreational Department, Glasgow City Council Direct Services Organisation:

Yes, it's a very apt name, I suppose. We have seven golf courses, four nine-holes, three 18, and that's more public courses than any other city, although Aberdeen comes close. That's where I come from. But the golf's a lot more expensive there. I've only been here just over two years, and I used to play a lot of golf, not so much now. But I've played all the courses we have, and I must say I was impressed. Some are very good, undoubtedly championship standard, and we hope to attract some competitions in the future, get some professionals to play, that sort of thing.

Lethamhill is 18 holes, and I suppose it's the flagship of the Glasgow public courses. You get beautiful views from the top, and it's not easy. It's a par 70, but the Scottish Golf Union have been round recently and there's talk of it going up to a 72. The 18th is probably the best hole on the course. It's quite long, just under 500 yards, and a par four. It's right-angled dog-leg over that huge mound in the middle, with trees on the right. You can either go over the trees, or hit short on to the apex of the dog-leg, then batter it straight down the fairway to the green. We have Hogganfield Loch on the right, which is still part of the Glasgow Parks Department, and it's quite scenic. There are rowing boats on the loch in summertime and the MV *Glasgow* gives trips around it.

We definitely have a lot of hackers playing on all our courses. We don't want to discourage them, because this is a large city, and we want more people to play golf, too. We're going to start coaching programmes at the nine-hole courses, so that people can gradually progress on to the larger ones. According to the Sports Council, we're actually lacking courses given the number of people who want to play golf here. The city council has approved a sports and recreation strategy which has set out major improvements for golf in Glasgow, including new waiting-rooms, changing facilities, cafés, pro-shops, and here at Lethamhill a golf driving-range and practice areas. Golf is safe in Glasgow City Council's hands, definitely. There's just no question of these courses being used for housing, being sold off. These places are enshrined in the leisure culture of

Glasgow, and anyway the council has a policy of not building on green space. And the courses are very busy. There would be an absolute uproar. Glasgow has over 70 parks, you know. More green space than any other city in the world, and that's how it will stay.

Glasgow has a reputation for being a crime-ridden city, and the golf courses are huge open spaces. Round the back of Letham-hill there's the Ruchazie housing scheme, and some of the youths do come across and steal golf balls. Occasionally, they do steal golf clubs from customers, but we are trying to combat this, with security checks by our park rangers, and the problem has certainly decreased over the past six months, I would say. We don't let them ride motorcycles over the courses. We don't allow vehicles.

We have special tee markers which we use for competitions, but we don't put them out for normal golf. We're nearing an agreement with a company for sponsorship which will provide tee markers. People don't steal them, but they do tend to get damaged. A certain number of people use them for practice shots, for practising drives and the like.

I've never heard of dogs stealing balls on any of our courses, but I do know of a dog playing football at Crown Point Stadium. In fact, he's probably the best player there.

Littlehill is just on our side of the border with Bishopbriggs, just before you go out of Glasgow. It's a par 70, like Lethamhill, but it's not as hard. It's shorter. Stobhill Hospital is very handy in case of accidents. The last hole at Littlehill is called Aff Furra Pint, but we don't have a licence for the pavilion, which is quite an impressive, 1920s building. There is a pub just down the road.

Linn Park, on the south side of the river, has an experimental booking system, and that seems to be working quite well. We're hoping to extend that to the other 18-hole courses if it's successful. At the moment, you just turn up, pay, wait and play.

Ruchill, well, Ruchill we have had some problems with. The pavilion was burned down, and we don't have flags out on the greens, normally, except for competitions. They get stolen. It's actually on free play at the moment, but it's a lovely wee course, quite testing, with marvellous views out to the west, and quite safe. It's on full maintenance cycle, so it's kept up to scratch, greens mowed and that sort of thing. You can have a relaxing game of golf there, and while it is the cheapest golf in the world, that won't be forever. We're going to put in a new pavilion as soon as possible. Maybe somebody burned the pavilion down just to get a free game of golf.

No Helicopter Spraying

John Hepburn, Golfing and Recreations Manager of the Parks and Recreational Department, Glasgow City Council Direct Services Organisation

These midges are a seasonal thing, because we're so close to Hogganfield Loch. I'm assured it's seasonal. There'll be no helicopter spraying. It wouldn't do our greens any good.

Excerpt from Glotta (A Poem)

Humbly inscribed to the Right Honourable the Marquess of Carnarvon, by Mr Arbuckle, Student in the University of Glasgow, published in 1721

> *The hastening flood at length to GLASGOW speeds.*
> *Its NORTHERN bank a lovely Green displays,*
> *Whose e'ery Prospect fresh Delights conveys.*
>
> *In WINTER too, when hoary frosts o'erspread,*
> *The verdant Turf, and naked lay the Mead,*
> *The vig'rous Youth commence the sportive War,*
> *And arm'd with Lead, their jointed Clubs prepare;*
> *The Timber Curve to Leathern Orbs apply,*
> *Compact, Elastic, to pervade the Sky:*
> *These to the distant Hole direct they drive;*
> *They claim the Stakes who thither first arrive.*
> *Intent his Ball the eager gamester eyes,*
> *His muscles strains, and various Postures tries,*
> *th' impelling Blow to strike with greater Force,*
> *And shape the motive Orb's projectile Course.*
> *If with due Strength the weighty Engine fall,*
> *Discharg'd obliquely, and impinge the Ball,*
> *It winding mounts aloft, and sings in Air;*
> *And wond'ring Crowds the Gamester's Skill declare.*
> *But when some luckless wayward Stroke descends,*

Whose Force the Ball in running quickly spends,
The Foes triumph, the Club is curs'd in vain;
Spectators scoff, and ev'n Allies complain.
Thus still Success is follow'd with Applause;
But ah! how few espouse a vanquish'd cause!

CHAPTER TWO

Indicating Line of Play

SOMEBODY, presumably Bob with the much-tipped help of James, had put me to bed in one of the Hilton's standard rooms. The Japanese floor, with its special beds, air-conditioning and Shintoesque trimmings, had obviously not been thought a necessary added expense. I woke to the telephone ringing. 'Mr Palmer, this is reception. This is your early afternoon alarm call. It's 1.30 p.m. Would you care for some lunch?' No trace of irony in the well-modulated, management-trainee home-counties voice. I muttered something incomprehensible into the mouthpiece, including, I hoped, the words 'coffee' and 'orange juice', and slumped back on to the bed. I still had on my Boss suit, which was stained with grass and mud around the ankles and knees. My shoes were nowhere to be seen.

They appeared with the coffee, shined to perfection, along with orange juice, warm rolls, and a message written in Bob's spidery writing on Hilton notepaper. 'Call in if you wake up' was all it said.

I was becoming really sick of being sick over carpets and furniture and indeed myself, so after the room-service waiter had left the tray on a bedside cabinet and my shoes by the door, and after I had made no attempt to tip him, I lurched out of bed for the bathroom and threw up there. I then drank two tooth-glasses of cold water, and lay down again on the bed until the room stopped spinning. Which took about half an hour. Fortunately, the coffee was in one of those fancy plastic Thermos jug things, and was still palatably warm. I deliberately drank and ate everything on the tray. Enough was enough. It was time to straighten a few things out, and I was as well starting with myself, and a breakfast. Or rather, lunch.

I taxied back to Wilton Street, still flushed, pouchy about the face but reasonably steady, and found the flat hoovered and as immaculate as a house can be when someone has tried to play psychopathic auto-destruction golf within its portals. Tuesday. Oh God, yes, this was the day Marlon came from The Office Cleaning Executive to deal with my sordid solo living habits. We used OCE at Pitch and, for an extra consideration and a monthly bung of £50 out of petty cash, Marlon sorted out my flat weekly as well. He was a philosophy graduate, would-be rock musician and extremely thorough cleaner. Honest, too. He'd had a set of my keys for the past nine months, when I began admitting that I was either unwilling or incapable of coping with a life which included dusting. He was prone to leaving notes for me if I was out when he left, so I began searching for the current one. Given the horrendous mess I'd left him, I expected a corker. Apart from a few lumps knocked out of walls, the place was pretty immaculate, although it smelled of carbon tetrachloride and dope. Marlon toked as he worked, which was fine by me. I occasionally shared a joint with him, though of late I'd found that it simply escalated my anxiety and paranoia, leaving me with a raging thirst, hunger and pathological worry over being raided by the cops. They had dogs which could smell it days after you'd been smoking. I knew this for a fact. Micro-amounts of ash could have you prosecuted. I'd never see my kids again . . .

The square of white card, with the printed heading THE OFFICE CLEANING EXECUTIVE HAS BEEN, SEEN AND CLEANED YOUR MACHINE, had the following lines blocked out in ballpoint capitals:

> It is essential to be drunk all the time. That is all: there's no other problem. If you do not want to feel the appalling weight of Time which breaks your shoulders and bends you to the ground, get drunk, and drunk again.

I crumpled the card and threw it on to the now-pristine carpet. If I wanted some junior sage's third-hand Baudelaire I could find it myself, in the Penguin Classics edition I'd bought at university, when I was obsessed with Bob Dylan, and his throwaway references had sent me to Rimbaud, Baudelaire, Ginsberg and other creatures very strange to a student of accountancy. Not that I'd lasted long at that.

Marlon had put my golf clubs away in the hall cupboard, the old blue leather bag cracked and scuffed, the shiny heads of the irons battered by years of use and recent abuse. I picked out the four wood, a real wood, not one of those metal things they use nowadays. This one was laminated, with red and white plastic inserts on the face. I remembered the clubs I'd bought as a youngster, wooden shafted, a driver with a metal plate on its face, an old brassie with a green, verdigrised bottom. I'd traded them for three steel-shafted Jameson irons and a Dunlop driver, springy and whippy and my pride and joy. It was years before I realised how valuable that old set of hickory-shafted clubs had been. Slowly, I slid the driver back into its bag. No more destruction. I tottered into the bedroom and flopped on the bed.

It was 7.00 p.m before I wakened. I had my second shower of the day and changed into a repulsive but very comfortable cotton Umbro tracksuit. The answering machine was winking its sly conspiracy that people had been calling, and it knew who, and I noted that the estimable Marlon had muted the phone's bell. What a thoughtful guy. Maybe I should marry him.

I ignored the Answercall and slouched into the lounge. Both the telly and the stereo had escaped the attentions of my golfing blitzkrieg, somehow. I couldn't face the prospect of the world outside coming slithering in through the 26-inch Nicam-stereo Sony, so I browsed through the shelves of now obsolete and old-fashioned and redundant and much, much loved 12-inch vinyl LPs, and picked out the Flamin' Groovies *Shake Some Action*. Only the title track is listenable, but that's because it's one of the best single rock'n'roll songs ever written, performed to slack-jawed perfection. The rest of the album is good, but flaccid and pale compared to 'SSA' itself. I fired up the prototype Pitch Black, 50-watt-per-channel RMS amp, opened the perspex lid of the Linn LP12, an old one, with only the

41

Valhalla electronic speed stabilising mod and the special bearing oil, switched it on and let the heavy platter come up to speed. Then I reverently placed the LP on the felt cloth, and lowered the Ittok arm with its venerable Asak cartridge on to the record. The big Tannoy monitors, rewired internally and with customised tweeters, rumbled and spat a little with the worn record, then detailed that marvellous, distant, echoing guitar which introduces the song. 'I will find a way . . . to get to you someday.' Perfect. Then that chorus, volume up, staccato, sullen, desperate: 'Shake . . . Some action's what I need . . .' I let the song run out, then lifted the arm off the record. Tears. Too much hope in that song. Thumping from upstairs indicated that Mrs Braithwaite was having a good time.

The turntable was plugged through the special input circuit I'd had Bob wire into the prototype Pitch Black for my own use; production versions had CD inputs only, carefully tweaked to imitate the easy, infinitely listenable warmth of black vinyl played on a really good system. Because the fact is that CDs, scratchless and lovely to hold though they are, sound crap without some electronic smoothing of their digital soundwaves. And that's what the Pitch Black does. Better, thanks to Bob, than anything else currently available.

I telephoned for a pizza, asking for a couple of cans of Coke with it, diet no-caffeine Coke. No more alcohol. No more drugs. I was going to keep straight for a while, let the poison out of my system. Deal with this Belinda thing, sort out what to do about Patti and Paul. When the pizza arrived, I found a copy of *The City*, a free, advertising-fuelled non-newspaper, lying on the doorstep. Over rapidly cooling pepperoni I skimmed it. PR bullshit, mostly. Their sales reps had been on the phone every week for the past two years, trying to get us to take out space, promising editorial coverage. It wasn't our scene at all. In the inevitable slew of car advertising, my eye was caught by one discreet box from Gordon Lazarre Motors in Whiteinch. Gordon was an old pal, a fellow hi-fi nut who had haunted obscure shops along with me and one or two others in the late 1970s and early '80s. He'd set up a small classic-car operation, mostly dealing in restored British sports cars such as Michael's Midget. His stuff was solid, reliable, and he gave good, cast-iron guarantees. It was rare for Michael to have no complaints, and he didn't. I'd considered getting rid of the Sierra, or getting something old and interesting just for leisure purposes, but I'd been a busy family businessman, and then a worn, rattled, frazzled and paranoid divorced businessman, and I had the music and the boys' toys at home. The Sega, hardly used, the Mac with CD-ROM and all the multimedia bullshit, again played with only rarely. The Scalextric set, ostensibly for Paul but . . . no. No, I wouldn't think about that. Couldn't, not safely.

Among Gordon Lazarre's clipped descriptions of MGBs, a Daimler Dart and a Triumph TR6, was something odd. 'Kawasaki Z650. Excellent, low mileage, 1981.' A Kawa Z650. I'd had one, back when I was footloose and financially unworried, dropped out of university and shaking accountancy out of my lengthy hair, selling records in the city-centre branch of the Listen Records chain. The one I'd had was old, a 1974 model with rotting wire wheels and cam chains which rattled like a kid scraping a stick along park railings. But it went like stink, nevertheless. I remembered the rush, the sheer visceral grinning thrill of high-speed squirts up the Loch Lomond Road, out into the country, up into the hills, Glencoe, that sense of oppression you get there, especially on a bike, how tiny you feel. Wild nights in the Clachaig Inn, with girls who weren't Belinda. Two of its four cylinders had seized solid one night on Great Western Road, out near Anniesland in the wet, with me half-drunk and a girl called Rosie on the pillion. I'd caught the resultant skid on the clutch just in time, but Rosie had not appreciated having to walk home. I'd ended up selling the thing for scrap.

My head was still nipping from the sustained drinking, but the music and the food and the Coke had left me capable of dealing with whatever horrors lay on the answering machine. I switched the phone's ringing tone back on, rewound the tape, and heard Bob, a cheerful Bob, telling me not to worry about coming in. Fuyaki had called, they were drawing up a provisional manufacturing agreement, and he was interested in some kind of reciprocal representation deal for the finished Pitch products in Japan. 'They flew to London this afternoon. He says to thank you for your tour of cheap golf courses, and says you must come to Tokyo for an expensive round with him, during daylight but with plenty of whisky. Togaki, I think he said.' So the excesses of the previous night had not ruined things, it seemed.

There was a message from Michael, wondering how I was, and inviting me to dinner. And Belinda, bright and businesslike. 'Can you call me, Arnold? I think we have things to discuss. Oh, the children said . . . hello.' And in the background I could hear Paul's giggling shout. 'Hello, Arnold!' Hello *Arnold?* Who was I, some kind of bloody pretend uncle? Christ, maybe they were already calling the hideous Victor 'Dad' and 'Daddy'. My blood ran cold at the thought. The taste for whisky rose in my throat, but I went to the stereo instead, picked out Richard and Linda Thompson's classic depressive masterwork *I Want to See the Bright Lights Tonight*, and

43

let the pathetic tears come. 'My Love Has Withered and Died'. But tonight I was going to behave. Absolutely no indoor golf.

It was a railway arch gone upmarket, with glittering security shutters neatly retracted and one of those carefully executed signs meant to exude quality and distinction due to an excessive use of gold leaf. Naff was the word. Inside, it was showroom and service station combined, immaculate, temperature controlled, lined in plastic and well lit. But upmarket or no, Gordon Lazarre had gone slightly sleazy, absorbing some of the car trade's inevitable greasiness. Perhaps it was his way of dealing with the slings and arrows of outrageous hassle which go with a growing business. Maybe I'd gone greasy, too. I caught my reflection in the polished windscreen of a red TR7, never a popular vehicle and too ugly to really cut it as a classic car. My hair was greasy, or looked it from the Brylcreem gel I was in the habit of using. I kept it short, slicked back, and the shortness at the back and sides was revealing more and more flecks of grey. Or white. Call it silver, maybe. As for the areas of scalp becoming increasingly apparent . . . Phil Collins used to claim he had always had a high forehead and a double crown. Me too.

'Arnold Evelyn Palmer, bless my cotton socks.' Something of the pre-lubricated Gordon came through in a crooked smile. He leaned against a Lancia Delta HF Turbo Integrale, smoking a Lew Grade cigar, grinning. 'The man for whom fidelity is a high priority.' Ouch. Though I had been faithful to Belinda, at least in practice, at least physically, and since leaving had found the whole process of dealing with women in the hope of sex or affection or even both, wearisome and boring. I was too old for romance, that teenage conceit. That 'fidelity is a high priority' was a line from a particularly naff piece about Pitch on the BBC's local news programme. You could hear the sub-editor's brain creaking.

'Hi, Gordon. How's life in the upmarket scrap-metal business?' He lightly hooked his hand through my arm, and led me into a wood and glass office which had been built at the far end of the arch; it was decidedly plush inside, with a leather settee, no less, and an impressive, Mussoliniesque desk. I sat and squeaked uncomfortably while Gordon lolled in a captain of industry chair.

'Not bad, not bad. Nostalgia keeps us going, and the big boom is a goner, so more people can afford to wallow in their past. The number of grown-up boys who simply want to own their dad's cars, show them and everyone else that they're bigger and better and more successful than papa . . . Anyway, what can I do you for? Getting rid of that crappy Dagenham dustbin? How about a nice Rover P5? Suit your position in life. I bet your . . .'

'My dad didn't have a car, Gordon. But yeah, I suppose nostalgia is why I'm here. Do you still have the Z650?'

He thew his head back, sighed, laughed. 'Oh, my God. The reborn-biker syndrome.'

'Does everything have to be a syndrome, Gordon? Is it boys outdoing their dads or mid-life crises and nothing else?' I was getting a little too tetchy. I could hear it in my rising voice.

'No . . . well, yes, actually.' He smiled. 'Come on, Arnie. permit me my ration of car dealer's bullshit. It comes with the territory. What do you think of the moustache?' I looked at him. Tightly knotted neon silk tie, Next suit, puffy round the eyes, lank hair. What had happened to him? Something similar to what had happened to me, I realised: life in all its crapness. He raised his eyebrows quizzically, frowned. 'Kawasaki Z650 C3, 23,000 miles, 11 months MOT, taxed October, one owner from new, dead – coronary thrombosis, apparently. He also owned a Jaguar S-type, immaculate, unrestored, an MGB GT roadster, badly restored, full of bloody pudding but a goer, and a Triumph Bonneville, which has already been sold. To me, actually, as I, too, am searching for my lost and much-yearned-for adolescence. We're acting for the estate.' Gordon leaned forward dramatically. 'So, can I interest you in your youth, sir? Shall we say, oh, £1,500? Or £1,400 and a free amplifier?'

'The Pitch Fork costs £500, and that's cheap at the price, mate. I'll give you a discount on a Black, if you like. £700 to you. What have you got, anyway, these days?

'Ah. Well, truth to tell, I got sick of the whole hi-fi thing, mate. Bought an all-singing, all-dancing, remote-control Aiwa music-centre, to be precise. Or honest. But if you were to hand over a nice Pitch product, I'd be tempted to get back into it. Much to Lianne's disgust, probably. Spoil the décor. Lianne. She's the wife, by the way. Her, so to speak, outdoors. She's probably playing golf as we speak out at Pollok.' Golf. There was no escape.

Everyone wanted a cheap or free amp. From deaf journalists to petrol-pump attendants. But £1,500 for a 13-year-old Japanese bike? 'God, I thought it would be cheap. I had one way back and it only cost £150. It was wrecked, right enough, but these are ordinary Japanese rice-wine specials, for goodness sake.'

'Not any more, mate. 1970s and early '80s Japcrap is now very collectible, if it's the right piece of machinery. Plus, if a bike's over 13 years old you get classic insurance, which at today's prices is a real godsend to the would-be Mad Maxes out there on the streets. Anyway, come and see it.' He heaved his considerable bulk out of the Robert Maxwell chair, a parachute of fat falling down inside his shirt front. 'The Bonneville's at home, just sitting in the garage. Sometimes I start it up, run it for ten minutes, and just listen to it. Other times, if it's dry, I'll take it round the garden. It's just a delight, part of Britain's bloody heritage, mate!'

'Why don't you take it on the road, Gordon?' He smiled sheepishly.

'Don't have a licence, mate. Only able to ride tinpot 125cc affairs on a car licence these days. Two-part test, treat you like a ninny. No thanks. I might fail.'

We left the office, and the smell of garages, defeated in Gordon's leather and wood cocoon by air fresheners and the Great Smell of Paco Rabanne, overwhelmed me: oil, wax, petrol, exhaust. The scent of male fantasy. The space had an inspection lift and all the accoutrements necessary for repairing the Space Shuttle. It was surgically clean, and the only mechanic on display, standing next to an old British racing-green Lotus Elite, had on pressed white overalls, not an oil stain in sight. We passed through a heavy metal door in the side of the workshop, and entered what was obviously the next arch. It was chock-full of the past: Jaguar, MG, Riley, Austin-Healey, Daimler, Lotus, Triumph; cars ranging in state of preservation from the concours to the collapsed. Between a rusty Frog-eye Sprite and an E-type Plus Two stood the Kawasaki. It looked brutal. Dark blue and glinting in the fluorescent reflections of all the other machinery, the Z650 seemed immaculate, crying out for . . . for me. I knew I had to have it. Gordon flicked on the ignition, pressed the starter button once. A great, staccato, smooth roaring filled the arch, a kind of refined hooliganism among all that four-wheeled neo-classicism, that moneyed wallowing in four-wheeled comforts from the past. The sound of a motorbike, a big one. Two fingers to authority, safety, adulthood . . . no matter how old you were, once in helmet and leathers, you were a teenager on a bike. And policemen always called you 'son', no matter that you were some 60-year-old high-court judge on a BMW. The motorcycling myth: escape, freedom, wildness. Potent, though. And irresistible.

Next morning at 9.00 a.m. I was heading north-west out of Glasgow into a morning of half shadow, half hard, breaking light and the beginnings of heat, threading through the traffic, butting into the rush hour coming in the opposite direction like a surfer heading out to sea. For May in Scotland, it was extraordinary, breathtaking weather; perfect for the beginning of a journey; ideal for motorcycling.

Gordon had finally taken £1,200 and a trade discount on a Pitch Black for the Z650. I'd spent the rest of the day in a whirl of motorcycle accessory shops, buying into the myth with a vengeance: leathers, black fibreglass Arai helmet, proper gloves armoured with Kevlar, Frank Thomas Boots. Insurance was a matter of a telephone call, and then I took the Sierra to our factory in Clydebank. I was going to take some time out, I informed Bob. He seemed relieved.

'Thank God for that,' he said. 'Well, I mean . . . anyway this is as good a time as any. We've got a lot of technical work to do on the Pitch Black production schedules, so when you come back you can get the marketing plan sorted out, think about advertising . . . even listen to the finished article, if Fuyaki and the Itsuoko people can come up with the electronic goods in time. Go on, you need a break. You deserve it. God, all that falling about on golf courses was a bit out of order on Monday night, wasn't it? Still, Fuyaki seemed to like it. When you come back, we'll head out to Japan, you can play some golf with him. Glad I dragged you out of your hell-hole. It worked out.' He looked perky, old Bob. Decidedly glad to get rid of me. Maybe he was hoping it would turn out permanent. Was that a smile on his face when I told him I was going touring on a motorbike? Dangerous things, motorbikes . . .

I phoned The Office Cleaning Executive and told them to give Marlon a holiday from my polluting instincts and Baudelaire for three weeks, then parked the Sierra in Wilton Street, walked down the subway and took Glasgow's miraculous toy underground railway, the Clockwork Orange, into town. In the olde-worlde ambience of Greaves Sports I bought a collapsible Wilson golf bag in green nylon, a dozen Maxfli balls, some tees, a Foot-Joy glove and a pair of Stylo Oakdale golfing shoes, the first I'd ever owned. No Pringle sweaters, though. Because my plan was to pursue a vision of golf where those Faldo-bless woollens were anathema. OK, in Glasgow, public, cheap golf was available but it was overwhelmingly over-subscribed and the courses were worn down with use. There had to be places where golf was available to anyone, cheaply and quietly, without hassle or hostility or sneering observers. I couldn't handle that. The east coast was where all the big championship courses nestled their linksland dunes into the North Sea's embrace. That was where real, good golfers, ones with official handicaps, powered trolleys, little furry things on the top of their woods . . . that was where they played. And at the likes of Muirfield, the élite enlisted, if they were deemed suitable and weren't hiding some horrible secret, such as being female, in the nearest equivalent to Mr Fuyaki's Japanese nightmare, only with all the inherent snobbishness of a boarding-school officer class and near-masonic secrecy writ large. I'd once been told that while the origins of golf in Scotland could be traced to rough games along the traditional common linksland at Musselburgh, Leith and St Andrews, and on Glasgow Green, its development during the seventeenth and eighteenth centuries had been shrouded in secrecy because of a close association with Freemasonry. All documents relating to this had been destroyed when golf began to move back into the hands of the common people towards the beginning of the nineteenth century.

No one ever talked about west-coast golf; maybe there wasn't much, or it wasn't very good. But the really wild corners of the Scottish landscape were all there, and I was sure there had to be some secret, hidden havens of golf there too. Machrihanish was famous, away down at the tip of the Mull of Kintyre. People said it was the great lost championship course of Scotland, and virtually undiscovered. I thought I'd start there, see what happened, see which way the wind was blowing.

So I took a taxi out to Whiteinch, leatherised myself, and gingerly navigated the big bike around various backstreets before taking the beast out on to the Clydeside Expressway for a clockwise burn-up, a return to the stupidities of youth: Expressway east, over the Kingston Bridge south, M8 west, Clyde Tunnel north . . . a delirious, high-speed test run to see if I could still ride bikes and which was spoilt only by the moronic behaviour of certain lorry drivers and a brief shower of rain. The old Kawa could out-accelerate virtually everything on four wheels, despite its age, and sit at a steady 90 mph without any problem save the usual sensation that your arms were about to be torn off the handlebars by your own personal hurricane. Back at the flat I packed an old Wynnster rucksack and bungeed it on to the bike. Attaching the golf clubs, in or out of my new Wilson bag, proved more tricky, but eventually I decided to settle for a driver, three, five, and seven irons, pitching wedge and putter. In the bag, with the base jammed against the rear footrest, two elastic ropes held the clubs secure against the side of the bike. And the bag's hood would stop it filling up with rain. I hoped. I locked up and left, feeling that *Easy Rider* urge to throw away the keys and my watch. But I didn't.

I stopped at Arrochar, exhilarated, but cold and stiff from the unaccustomed business of clinging to a lump of fast-moving metal in the open air. In my new leathers I creaked and squeaked, and I wondered if I looked cool or just another middle-aged menopausal male with a Brando fetish. The lady in the the olde coffee shoppe served me without a qualm. 'Sprechen Sie Deutsch?' she asked in a Somerset accent. I told her I didn't, that I was Scottish.

'Oh, we get loads of Germans in here on their bikes, lovely

they are, great big Harling Davidson and BMWs, all dressed in leather like you are, dear, very polite, most of them. 'Course, there are always exceptions.' And she looked hard at me. I was Scottish, in Scotland. Therefore probably not to be trusted.

Her coffee and cake were good, though. I sat at one of the little check-clothed tables and wrote three postcards: one each to Belinda (a Highland cow; very apt, I thought), Patti (Loch Lomond from Tarbet) and Paul (Inversnaid Falls). Each said simply that I was going away for three weeks, and that I'd see them as soon as I got back. The ones to Patti and Paul were signed 'love, Daddy'. The one to Belinda I left unsigned. She'd recognise the writing.

I stopped in Tarbert, Loch Fyne, not to be confused with Tarbet, Loch Lomond or Tarbert, Harris, for a lunch. Tarbert is an exquisite, perhaps too exquisite village, hooped around a harbour so picturesque you distrust it. Or I did, anyway. When I got closer to the houses and hotels, the gift shops and newsagents, the flaking paint and slight genteel shabbiness became apparent. Also the sound of English voices, the 'white settlers', seduced from their high-equity southern properties by the prospect of scenery and cheap housing. I made the mistake of ordering a cappuccino in the C'a D'Oro café, a classic 1950s throwback Italian ice-cream and coffee shop. Instead of espresso capped with frothy milk from the Gaggia machine gleaming on the counter, I got nondescript coffee topped with synthetic St Ivel 'cream' from an aerosol can. It was salty and undrinkable. I drank it anyway. The bacon rolls were good, crispy and not too greasy. Nearby was a little half-hippy girl with yellow ribbons in her Volkswagen-advert curls. She was, maybe, four. Her mother chain-smoked roll-ups, and I felt a sudden pang, a sharp desire for a cigarette, given up a decade previously. Motorcycles and cigarettes – a dying combination. I resisted, heaved my stiffening, leather-clad bulk outside, and headed south.

Kintyre is a long, drooping-penis-shaped peninsula which dangles south until at its tip, the Mull of Kintyre, it is only 12 miles from Ireland. It's only one of about a dozen locations in Scotland where Columba is thought to have first arrived with Christianity in his kit-bag – and, some say, the first recipe for whisky. Kintyre is strewn with ancient settlements, and ranges from heavily wooded hinterland to dramatic cliff scenery, from exquisite beaches to truly doom-laden hills.

Campbeltown, 120 miles from Glasgow, was an hour from Tarbert along a spectacular and very smelly – from the rotting seaweed on the foreshore – coastal road, the A83. And yet this was still Strathclyde Region, the same as Glasgow, and identical regional-authority signs kept popping up, defusing any sense of being in a wilderness. I clearly wasn't. The RAF station at Machrihanish meant ease of access to this otherwise remote area had been paramount, pre-glasnost, and this was a traditional stamping ground for west-central Scotland's holidaymakers. It felt a bit like Blackpool, only smellier. I was tired, slightly disappointed, frazzled by one or two hectic encounters with blind car drivers, and Campbeltown hit me like a hallucination. It was full of large, ornate and clearly empty buildings. A huge bay, the famous Campbeltown Loch, mirrored the sense of decay. Once the whisky metropolis, home to dozens of distilleries, just two are left now, and only the decaying riches of the past spirit barons remain to indicate what was once immense prosperity. Wearily, I pointed the Z650, which had not complained once since leaving Glasgow, in the direction of the B843 and Machrihanish six miles away.

It's not a dump, and yet there's something very seedy about the place. Something jerry-built, uneasy. A straggle of houses, a pub, a converted former hotel, the golf course and its clubhouse. All the signs of military fallout, somehow, the same feeling you get in places like Lossiemouth – of temporary residents and fast bucks badly distributed. The carpark for the golf course, which looked exquisite in the blurring, golden light of a fine, if blustery afternoon, was full of large, shiny cars, hired by the look of them. And as I trundled the bike to a rest, I saw a group of blue-rinsed ladies dressed to blind and maim come out of the clubhouse door. When I removed my helmet I heard them speaking.

'Gee, Ethel, isn't this just the most darling gawlff club you ever did sayee?'

'Sure Gladys. Sure am glad we took that Golfing Safari tour you saw advertised back in Long Island. Who'd a thought we'd end up in this place? And so hospitable, oh baby, didya see that guy in the kilt in there? Wowee, babe . . .'

Odd. This was supposed to be an undiscovered course. But it looked like a serious piece of golfing, undoubtedly a classic links layout, wonderfully situated, although the RAF station's runway was slap next door. I wandered over towards the first tee, seaborne on a sand-scoured promontory. God almighty. It was stunning, horribly intimidating in its uncompromising coastal sweep. Coward's choice was to avoid the tempting batter – what, 250 yards – straight across the beach to safety on the far part of a dog-leg, and clip the ball safely right for 100 yards or so. And there were people around, ready to jeer in silence. I eyed the expensive cars in the carpark, the large number of brightly clad, probably Pringled figures out on the course, the four American ladies who were now standing by a white Mercedes limousine, the kind which has had an extra three feet welded into it.

'Wait'll we tell the girls at the country club back home, Wendy. And Bill, from the Pinewood Bay Golfing Heritage Society . . . God, he'll go crazy when he hears about this place, and that we met Freddy from the Lake Justerini Golf Museum here. Jesus, he'll wet himself . . .'

I put my helmet back on, started the bike, and slowly left the carpark and Machrihanish behind me. This was clearly tourist-track gold. The course looked more than difficult, far too classy for my meagre talents. My uselessness would be all too obviously displayed, always assuming they let me on without a handicap certificate. And £22 a day was, well, slightly dearer than Knightswood.

The Campbeltown tourist office found me a bed-and-breakfast, run by a Mrs Pringle, presumably not of the sweater clan. Her house was clean and smelled of air freshener, fried bacon and fabric conditioner. I de-leathered, showered, and then wandered into the centre of this weird half-town, half-village, eventually finding a surprisingly sophisticated wine bar called Eaglesomes, which turned out to be part of the Springbank Distillery empire, along with the town's only delicatessen. All civilised life seemed to lie within the distillery's orbit. After a reasonable lasagne, I ordered a pint of fresh orange and lemonade in the public bar of the Royal Hotel, drawing some peculiar glances from other customers. I was, their eyes judged, clearly some kind of weirdo city child-murdering psychopath. Fresh orange and lemonade, indeed.

'Not from around here.' The statement was flat, unarguable, spoken by a beetroot-faced man in a deerstalker and tweed jacket, both of which appeared to have faced many an attack from an enraged power-tool operative. A wispy, stained moustache sprouted from his upper lip.

'Err . . . no. Glasgow. On holiday, actually. Golfing.' He looked as if he would be more impressed with golfing than motorcycling. He was standing at the bar staring straight at the gantry. I was only guessing that I was the object of his conversational gambit, if that's what it had been.

'Machrihanish?' The accent was Glasgow, originally upmarket, but somehow coarsened. He was drinking lager, sipping it cautiously, as if unsure what damage it was likely to do.

'No. Well, I mean, yes, maybe. But I went down for a look, and maybe it's a bit beyond me. I don't know. I'm really not much of a golfer.' I sipped my fresh orange and lemonade. The lemonade was flat, but so far my teetotal resolve was holding. Nearly three days. Not bad.

In a sort of convulsive attack, the man jerked the pint of lager high above his mouth and tipped it down. His head was already almost horizontal, lips twitching slightly. His throat worked, his chest heaved, and within a few seconds the entire pint of yellow beer had vanished, leaving only a few flecks of foam attached to the glass. Gasping out a whistling belch of relief, he slammed the empty glass down on the bar, slid off his stool, revealing himself as very short, about five feet, and moved towards the door. He stopped, though, and turned back to me, cocking his head to one side, so that the deerstalker, had it not clearly been held on by years of attachment which had probably merged his hair and the tweed, looked perilously close to slipping off. He belched again, the tone lower, more ruminative. From the pits of his jacket he produced an old pocket watch, its glass face badly cracked. He glanced at it, then thrust it back into the hairy, sagging pouch which had once been a pocket.

'Dunaverty,' he said, then ferreted out the door without another word.

I finished my dull drink and went back to Mrs Pringle's. Dunaverty. I'd never heard of it. Next morning I asked my landlady about it over the heart-attack breakfast I was tucking into with genuine biker's gusto.

'Aye,' she said, her candyfloss Persil perm bobbing. 'It's a golf course. At Southend, just down the road.' A golf course. Uh huh. Maybe there I'd find what I hadn't at Machrihanish.

It was dull, windy but dry. The road to Southend, right down at the southerly tip of Kintyre, hence the name, snaked through fragrant farmland, until suddenly there was the sea, a wide sweep of silver sand, a hotel, the Argyll Arms, some houses amid the fertile fields, and a bizarre concrete pseudo-castle, also a hotel. I trundled the Kawasaki into the golf club carpark and switched off the engine. There was no one else there at all. The wind buffeted and tumbled around my ears, with the sound of a heavy surf melding into the unearthly chattering of skylarks. I could hear the sailing-boat slap of the flag on the eighteenth green, and I felt suddenly eager to hit some balls around the course. It was clearly very well cared for, a classic links, laid out between huge sand dunes and the beginnings of the serious farmland. And as the sky cleared, momentarily, over to the west, I caught a glimpse of a darker shadow on the horizon. Ireland.

I went into the modern, apparently deserted clubhouse to

change and search out a score-card, my clubs having survived the trip from Glasgow unscathed, although the bag had acquired a layer of road-grime. A pile of score-cards lay on a shelf; a notice indicated that play was £10 per day. I extracted the cash from my wallet and placed it in the box provided, the honesty box. God, I wondered how long that would have lasted on a Glasgow public course. I took off my leathers, keeping on a Helly-Hansen fleece jacket, inserted my feet into my new Stylo golf shoes, and was ready. This, then was where the pilgrimage began. I walked out towards the first tee. The course's par is 66, with a standard scratch of 64. It looked, with the wind hirpling in from the west, far more difficult than those figures indicated

The stinging, unsettled air buffeted me as I teed up the ball and got ready to drive off, down towards a square, rocky headland. It was then I heard the unmistakable clink of golf clubs behind me, and turned to see that medically attached deerstalker from the previous night, atop the same boiled-ham face, but now carting a set of top-of-the-range Mizuno Tour clubs, and dressed in . . . a Pringle sweater. A yellow Pringle sweater.

'Aye,' he said. 'Fancy a game, then?' I nodded in mute amazement.

He said his name was Jimmy, but gave little clue about his livelihood or indeed anything personal at all. I looked back at the carpark, but could see no sign of a car. 'Dram a hole, then, OK?' His lips were pursed in enquiry. I shrugged assent. 'Name?'

'Arnold,' I replied. He motioned me to play. 'Down to Dunaverty Rock, eh? Fire away.' I eyed the ball nervously, then the headland which I now realised was Dunaverty Rock itself. This was it.

The first hole at Dunaverty is called Strangs, a 318-yard par four which saw Jimmy win with a tentative, three-putted six and me shame myself with an eight. Despite the wind, I recovered at the second, Garrach Dhu, a par-three 157-yarder, to scramble a bogey off a three-iron tee shot. Jimmy got a par, and from there on in he just got better and better. I fumbled around, playing badly, playing well, but lost in it. Lost in the big sky and the wind and the business of trying to make a pendulum out of my arms.

Jimmy spoke very little, as we traversed the undulating dunes of Dunaverty. 'Dunes. Big Clet. Little Clet. Out there's Sanda, then Ireland. This is God's own, this course.' And he spat, forcibly. He birdied the fourth, and by the time we came to the 11th, the tee teetering high up among the marram grass, he was ten drams to the good. He permitted himself a smile.

53

'The Cleat,' he said. 'Look down there. Just look.' And the fairway fell dizzily beneath our feet, the Irish Sea crunching in to the left, a fine spray of sand coming in with the taste of salt on the wind. I'd noticed that the perennial erosion problems of a links course were having their effect on the sea fringes of Dunaverty, which is cut in half by a road and a wide tidal burn. It is a course which follows nature, and lets nature take a hand in its shifting status. I could see that the burn would flood on certain occasions, too. The square lump I now knew was Dunaverty Rock rose like a full-stop to Kintyre, to Scotland. Not another soul could be seen on the course. Jimmy and I were on our own.

'Keil Hotel,' Jimmy gestured with a Mizuno driver at the strange, castellated concrete building I'd noticed when I arrived. 'Hospital in the war. Kelly family ran it for many years. Not any more. Not a bad pub, though.' He hit a magnificent drive, left into the wind so it drifted back into the middle of the fairway. The metal wood made that distinctive 'chink' noise as he swung, in a deceptively casual, hooky kind of way, and made contact. I decided I would do at least as well. I stood above the ball, letting the driver have that extra inch of stretch it needs, let my knees flex, and then, just as my mind was filled with nothing but the sounds of the course, the sea, wind, skylarks, Jimmy's wheezing presence, the feeling in my legs and arms and a kind of pleasant fluttering in the pit of my stomach, the lock-gate opened and all the emotional sludge came tumbling blackly down: Pitch Electronics, the new amp, Bob's uncertainty about me, my fears about myself, Paul, Patti, Belinda, the fact that I hadn't had sex for almost a year . . . in what seemed like a micro-second the tidal swamp containing all of that flooded my being. I was away, lost, drowning, suffocating.

'Fine shot.' I was holding the driver, following the ball as it fell, perfection, next to Jimmy's, in the middle of the fairway; well, maybe slightly left. My knees felt weak.

'Jewel, Dunaverty. A jewel. Machrihanish? Ach, some of them tell visitors no' to come here, that this is a nine-holer. A nine-holer! Been here since 1889, 19 March 1889, the club has. Eighteen holes, a jewel. A jewel. A diamond.' He looked vaguely embarrassed at having spoken so much.We walked down to our balls, me recovering from that attack of strange, black transcendent despair. Golf. It empties you, leaves you open to that kind of emotional attack. Maybe it does you good, maybe it doesn't. I tried to shrug off the brooding bulk of the past, shake it down, away while I finished the round. I couldn't, though.

The 17th is called the Burn, and with good reason. A straightforward drive down a wide, open fairway leaves you with either a good iron shot and a pitch, or two mediocre irons on to the green. About 20 yards in front of the green is a 15-foot wide stretch of river, the Conieglen Water, as Jimmy gruffly informed me. Between the river and the green is a road. It's a hole of bland horror, deceptive in its initial ease. A reasonable drive left me attempting a three iron to the green. Into the river. New ball, drop behind the 'burn'. Muffed pitch; into the river; seven. Oh my God.

Jimmy had gone ahead, apparently indifferent to my plight, and from what I could see he had holed out for his par during my watery hiatus. When I finally clattered across an old wooden bridge, crossed the road and sank the ball for a nine, he had disappeared. There was no sign of him on the 18th at all, and by the time I reached the clubhouse, wind-shattered and dulled with defeat and ineptitude, he might never have existed. I owed him 17, pehaps 18 drams, so perhaps he had decided that this ignominy, not to mention expense, was too much to ask a mere visitor to bear. I'd kept my score, and his to the 17th, assuming he'd made his par, but adding up the totals was too much to stand, just then. Odd, though; he hadn't struck me as the kind of person to turn down the idea of 18 whiskies.

The clubhouse was still empty, so after changing and strapping the clubs back on to the bike, I trickled the Kawa round to the Keil Hotel, which appeared to be in the last stages before dereliction set in. I took off my helmet and wandered into the public bar, which remained fairly comfortable; worn but welcoming. A picture of a smiling, youthfully middle-aged lady cuddling an enormous trophy caught my eye. A similar one had been hanging on the clubhouse wall, with the name 'Belle Robertson, MBE' and an astonishing list of golfing successes. The name had rung faint bells with me, but ladies' golf has never been a fetish of mine. There was the list again: three times runner-up in the Ladies' British Open Amateur Championship, the first time in 1959, aged 21. Amazingly, it took 22 years for her to win the trophy outright, in Wales. The list went on. Scottish Ladies' Champion on seven occasions spanning 21 years, from 1965 to 1986; represented Scotland 18 times in the Home Internationals; played in four Curtis Cup series; captained the British team for two more; New Zealand Ladies' Champion in 1971 and 1978; Scottish Sportswoman of the Year four times. Good God.

'Aye, she's from here, you know. Still a member – life member in fact, at Dunaverty.' The speaker was an impossibly round man with a small, knobbly head like a potato, topped some sparse strands of hair. He barely reached my elbow.

'Incredible,' I said. 'Fantastic achievement.'

'Aye. No bad . . . for a woman, like. Well, I mean, it's all women's competitions and stuff, know what I mean? Golf, now, men's golf, that's a harder game, much tougher. But you, my friend, you're maybe more a biker than a striker of the, eh, the wee white ball, know what I mean?'

'Actually, I've just had a round at Dunaverty, and I wouldn't even be fit to lace the shoes of Belle Robertson.' Pomposity came easily to me under certain circumstances. I loosened my leather jacket. I needed a dram. 'By the sound of this, she would have given many a male tournament player a run for his money.'

'Ach well.' The diminutive ball-shaped man was zipping up an anorak, moving towards the door. I caught the reek of gin on his breath. 'I'm no much of a golfer, me. Follow the fitba', like, but that's it. Golf, well, they talk aboot it all the time in here, like, but well, I find it pretty boring, know what I mean?' I shrugged, went with relief to the bar and ordered a large Springbank. One wouldn't hurt me, and I was sure my driving would improve. My motorbike driving, that is.

The woman on the next stool along was accompanied by a small Jack Russell terrier, and was daintily sipping a tomato juice, as far as I could tell unfortified by vodka. She was in her mid-forties, wind-scoured, ramrod-thin and carrying the remnants of long exposure to a tropical sun. Chain-smoking Dunhills, she offered me one, and grimaced when I refused. 'Healthy, clean-living motorcyclists! Whatever next?' The accent was middle-class Edinburgh, pleasantly deepened and burred by decades of cigarette smoke. Her name was Annie Bankhead, and she had retired, she said, to Southend, after years as a senior nursing sister in Kuwait. 'Family inheritance. Holiday bungalow, enough to live on, play a bit of golf . . . came here every summer when I was a child. Nostalgia, I suppose.' She loved Dunaverty, using the same word as Jimmy to describe it. 'A jewel, a real jewel. Ignored the whole time, of course, because of Machrihanish. Have you been there? It's a dump, you know, the village: threadbare and with some real problems. Still, the course is great, but they're more than a wee bit full of themselves. Dunaverty's more like golf ought to be. And once you've played here, you always want to come back . . . and stay. Like me.' She smiled and sipped her tomato juice in a cloud of blue smoke; blue and red and the faded orange of her henna-laden hair.

'I struggled round this morning,' I revealed. 'Just a hacker, really, well over the 100 for the course, but it's a wonderful links.'

'Did you go round yourself? It can be difficult to find your way about if you're on your own?'

I told her about Jimmy, the man with the Mizuno metal woods and the impacted deerstalker, the straggly moustache, the Glasgow accent and an impressively efficient method of drinking lager. She wrinkled her brow. 'Jimmy, you say? No, I don't know who that could be. Peter!' The barman, a young lad in an REM sweatshirt, looked up from his glass-polishing. 'Know any Jimmy from here or Campbeltown, deerstalker, lager, scratch golfer?' Peter shook his head. 'Never seen him in here.'

'Oh well, never mind. It's just that we were supposedly playing for drams, one a hole, and he beat me fair and square at every one.'

'I wouldn't worry about that,' said Annie, draining her tomato juice. 'If he's not here, he's missed out. Buy me a large Bloody Mary instead.' I obliged. So. The tomato juice was not what it seemed. I moved on to mineral water. My rucksack was still at Mrs Pringle's, and I wanted to be heading north, on beyond Campbeltown before the day was over. My self-discipline surprised me, especially as the warm glow induced by the smoky, salty seaweedy tang of the Springbank was very, very pleasant. I practised my much-disused flirtation skills on Annie, and left as the bar began to fill up at lunchtime with farmers and some evident tourists. Before I left, I called Peter over and gave him £30.

'Put that behind the bar for Jimmy: deerstalker, red faced, drinks lager,' I said.

Peter took the cash, gingerly. 'Annie!' She peered through her cigarette smoke, slightly woozy now from the vodka, maybe. 'You're a witness. See they keep that for Jimmy!' She laughed, raised her glass.

I stood in the hall, outside the rising hubbub of the bar, and prepared to face the dulling, greysheet day onboard the Z650. As I was zipping down the sleeves on my leather jacket, Annie emerged from the bar, walking delicately, but straight, surprisingly tall, the Jack Russell, whose name was, surprisingly, Jack, toddling behind her on a red-leather lead. When she reached me she grasped my arm, turned me to her and blew smoke sideways over my shoulder. Then she pulled my head down to her ashtray mouth and kissed me on the lips, a liquid, smoky snog, high in hydrocarbons. I was, to say the least, surprised.

'Don't worry, I'm going,' she said. 'I just fancied kissing a biker. Something I've never done. Or at least, not for a long time. By the way . . . this . . . Jimmy. You say he just sort of vanished?'

'Yes. When I came to the 18th tee, there was no sign of him.

He'd gone ahead of me at the 17th.'

'Well, if it wasn't for the Mizuno clubs, maybe you saw a ghost. Have you heard about Jimmy Lyon? No, of course you haven't.' I was smiling doubtfully at her. 'Don't grin like that. I'm not that pissed.' And, standing in the hall of the Keil Hotel, she told me about Jimmy Lyon, from good Glaswegian stock, who at the end of the nineteenth century had become an imbiber on a grand scale. 'It was Angus MacVicar who told me this, by the way. You know Angus? He's in his eighties now, but he's famous, or was. Wrote hundreds of books, science-fiction, a thing about here called *Salt in My Porridge,* which had dozens of sequels, made him a star, and he wasn't young when that came out. Nice man, delight, knows everything about Southend, lived here all his life, and still plays golf every Wednesday. They have a club called the Geriatrics. Anyway . . . '

In the 1870s Jimmy Lyon, it seemed, had been placed on the island of Sanda, off Southend, to dry out. He was an obsessive golfer, and had constructed a few holes to ease the troubled hours, calm the DTs. But his escapes to the mainland had become more and more frequent, and, on joining Dunaverty, with its handily positioned hotel, he proved to possess a brilliance unmatched in Kintyre. 'He was club champion, I think, oh, something like three times in four years,' said Annie. Jack the Jack Russell was whimpering at her feet, but she took no notice. 'He got seriously into the whisky again, though, and apparently he played even better when he'd had a dram or two. Said it was something like . . . like, oh, I can't remember . . . I know! Sober, the hole was a flower pot. Two drams and it was a bucket. He could supposedly drive a ball over the Ugadale Arms Hotel in Machrihanish off the face of a pocket watch.'

'So what happened to him?'

'He disappeared. Just vanished. Angus says his health deteriorated, and his family had him taken away from Sanda. No one ever saw him again, although there have always been strange stories about his ghost . . . but then, ghosts don't have golf clubs, do they? Strange thing is, the trophy they play for here, annual matchplay prize, is called the MacCallum-Lyon Trophy. There was a professor MacSween was captain here in the early 1970s. One day he found a set of ram's horns mounted in silver in an antique shop, in Glasgow, I think. There was an inscription, saying it had been the captain's prize to the Dunaverty champion in 1898. The champion in 1898 was Jimmy Lyon.'

I was still smiling. Annie's face tightened. 'Och, no imagination, some people. I'm off. If your Jimmy doesn't turn up to claim his drams, by the way, I'm going to tell Peter you came back to my house and made passionate love to me over a period of days, and that we agreed I could spend the cash on any deserving cause, such as vodka and tomato juice for yours truly.' She grinned again. 'Don't worry. I'll see you sometime, maybe.' And with that she was gone, the little dog waddling in her wake. I noticed that she had extremely good legs, something in these post-feminist times you're not supposed to acknowledge. An easy guilt to absolve yourself from, though.

I mounted the bike, put on my helmet and started the engine. In its raucous throb I could hear Jimmy's Glaswegian tones, and I remembered the pocket watch with the smashed face, the one he'd produced from the pocket of his tweed jacket back in the Royal Hotel in Campbeltown. Supposing he'd teed up a ball on the watch . . . but it was ridiculous. Ghosts didn't use metal woods. Or drink lager.

LOCAL RULES (Revised May 1992)

1 SUNKEN LIES: A ball plugged on the fairway, or lying in a rabbit scrape/ rabbit hole, or scrape, hoofmark, tractor road/tractor run, anywhere on the course, may be dropped immediately behind without penalty.

2 When a ball lies in or touching dung, or if the dung interferes with the player's stroke or stance, the ball may be lifted and dropped immediately behind without penalty. The ball may be cleaned.

3 OUT OF BOUNDS: A ball driven into the Machribeg Field at the 1st c 2nd holes, or into Brunerican Field at the 13th, 14th or over the river at tł 15th hole, or in and over the small ditch at the 17th shall be out of bound No entry is allowed to Machribeg Field. The fence between the car park, tł club house and the course is the boundary fence. A ball played through tł fence on to the car park or surrounds of the club house is out of bounds. A ball in play but close to the fence may be lifted & dropped at the penalty oi one stroke.

4 HAZARDS: The shore is a hazard. (The ball may be played as it lies or dropped at point of entry under penalty of one stroke). The river at the 15th & from the end of the out of bounds at the 17th hole to the sea, is a Water Hazard. If a ball comes to rest on the green side of this fence at the 17th hole, thus preventing a backward movement of the club for the stroke in the direction the Players wishes, it may be lifted to the side - not nearer the hole - without penalty.

5 FENCES ROUND GREENS & TEES: are immovable obstructions. When a ball lies near or under a fence round a green the Player may elect to have the wire held by his fellow competitor to enable him to play tłr shot, or he may use his equipment, or he may take the ball two club lengths away from the fence - not nearer the hole - without penalty. Should a ball strike a fence near a green to which the Player is playing it may be replayed without penalty.

6 OVERHEAD WIRES If a ball strikes any of the overhead wires, or poles supporting them, it may be replayed without penalty.

7 5th HOLE: A ball lying between the river and the tractor track crossing the fairway (but not on the shore) can be lifted and dropped - not nearer the hole - without penalty. A ball lying against the fairway fence may be dropped within one club length without penalty.

NOTICE *Players please ring the bell on leaving the 12th green to indicate to approaching players that it is safe for them to play on.*

Severe Gastric Disruption and its Application in a Golfing Context

Angus MacVicar, author, Southend resident, member and past captain, Dunaverty Golf Club

I'm a Southend native through and through, and I'm very proud of this golf course. It's wonderful. It probably has the finest scenery of any golf course in the west of Scotland. And it's an 18-hole course, in spite of what appears in some guidebooks. That is on account of Machrihanish. Our neighbours are always trying to do us down. There's no bad blood, not at all, we're all very friendly, although this year we have managed to beat them in the annual competition between the clubs. No, I would say this is one of the finest, most scenic courses in the west of Scotland. When you stand there, looking out at the Antrim hills across the North Channel . . . it's wonderful! It raises the spirits, even if you take an 11 at a hole.

It's a low-par course, 64, and I can boast about having shot a 66. I have to admit it's a par 64, though. I started playing golf when I was 11, and I became a member in 1925, when I'd have been 17. The subscription then was only ten shillings, with an entrance fee of five bob as well. Since then, I've seen both the subscription and my handicap go inexorably up, hand in hand. I played off five at one stage. I had a handicap of 18 when I was 65, but now I've hit the top peak – 21. I'm 86 now, and I still play regularly, and though my handicap is probably nearer 32, this is a nice kindly club and it's still officially 21. I play every Wednesday and as many other days of the week as possible. As far as I'm concerned, golf is therapeutic both mentally and physically. I've been writing all my life, hunched over a typewriter, and these days I've got a touch of cervical spondulitis. Over the years it's been a great thing, to get out on to the course with my friends, in the fresh air. You forgot your stress or distress as a working man – and exchanged it for a different kind of stress and distress!

I've always been interested in local history. The first hole is played straight towards the rock of Dunaverty, which was the scene in 1647 of the massacre of the MacDonalds by the Campbells, their ancient enemies. It happened in Glencoe and it happened here too. At that time the Campbells were part of General Lesley's Cromwellian army, the republican army trying to do down the MacDonalds. Just beside the first tee, there's an ancient enclosure which contains the bones of the MacDonalds. It was a massacre. At one time, before the war that would have been part of the course, and in that big bunker on the left-hand side of the eighth fairway, many of the MacDonald bones have been found.

I have had some awful moments on this course. Once, in a monthly medal, I was standing on the 13th tee and across this hollow lay the green. You can reach it with an iron, but to the right of the green were whin bushes; to the left hand were whin bushes too. I hit a shot into the whins on the right, and by the time I'd emerged from those whins and holed out, I'd taken 14. That was a desperate business, and I was feeling in great form, too! But you know my best round? I had a 66, you know! It's stuck in my mind that during that round I had diarrhoea, and that explains the play. I wasn't thinking about my swing, I was just thinking about getting home. It is a very vulgar thing to say but it may have improved my stance.

I always did working hours as a writer, always wrote in a strictly disciplined way. Three hours in the morning, three in the afternoon. In the wintertime, most of my golf was on Saturdays. I'm too old and dim to write now. The success that came with *Salt in My Porridge* . . . but I've written lots more books than that, you know! *Salt in My Porridge* was a labour of love, really, to give a sort of family history and tell how much I owed to good family life. It just happened to take off. But I've written one called *Golf in My Gallusses*, too, you know! You know what gallusses are, of course. Braces! In those days boys had no belts, and we started golfing in our braces. It was all right, though. I always thought it helped to keep our swing under control.

I once had a memorable round of golf with Duncan Watson, who was nicknamed in his later years 'Mr Dunaverty' by visitors. He was club master and professional, and began his professional association with the club in 1924, when he was asked to supply tea and sandwiches for the competing teams in the MacNeil Cup. He was a very old friend of mine and a marvellous golfer. He was injured in the First World War, and he died sadly in 1976. He had a beautiful swing, and on his 75th birthday we went off after work to play a few holes. Anyway, we decided to have a medal round, and take his score. He went round in 75, a 75 on his 75th birthday. I was very proud of him.

How to Win a Camel

Margaret McIntyre, past ladies' captain, daughter of Duncan Watson

My father was associated with the club for over 50 years. By the time he died, aged 79, he and the club were synonymous. He was club steward, a kind of professional, and he had a tea room and golf shop, looked after the clubhouse, gave a few lessons here and there.

There is a very friendly rivalry between us and Machrihanish. We play for the camel, of course. A certain lady presented a camel to the club, and it's played for by Machrihanish and Southend. No, not a real camel. It's in a frame. I have to admit it's seldom seen the sand down here – it's spent most of its years in Machrihanish.

Belle Robertson is our most famous lady member – our most famous member. We're very proud of her, and of the fact that she's always kept Dunaverty as her home club when she could have chosen one of the better-known ones. She was world number one for a time. She plays to a handicap of two, and she's past 50.

The old clubhouse was just a corrugated-iron building, very small, but there was a marvellous atmosphere. We seem to have lost that. It's very nice having all these facilities, but maybe we have lost some of the character, in a way. I've stopped golfing for the moment.

CHAPTER THREE

Loose Impediments

THE Carradale Hotel is a pleasantly manic mixture of wonderful food, owners who really want you to have a good time ('as long as we can have a good time as well') but who won't kow-tow to anyone, a rambling building in the midst of what appears to be continuous upgrading, and comfortable rooms. The whole set in a working fishing village which combines beauty with a kind of visceral, we-don't-need-tourists-really sullenness, epic, neo-Victorian views of Arran's peaks and purpleness just over the water, and, right next door, a nine-hole golf course which is both pretty and pretty tough. Approaching the top of the drooping male organ which is Kintyre, near the Claonaig ferry to Arran, Carradale nestles in the midst of commercial forestry, not quite as isolated as it likes to make out.

Proprietors Marcus and Mo Adam, formerly of London and the grinding world of corporate exhaust-fume-breathing, are by no means the usual flavour of despised home-counties incomer. Marcus is no Basil Fawlty, and yet he has a sense of humour clearly nurtured on Python and its spin-offs. His tongue has a serrated edge, and you're expected to give as good as you get.

'Is that all right?' I asked him at one stage while I was ordering mashed potatoes instead of roast.

'All RIGHT!' He roared. 'All right? God, that really annoys me, people asking if something's all right. This is a hotel, you just say what you want, and if it's not all right, we'll soon tell you. No faffing about. I can't stand that sort of thing.'

It's a family hotel, where you're likely, in a quiet period during May, to find yourself sharing the Adamses' bottle of wine, eating in the lounge, killing bottles of Springbank with the owner and yarning about deep-sea yachting, the hotel's excellent paperback library, and the pleasure of staying somewhere lacking in both pretence and expense. It was, I have to say, a real find, and just a matter of blundering into Carradale on the bike and stopping at the biggest building I could see.

The back road from Campbeltown up the east side of Kintyre is a corkscrewing nightmare of unmaintained tarmac which nevertheless reveals some of the most spectacular views in Scotland. There are some amazing historical sites, only one of which I stopped to examine. The huge carved stone figures at what remains of the Saddel monastery are truly surprising, not least because you get to them by parking in the middle of a small council estate.

'Just wait until they start this ferry service from Campbeltown to Northern Ireland,' said Marcus, on my second night. I couldn't resist seeing what the young Glaswegian chef, Billy Morrow, had cooked up for dinner, after perfect noisettes of lamb the previous evening and superbly crunchy veg. Eaten, incidentally, alone by a log fire in the lounge. The only other guests, two Spaniards called Pedro and Jesus, were out hunting small Sika deer, courtesy of the Forestry Commission. 'That ferry could really increase our business by 100 per cent, if not more.' The locals I met in the pub obviously consider the Adams family somewhat outlandish, but there is also respect, and affection. Possibly because of the installation, in the hotel's public bar, of satellite television, enabling live sports broadcasting to reach anyone in Carradale who cares to imbibe. And they do.

Breakfast was a riot. Mo, much given to giggles, took my order for kippers, and then I could hear much good-humoured shouting from the kitchen. Was there a problem with my kippers?

'Oh no,' laughed Mo. 'Only that you're the only one eating breakfast. The Spaniards have been out shooting since five, and God knows what they'll want, if anything. Yesterday they just ate the sandwiches they'd taken with them, here, still wearing their wellies.'

At this point Marcus emerged to tell me that Pedro and Jesus had been none too successful in their attempts at killing harmless imported Japanese deer, once purely decorative aspects of Victorian country-house living, to be seen wandering delicately on the coiffed lawns.

'First their guns got lost. They were sent to Geneva by mistake, and when security X-rayed the cases, which were of course locked, they found they were fully loaded with a round in the breech. Naturally, every alarm in the airport went off.'

The rifles had turned up eventually, but the Mediterranean languor of Pedro and Jesus, clearly moneyed señors on a spree, had carried off the delay without tension. Since then, a singular lack of success in blowing away any Bambi clones had also been taken well.

I was enjoying my undyed kippers when in they came, Pedro and Jesus, grinning from ear to ear and once more without any blood on their rather grimy hands. Rifles parked on the sofa, their eyes lit up when they saw my kippers.

'Aha,' said Pedro, or words to that effect, 'feeesh!'

He and Jesus eyed my plate longingly. My offer of a morsel so they could taste this classically Scottish delight was seized on immediately, whereupon Mo came in.

'You could have some of your own, you know,' she admonished the duo, one bearded and squat, the other tall, thin and devoid of even the merest smidgin of English. Soon they were up to their eyes in smoked herring, and I had another plateful of the superb fish to compensate for their attentions. Thoroughly kippered, I was ready to shoot some golf.

Thirty seconds scrunching round the gravel drive took me to the Carradale clubhouse, unchanged since the 1930s and a small masterpiece of nostalgia in worn wood and corrugated iron. Inside, there was a tiny room with a low bench running round each of its sides, and securely locked lockers for local members. An honesty box was attached to the wall nearest the door. Six pounds per day. It seemed like a bargain. I picked up a score-card from the pile, dishonestly shoved two one-pound coins into the box and turned to leave, just as the stormy, pearlescent light streaming into the club-house was suddenly extinguished by the arrival of a bulky figure which filled the doorway. 'Aye pal, how's it going?' The voice was Glaswegian, scored and rutted with glottal stops and a smoker's long-term inhalations. The face, wide and pitted with outgrown acne, was adorned with Ray-Ban Aviators, and the big body in what looked like an expensive Italian equivalent of the dreaded Pringle. No nasty patterns, just pastel shades and the look of casual quality. The figure spat on the clubhouse floor. The result looked like some-thing living, as if he'd just expectorated some kind of pulmonary parasite. I swear the brown, streaky phlegm wriggled once after it fell on the worn, stud-scarred wood. 'H'much is it, then?' Light leaked around the Bulk as it moved towards me, light on its feet, which were shod in expensive Dexter golf shoes. 'I just came down from Glasgow, get a wee game, quiet like, y'know? Heard about the place, like. Six quid? Don't have any change, but what the hell . . .' He reached for his wallet, which bulged like an American triple-decker sandwich, flicked out a £10 note and stuffed it into the hon-esty box. 'Fancy a wee game, then? Seein' as you're here, and I'm here, seems daft no' tae . . .' He took off his shades, revealing coal-chip eyes set in an odd criss-cross of fine white flesh. Scar tissue. I looked at his hands, surprisingly small. Sure enough, blue smudges on the knuckles. I could guess what they had once said. 'LOVE' on one hand and 'HATE' on the other. Or possibly 'HATE' on both. I shrugged.

'Sure. What do you play off?'

He smiled, revealing even, modified teeth. 'Och, I'm no sure. A lot. I've just taken this up, sorta to relax, get my mind off work, that sorta thing, you know, like. How about a fiver a hole?' A fiver a hole. God, I usually placed bets only on the Grand National. But why not? I was on holiday, or something. Live dangerously, and what was £45 to lose if the worst came to the worst. This guy was probably an emissary sent to punish me for thinking I could get away with putting two pounds in the honesty box. His tenner had made up the correct amount for both of us, so all I could do was ride with it. Besides, maybe, just maybe, I'd win a few holes. Anything was possible.

We walked out to the first tee, me with my paltry selection of travelling clubs, the Bulk trundling behind a huge leather bag on a battery-powered trolley which gave out a kind of protesting whine. It looked as if he had the entire Titleist range in there.

'Fred's the name, by the way.'

I suddenly didn't want the whole 'oh, Arnold Palmer, that's apt' rigmarole so decided to apportion myself another name. Unfortunately, what I came up with was even worse than Arnold. 'Severin.' Jesus Christ. Where had that come from? He grinned.

'Ah well, Severin. I suppose you could be Sevvy, eh? Sevvy Ballya Stairrods, as we call him, eh? Then I'll be Fred Couples. Love watching the gowff on the box, so I do. Relaxing. That's what I need, see, relaxation. Even went to get hypnotised, like. Hypnotherapy. Tellt me to find my own special place, close my eyes and imagine I'm there, like, the place I was happiest in. So I'm lying there, thinking, and, like, I'm on a golf course. That's the place, I'm a wee boy and I'm on a golf course. Which is pretty weird, 'cause where I was brought up, no way was golf sorta encouraged. But anyway there I am, and I've just hit this perfect shot, just perfect, up and away and hundreds of yards, miles. And when he snaps me out of this trance business, I'm feeling good, quite calm, but thinking, where the hell was that? And finally I think back and it must've been Linn Park, just next to Castlemilk where I was brought up, and suddenly I was right there; livin' it. One time me and Mick McFadyen nicked some clubs off a guy, just sorta took them and ran off. And we went back, oh, weeks later, at night, the light nights, but no one around, like, and got out the balls and began to hit them, just sort of battering them about, like. And one time I just hit it perfect. Christ, it felt so . . . so fuckin' . . .' he shook his head. 'Anyway, now I've got to relax. That's my special place, but no way am I going to Linn, though it's gone upmarket now. Too exposed. Too many . . . anyway, I might join a club, once I'm up to standard. See how I get on. Had a lesson or two, out at the Normandy golf range . . . that all right, a fiver a hole? Makes it interesting, eh?'

The course looked well cared for, at least from the first tee, a rocky, undulating little test of both stamina and skill, reaching out to a headland and the rocky cliffs of this part of Kintyre. In the distance, the Disneyland peaks of Arran reared across the water.

The first hole was called Hazelhill, a 159-yard par three. Gusts of wind came belching towards us from the sea, and the sky was grey enough for Fred not to be wearing his expensive sunglasses. I took out my three iron and hit a reasonable, hooky shot which remained safe in light rough. Fred took three off the tee, also using a three iron, and finally topped the ball 20 feet down the fairway. His first ball had gone an inch, that heavy head whipping up on the moment of impact, huge amounts of nervous energy being piled into a brutal, whippy swing from hell. I offered him a chance to take it again, but he glowered at me. 'No a betting man, eh? This is money, pal. Should be smiling from ear to fuckin' ear.'

So I let him get on with things, until a caber-tossing swing and jerky head let him off the tee at last. 'Good direction, Fred.'

'Calmness, confidence, control,' he replied. He was frowning. His floppy designer haircut, which looked strange on that battered face, was being tangled and tossed by the wind, making him suddenly seem, despite his undoubted hardness and strength, lost and defenceless. 'Calmness, confidence, control. Relax! Fuckin' RELAX!' This was shouted out into the turbulent air like a challenge. The wind took no notice.

I took a five, respectable enough I thought, against that dyspeptic wind. Fred managed a nine, having lost the one ball he hadn't topped, a boomeranging seven iron which vanished into a clump of bushes. As we walked to the second tee, he pulled out a five-pound note and handed it to me. 'One up,' he said. 'I just need to relax, get my swing evened out, no try so hard. At least, that's what they tell me.'

'Keep your head down, Fred, and that's right, just let the weight of the club take the ball onwards.'

He glared at me. 'Money. This is for money. Remember that, my friend. No advice. I need to relax, but I need the edge. And it's honour-bound, pal, honour-bound in the world of wagers. Betting is the true mark of risk, of a man's worth. Mark my words, Sevvy.'

Having as a partner someone who was clearly a million times worse than myself proved an inspiration. I hammered a wonderful, 250-yard drive straight down the second fairway, expecting it to bounce and run on. Instead, it stopped as it hit the ground, with a discernible, sucking *plop!* noise. Fred hit a rather good drive, a bit low, but straight and maybe a 100 yards long. It was, however, his third swing at a ball which seemed superglued to a tee welded to a steel block beneath the Carradale turf.

Fred hit a four wood four feet, then made sufficient contact, desperately mumbling to himself 'calmness, confidence, control' as he physically trembled in the effort to keep his head still, to send a reasonably hard shot low across the grass. It not only refused to bounce, but came to a sudden halt just a few yards on from where my ball had met its arrestment. By this time I had an inkling of what had happened: the fairway was covered with large, soggy cow-pats. Peeking from one of them like the head of a rancid pluke was my ball.

'What are you going to do about that, then, Sevvy?' Fred was not laughing. It was a game about money, and my decision would have to be serious and correct. Cowshit on a golf course was a first for me. What was the right club to play? Maybe in certain places they had developed a shit wedge for such situations. What would such a club look like? The prospect of playing the ball from its odiferous, slimy, green lie was unpleasant. Lumps of cow-pat would undoubtedly go everywhere, and some would adhere to me.

'I think you're in the same boat, Fred.' I peered ahead, then walked the ten yards or so to where the Bulk's ball had landed. There was a crater in a cow-pat, but no sign of the ball.

'Oh no,' said Fred, 'lost ball. I'll just play another. But you'll have to go for yours. That's golf, innit? Play it wherever it lies. You got to do it, man.' I looked for a spark of humour in his anthracite eyes. There was none. He had decided to sacrifice the money for vindictiveness. I wondered what it was Fred did that he had to relax from so badly, but it seemed risky to ask. I took out the score-card in search of the relief it was clear Fred was determined not to give me. Suddenly, I felt vaguely afraid. The list of local rules stretched through out of bounds, water hazards, immovable obstructions and, oh, blessed, blessed 'relief from tractor marks, hoof marks and dung'. Dung, it appeared, was not classified as a natural hazard. Balls could be removed from dung without penalty, or moved if your stance involved over-proximity to ordure. It was the first time I had ever seen shit made an explicit part of the glorious game in anything but a metaphorical sense.

Fred was not noticeably impressed with the written evidence of my salvation from excremental suffering. He shrugged his shoulders and turned away as I scooped my ball out of the cow-pat with my wedge, then gingerly wiped both ball and club with some grass. The smell wasn't as bad as I'd expected, and I found stray thoughts rampaging through my brain, effortlessly associating themselves forever with this moment, with this act, this pile of shite. The thoughts were all associated with Belinda. When I at last had a ball capable of some aerodynamic integrity, I swung and hit a five iron with venom and violence and a head which jerked up before the club head hit the ball. By some fluke, I topped the ball so much that it spun backwards an inch. Fred's quarried face crumbled into a grin, revealing those improbable teeth once more. 'One step forward, eh? Two back and all that. Springsteen song. I'm a big Springsteen fan.'

'One step up, actually.' He looked puzzled. 'It's "One Step *up*, Two Steps Back", from the *Human Touch* LP. Or maybe it's *Lucky Town*, it's all one anyway. Should have been a double album. Not "One Step Forward", anyway. Big Bruce. Him and Alex Harvey, only two pop singers worth listening to.'

He turned away, shutting me off with that basilisk concentration, dropped his new ball, and hit, by some wild fluke, a smooth seven iron which landed about two feet from the pin. I took a further four to get down, which meant I won the hole by one stroke, and from that point on Fred became, if not relaxed, at least less threatening. Perhaps he had simply decided not to kill me.

By the time we got to the seventh hole, Port Righ, I had won five and we had halved one. I was £25 richer than I had been before we had set out, but Fred's humour seemed to be growing with every fluffed shot. And he was bad, so much worse than me it was embarrassing, but terribly conducive to confidence on my part. Having said that, our scores were not exactly a mile apart, except for that amazing nine of his at the first. As we clambered up to the raised tee at the seventh, Fred clapped me on the back and muttered. 'Ach, I tell you, I'm actually feeling relaxed all of a sudden. Just that one good shot, that seven iron way back at the second, it was like a kind of, I don't know, trigger or something. Calmness, confidence, control, like. Playing better, too, eh?' I nodded. Then decided to chance a question.

'So, Fred, listen, what sort of line are you in?'

He looked straight at me, and said, 'Och, just business. I've got various interests, know what I mean?' I thought I probably did. He didn't seem inclined to expand on what his 'various interests' were.

The seventh at Carradale is a really vicious little hole, an excruciatingly difficult but rather lovely par three of 164 yards, with a rocky cliff shore on the left and some suburban-looking bungalows to the right. The green lies right on the edge of the bay, which is presumably called Port Righ. I took a nine, and lost two balls. Fred lost three balls and had a 12. It was at this point that we both decided we'd had enough, something expressed initially by mutual shrugging and club abuse.

'Cramp,' I said at length.

'Och well,' replied Fred.

That was that. We walked back to the clubhouse, me with a pocket bulging due to a sudden influx of £5 notes, and Fred looking, well, relaxed. 'Self-hypnosis,' he said as we walked along, his electric trolley whining merrily in front of him. 'Or auto-hypnosis. Costs me £70 a session to learn, and my God, I think this is the first time it's worked. And that good shot there at the second, that seven iron . . .' He shook his head, smiled. 'Brilliant. That's the moment, intit? Special. Bloody special. Like back then at Linn. Ever been there?' I assured him that I had, way back. Way, way back.

I treated Fred to lunch at the hotel, thinking it was the least I could do, having relieved him of £30. There was a bottle-green Ford

Escort Cosworth in the carpark, its impossibly low front lower air-dam smashed and twisted. 'Came over from Arran,' volunteered Fred. 'Ferry from Ardrossan, then Lochranza to Claonaig. Steep wee ramp at this side, the Claonaig side; gave the Cozzie a bit of a bang. Still. Fixable. Ultimate car, that thing, you know. Best always to buy the ultimate car from some big company, cause they know what they're at, don't they?' Bloody hell. I hadn't realised you could hop across Arran to Kintyre. If I'd known, I could have avoided that long trip up Loch Lomondside and over and down. But then, I've always hated Arran with its weird combination of retired colonels and post-hippy torpor. Not to mention its theme-park compactness and feeling of being rather overly picturesque for its own good.

Over a succession of mineral waters for us both, home-made, excellent Scotch broth and fresh salmon rolls with tossed salad, I probed. I did not divulge my own business, even when Fred began to describe, lovingly, his own boy-toy sound system: 'Oh aye, I've got a programmable CD, remote control, one in the bedroom, one down in the lounge, and a sorta portable thing in the kitchen. Hefty. Loadsa bass. I got something hefty installed in the Cozzie too. Want to hear it? I've got that Springsteen CD wi' me.' I assured him that I didn't. Ferocious, bass-heavy car stereo systems are all right when travelling fast over a road surface with a bass frequency which needs disguising; but static in a carpark with the engine switched off is bad for the chest cavity. Besides, this daft notion of big-bass-equals-good-hi-fi . . . it's crap. What you're trying to do is get the information off the record or the tape or the CD as accurately as you can, or at least pleasantly. Which means, as far as Pitch is concerned, a bit of jiggery-pokery to smooth out the digital jaggy bits you get from CDs. But whacking great skull-crazing bass is only right for reggae and certain kinds of Techno. Anyway, I didn't want to try and explain all this to Fred, so I declined his invitation.

Apart from the number and size of his gadgets, I got very little out of Fred. He was married, had two sons, both at Kelvinside Academy, he informed me proudly. Lived in Bishopbriggs. And that was it. 'I'm just going to get a bit of experience at the golf, get it up to pace a bit, before I face my mates at their clubs, bloody posh clubs, buy your way in no bother, but you don't want to make a fool of yourself. Calmness, confidence and control is all very well, I mean, but . . . you know.' Why didn't he get some more lessons, I wanted to know. 'Ach well, you know . . . I think you can get on better just sort of learning, on your own, like. Picking up a few hints along the way.' He had, he said, played once or twice in Arran before hopping on the ferry to Carradale. He'd thought of

71

Machrihanish, had heard it was a great course, but maybe he wasn't quite ready . . . 'Besides, I have to get back. I'll catch the last ferry the night from Brodick if I don't smash the Cozzie's front end coming back from Arran.'

My imagination was running riot. He was a drug dealer, heading back to mastermind some major importation of cocaine . . . maybe that was his reason for being in Kintyre, a search for suitable landing points. Weren't the customs and excise always patrolling this neck of the woods, stopping and searching yachts? Parcels of marijuana were always floating ashore, weren't they? Or was it bank robbery, pimping, car theft? At last Fred got up to go, the Bulk at last on the move. 'I'll pay,' he said. 'Let you treasure your winnings, eh?' I insisted, though, getting Marcus to add our lunches to my room bill. 'Listen, when you're back in Glasgow, if you ever need any . . . you know. Just give us a call. Maybe we can shoot a few holes as well. I found this morning really sorta relaxing, you know? That shot made it for me.' And he handed me a business card. I sat in the lounge bar, sipping my mineral water as the Escort Cosworth's throaty roar echoed faintly in from outside. On the card was written VICTOR FREDERICKS LTD, FUNERAL DIRECTORS, UNDERTAKERS AND EMBALMERS. I decided to risk a sweet, and immersed myself in bread-and-butter pudding, followed by coffee, and, I couldn't resist it, a large Springbank. I was, after all, in Kintyre, home of that wondrous dram. It was only then that I looked at the business card again, and realised that Victor was the name of Belinda's boyfriend, and that he was an undertaker, too.

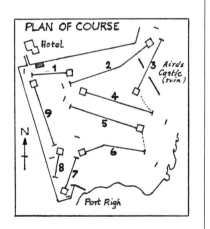

LOCAL RULES

OUT OF BOUNDS (Rule 27)
The Clubhouse enclosure; over any wall or fence to the left of the 1st, 2nd, 3rd, 8th and 9th holes; the sea at the 6th hole; over fences to the left of, right of and behind the 7th green.

WATER HAZARDS (Rule 26)
6th hole: Any ditches marked with yellow stakes are water hazards; any ditches marked with red stakes are lateral water hazards. A free lift and drop may be taken from open drains not marked with stakes.

IMMOVABLE OBSTRUCTIONS (Rule 24-2)
Shelters; the marker posts in the rough at the 2nd and 6th holes; electricity poles; made-up paths leading to the 2nd green, 4th and 6th tees and from the 7th tee; any posts and wires surrounding any green.
When a ball lies close to or under a fence-wire round a green the player may elect to have the wire held to enable the stroke to be played.
A ball striking a post or wire round a green while in forward motion towards the flag may be replayed without penalty.
A ball striking an electricity pole or wire at the 1st hole may be replayed without penalty.
The wall crossing the 2nd and 3rd holes is an integral part of the course. A ball lying close to the wall must be played as it lies or declared unplayable (Rule 28).

RELIEF FROM TRACTOR MARKS, HOOF MARKS AND DUNG
A ball lying in an animal hoof mark or tractor mark or rut may be lifted and dropped immediately behind without penalty.
If a ball lies in or is touching dung, or if dung interferes with a player's stroke or stance, the ball may be lifted and dropped immediately behind without penalty. The ball may be cleaned.

It Just Bounces Off

Robert Strang, greenkeeper, Carradale Golf Club

We get an odd one misusing the honesty box, rarely, but right enough, we usually get them. What you're supposed to do is put your money in the box, fill up a pink slip and then just go and play.

It's quite a hilly wee course, but it's not too bad to look after; I find it quite easy, just keeping the grass down, and drains clear, and keeping the gorse, the whins in check. We've got some rabbits that can scrape the greens, but that's not too bad. The cattle go on the course, right enough, but they're no real problem. The greens are fenced off when the cows are on, and bits of the fairways, so it's not that great a problem. I remove the dung for my vegetable patch. These are the things you've got to face. The cattle weren't on at all this year, or hardly. And if someone hits one with a ball, it just bounces off.

Moderators, Goats, Cowshit and Robert the Bruce

Colin Oman, vice-captain, Carradale Golf Club, 1994

It's a bit unclear, really, how the club began. It was a family called Holmes, very wealthy people, used to come down here for three months each summer. They started playing, mowed wee bits of green and just began playing golf – but when it actually became a club is a wee bit unclear, lost in the mists of history. Nowadays we have members from all over Britain; they come from Devon, Cornwall, London, the Wirral. I think there's about 300 at the moment. People come from the cities of Scotland, as quite a lot of folk have caravans or houses in the area. Many of them have given up their memberships in the big cities and become members here, because it's very cheap golf.

The club is very much part of the local community, and it's

anything but élite. Most of the members are very ordinary folk. Fishermen and their families . . . they all play golf. The annual dinner and prize-giving is very difficult to get a ticket for. It would be terrible for Carradale if anything was ever to happen to the golf course.

The insignia of the club is the Crubhan Buoy, which you can see from the higher parts of the course. Out to the right of the course is a point called Goat Island. There are wild goats out there, and the story is that these goats arrived here with the Spanish Armada. From the second tee you can look over to Arran, to Blackwaterfoot, and down at Port Righ, that little bay, there's the cave that Robert the Bruce was supposed to have hidden in. And I've got the stone that Robert the Bruce is supposed to have stepped on, next to my front door.

Cattle are allowed to graze on the course in the winter, as the club does not actually own the ground. So we have preferred lies anywhere on the fairway. But if you land in a cow-pat, you're in big trouble. I would think you couldn't even clean your ball, you'd have to play another, because it would be quite messy. But it has never happened to me. We've had a fox on the course, which has been killing a few lambs recently. We've been having a few shots at him, but he seems to be quite a cunning fox. Not with a golf ball, but with a shotgun, I think. We had a wee dog here for a while who was coming on and stealing balls. It was quite funny, really.

I used to play this course with Jimmy Simpson years ago. He was off one or two in those days. Now he's the minister of Dornoch Cathedral and the Moderator of the Kirk. He's coming here in July and I'm looking forward to a wee game. I think he's playing off five or six now.

CHAPTER FOUR

Movable Obstruction May Be Removed

'HELLO . . . Belinda? Yeah, that's right, it's me. Listen, I'm taking a few weeks' break, just to . . . oh, you got the postcards, right, right . . . and the kids are fine? Oh really, good, good . . . what? Taking them to . . . oh, is he? Well, actually, it's partly because of Victor I'm phoning, because you'll never believe this . . . incidentally, he runs his own company, doesn't he? In Shawlands? Yeah, thought so. Well, the thing is, we met up, old Vic and I. Had a little talk. Not really your type, darling Bel, I wouldn't have thought. Bit of rough with a

Rolex, eh, dear? Discuss literature together, do you? The thing is, he didn't know who I was. Didn't know I was your ex, father to Patti and Paul, etcetera, etcetera. See? That's what happens when you remove all photographic evidence of my existence . . . so, yes, we had a chat. A nice wee chat, lunch in fact. Ask him about Sevvy in Carradale, and tell him he's crap at golf. Married, eh? That's a new one for you, my dear, sleeping with a married man. Apart from me, that is, but then . . . yeah, married with two kids, both at Kelvinside Academy. You must be his bit on the side, although how he manages to fit in taking out Patti and Paul I do not know, as well as his other two, that is . . . what? Oh really? When did you find out? So you just gave him his marching . . . yes, yes, of course. Well, that's what I was going to say, it's not on, him sort of *in loco parentis* . . . oh, you agree? So he's off licking his wounds, then, is he, off trying to settle down with just the one family? I see . . . So you're footloose and fancy free, then? You've what? Oh, come on, Belinda, we can . . . you bitch. What do you think the Child Bloody Support Agency can . . . you've got the bloody house, haven't you, what the . . . oh right, lost your fancy, Escort Cosworth, rich-man, two-timing, would-be-bigamist bastard . . . oh was he? Yeah, well I've had no complaints from . . . I'll fight you for those kids, you piece of used, white-trash scum. I'll hire the best lawyers in the land to get them off you, you and your . . . don't hang up, you . . . DON'T HANG . . . '

The telephone receiver in Oban's ferry terminal felt hot, was hot. I banged it down on the brushed-steel, vandal-and-ire-proof box which dully reflected some strange, alien form; not me. Couldn't be me, shit-hot hi-fi entrepreneur, salesman, confident, on-the-up-and-up me. That bastard Victor. Married, and not just screwing Belinda, playing happy bloody families with her and my kids. Lying. Everybody was lying. Now she was going to go the whole hog, and screw me for every penny she could get out of my not infinitely elastic coffers. Screw. Fuck. Why do we use those words to mean damage, destroy, diminish? She hadn't mentioned the company, getting her claws on some of that action, but that would come. It was inevitable. And then dumped old Vic, what does he do? Runs off in his penile-extension motor car to play golf and forget, satisfy himself with his invisible family number one up in Bishopbriggs. Bastard. He was just doing the same as me. In more comfort. Glad he smashed his spoiler though. Fred Couples, indeed. Sevvy. Arnold . . .

A Tannoy blared. I'd checked in an hour previously for the 3.30 p.m. run to Lochboisdale, South Uist, a trip which was scheduled to take an unbelievable nine hours. It was drizzling, had done all the way from Carradale, leaving me soaked and squelching in my leathers, like a chamois windscreen cloth. I'd stopped in Lochgilphead for sweets, something to replenish the blood-sugar the rain seemed to have sucked out, despite my wonderfully kippered farewell breakfast at the Carradale Hotel. In the shop a young man, stocky in a dark suit, smart but implacable, was speaking in clear, loud tones to a woman behind the counter. 'I've checked,' he was saying. 'You owe £1,350 . . .' He held a clipboard like a shield, only it was somehow threatening, too.

The woman, flustered, English and angry, insisted she had paid. 'I sent a cheque for £1,000 just . . . why are you doing this, this is disgraceful, embarrassing me here, in front of customers . . . ' He looked her in the eye, coolly, and said, without a hint of regret, 'I'm sorry.'

'So you should be. Now come back into the store and we'll sort this out.'

I paid a younger assistant for my Extra-strong mints and left. There were still traces of the ultra-rare Longrow malt I'd consumed with Marcus Adams the previous night, after another excellent dinner, the exact details of which . . . ah yes, pork had featured. Pork and plums . . . and an excellent cheeseboard. No, not pork, port, a wonderful vintage Sandemans . . . the main course had been chicken stuffed with . . . cheese, or something. I searched the crevices of my fillings for any unbrushed clues, but could find nothing but the taste of kippers and Euthymol.

The raw landscape between Lochgilphead and Oban, with its scrawny, native pines, commercial woodlands, scabby hills and all-pervading mist and rain, induced a kind of trance as the old Z650's Marshall four-into-one exhaust maintained a solid, staccato rumble, not even hinting at failure. Only a continually misting visor caused me problems, eventually leading to an abandonment of eye protection completely as I neared Oban. When I took my helmet off at the Caledonian Macbrayne terminal, I must have looked like someone who had just read *The Bridges of Madison County* while watching *Love Story* on video, peeling onions at the same time. With a blunt knife. I hadn't been in Oban since I was a kid. The coliseum crown of McCaig's Folly looked like a fool's cap, high on the cliff overshadowing the town. There was a real buzz about the place, and yet its wool-shop-larded main drag and rather down-at-heel flavour sat uneasily with the jammed traffic, busy harbour and endless clatter of parading tourists. The Gateway to the Isles.

'The vessel now alongside is the 1300 hours sailing to Mull . . . to Colonsay . . . to Tiree . . .' The announcements carried with them

immense, heady promise. Those Hebridean names, the ships, of
varying size and shape, sliding busily in and out of the harbour, to
be loaded with cars, lorries, braying cattle, mewing sheep, mooing
tour parties of pensioners. I spotted a restored 1950s bus, complete
with those little paper-shaded lamps on the reading tables, and its
load of white-haired, north-of-England city-dwellers, blinking in the
strong, big, watery light, their flat vowel sounds clattering on the
pier among the tunes of Gaeldom in native voices heading back to
the islands. Gaelic. Later night and mid-morning television programmes always seem to feature a load of women sitting round a
table battering a large lump of tweed up and down while singing
some unearthly, Arabic song. Or there was that one with the guitar-
playing children's entertainer who wore strange hats. And then, the
lovely Karen Cheekbones Matheson, singer with the divine
Capercaillie, although I'd heard that none of them could actually
speak the language fluently. We used Capercaillie on some of our
amplifier demonstrations, as Karen's voice was guaranteed to
impress at high volume, and could be turned nasty and gritty by the
wrong equipment. Not ours. Runrig I had actually been to see once,
at Edinburgh Castle Esplanade, and been thrilled by, bowled over by
that huge rush of sentimental '70s Gaelic rock in such a context.
Their records bore listening to once or twice a year, say at
Hogmanay, or on a Walkman when you were far from home. I
could imagine that expatriate Scots in Canada or Australia were
reduced to quivering mush by the merest throb of Runrig. Anyway, I
was heading into the heartland, a place where Gaelic was still actually spoken, was on the road signs, for God's sake. All I knew was
that a golf course existed in South Uist, at a place called Askernish.
It was in the tourist guide I'd picked up in Campbeltown. A little
flag next to Lochboisdale, and the word 'golf', also, rather coyly, in
Gaelic as 'goilf'.

At last, it was 2.30, and I sauntered over to the blue bomber, a
damn fine looking motorcycle, I thought, even with its odd load of
golf clubs and rucksack. A golfing biker? One of the elderly tourists
from the vintage bus wandered over and gave the Kawa a measured
stare. 'Norton, Triumph, Velocette, Sunbeam, BSA, Vincent. Bloody
right motorcycles, them bikes. This is what bloody buried them, this
Jap filth.' I grunted, and tried to ignore him. I didn't like to say that
it was abysmal, blinkered engineering standards and poor quality
control that put the British motorcycle industry out of business,
although I had to admit that those names had a tremendous romantic ring to them. Vincent Black Shadow, Black Lightning, Triumph
Bonneville, BSA Gold Flash. And the Brough Superior, which killed

78

Lawrence of Arabia, or, some said, was used to kill him by a British government afraid of his links with fascism. The old Britbike freak wandered away, muttering.

Gingerly, I took the Kawa down the loading ramp of the *Lord of the Isles*, to where two seamen in boiler suits waited to rope her to a stanchion. Was that really necessary, I queried, querulously? Suddenly, I realised I was going to sea. They looked at me solemnly. 'Well, it could well be. It could well be,' said one, in the sing-song tones of the islander. 'But on the other hand, it looks like a fairly calm crossing. Then again . . . ' he shook his head and gave that inimitably Gaelic intake of breath which may or may not indicate assent or disagreement or, in truth, virtually anything. We had a research engineer at Pitch who had been brought up in Stornoway, put through the nuclear-weapons training programme at Faslane, part-trained in America, and he still had the same trick. It drove me mad.

Upstairs, there was a poky bar, which was already smoke-filled and creaking with discussion in Gaelic and Hebridean English, and a café, where Gore-Texed backpackers and other tourists, including my snow-haired bussists, were gathering, ready for some tea. I shed my now digustingly clammy leather breeks in one of the toilets, revealing the almost-decent Umbro tracksuit leggings underneath, and settled myself into one of the reclining seats, stuck on the Walkman Pro and tried to ignore a frazzled, jerky TV picture as the Blue Nile's epic 'Tinseltown in the Rain' lit up my head with space, neon, darkness and city sparkle. Next thing I knew, the tape had run out and I was uncomfortably hungry. I'd grabbed some wallpaper paste sandwiches in Oban, but now it was, according to my watch, getting on for 5.30 p.m. The boat was about as steady as the average high-speed train, but a lot cleaner, and I was consumed with hunger.

The cafeteria offered standard fried'n'frazzled fare, out of which I picked haddock and chips as being the most appealing option. It was, I have to say, awful, but calmed the gnawing ache in my stomach. Outside, the sea was a dull aluminium, thick misty rain settling finely on the windows. A day of murk. I took out of my pocket a battered copy of an old, favourite book, picked up in Paddy's Market, simultaneously one of the great sights of Glasgow and its daily shame. This is where the literally penniless come to spread their meagre, pathetic possessions out on a sheet: a pair of shoe brushes, a teapot, a cigarette case, some knives and forks . . . in search of enough cash for maybe two tins of Carlsberg Special or some strong South African wine. But it is also where professional and semi-professional traders sell old clothes, books, and, indeed, almost everything you can think of, legal and illegal. It is becoming commer-cialised, inevitably, but is nothing like the tawdry pseudo-cultural par-ody performance that the Barras, its big-time weekend equivalent, has become. Anyway, it was at Paddy's I found *Scottish Life and Humour*, by W. Sinclair, published by Sinclair and Co., Haddington, in about 1880, a collection of rheumy old tales which, nevertheless, occasion-ally amused. On this long Scottish sea voyage, the archaic humour and language seemed strangely apt. I headed for the bar, ordered a large Talisker – that peppery, slightly unmade Hebridean malt, and settled down to browse through, or at least dip into, old W. Sinclair's creaky sense of humour. In the chapter entitled 'Fun' he goes on at length concerning golf, but his stories are hardly side-splitting today:

> In addition to monopolising the links and hitting people with balls, golfers have been blamed for using very strong language when they got into difficulties. This was very unfortunate for ministers, elders, and such like models whom the public should copy. The case is his-toric of the minister who said he would have to give it up. 'What, give up golf?' 'No, the MEENISTRY!' It was probably a member of his congregation who could not be an elder because he 'whiles sellt a horse'. History says nothing of his selling a man . . .

I found something oddly reassuring in this bizarre prose, this writ-ing without noticeable modern reference points. It was like science-fiction, or some strange, lost document from an alien culture. But Sinclair, writing probably in the 1850s, was in touch with some legends and practices now long forgotten. Such as, in his section 'Auld Farrant Customs', another, weirdly primitive reference to golf:

> On the summit of Benarty, in Fifeshire, there were formerly held games in which the Fifeshire herdsmen and those of the neighbouring counties were the performers. These came to the place of meeting accompanied by their wives, daughters and sweethearts; and there being no lack of provisions, the fete was kept up for a few days, the revellers bivouacking during the night. Their chief games were the golf, the football and the Wads – a pledge or hostage. They had a lively time while it lasted . . .

It reads like a translation from a runic inscription on a Pictish stone. Wads? Pledges and hostages? What was that, some kind of sexual, tribal game? And there was golf, some form of rough, hill golf, no doubt, a hacking, hurling, hockey type of game, possibly involving running and hard, physical contact, bleeding shins and heads. Half-shinty, in fact, that bloodthirsty Gaelic warfare disguised as a team sport. I leafed back through the book, searching for one of my favourite passages, as the Talisker began to take hold and a warm comfort spread through my body. 'Dafties and Gangrels' the chapter was called, written about the time Scotland's lunatics were being moved from the street corner and the protected family hearth-side into new institutions. The words of a present-day doctor in the Comores, a newly independent island state in the Indian Ocean, flashed back at me from some Sunday-supplement travel piece: 'Here we do not have psychiatric problems; we have evil spirits.' Some of Sinclair's folk were just one step away from that cultural outlook.

A curious character, 'Daft Willie Smith of Dornoch' used to haunt Crieff. He was a stickit minister whose head was supposed to have been turned by Greek. He used to wear a strip of tin, about half an inch broad, folded tightly across his nose, curled up at both ends like ram's horns. This was to prevent his nose from seeking snuff. His head was encased in a small net . . . in his hand he carried a cudgel, and in his eyes a dangerous gleam. Jenny Garrow described him as 'a wild creater yon – a real ettercap o' a bodie. He flees whyles on folk like an evil speerit'.

But the story which appeals to me most carries the inexorable logic of insanity, and yet – perhaps because of that – rings a bell in my own experience. 'The wisdom of fools is entitled to be proverbial. An inmate of an asylum was visited by a relative, who asked if the clock in the room was right. "If it had been a'richt dae ye think it wad been here?" was the unexpected reply.'

I was giggling over this surreal story when a cough above me broke into my politically incorrect amusement. 'Is this anyone's seat?' The voice was American, southern, maybe Arkansas, or that might have been the Clintonisation process my perception of the United States had undergone since the man who single-handedly put Grecian 2000 out of business, not to mention his unexpectedly attractive, not to say shaggable wife had taken over as first couple. (I know, a hopelessly regressive description of Hilary that, but let's face it, that is how we men judge members of the opposite sex we can know only through the visual media of television or cinema. Long ago my friend Leonard and I had evolved the simple three-level code for women: DS, DU and PSIP. All right, all right: Definitely Shaggable, Definitely Unshaggable, and Possibly Shaggable if Pissed. In real life, of course, with real women, we were reduced to mumbling embarrassment, drunken flirting and bee-to-a-honeypot sexual slavery – and slavering.) The owner of the American voice above me left me open-mouthed and gasping, but only for a second.

'No, no, of course not. Please . . . please sit down.'

She was around 30, tall, dressed from one of those US outdoor-type shops like LL Bean or Banana Republic, in kind of upmarket khaki fatigues, though with a brilliant turquoise mohair sweater peeping through from under the jacket. Thick, peanut-butter-coloured hair was tied back in a short pony-tail, and strong eyebrows marked out a high-cheekboned, humorous face. She looked like Hilary Clinton's tougher, younger sister on assignment for *Newsweek*. She was carrying a bottle of Becks.

'Phew, that's better!' She set the Becks down on the tiny, screwed-to-the-floor table and sat back, flexing her long back. 'Had a sleep in one of those what do you call them, couchettes, and Great God Almighty, my back can't take that sorta thing anymore. What's that you're drinking? Scotch?'

I nodded. The directness of Americans always astonishes me. Sipping the Talisker, I looked into the grey eyes with dozens of fine, leaf-like wrinkles around them. Maybe she was older than 30 after all. 'On holiday? Sorry, maybe that should be vacation?' She shook her head in a sort of half-nod, half-disagreement.

'Sorta. Back to the land of my forefathers kind of thing, family business to attend to. You? Biker? what is it, a Harley?'

I explained that I was trying to combine motorcycling with golf, in an eccentric attempt at escaping work and the world for a while, out on the edge of Scotland. 'Ah, yeah.' She looked thoughtful. 'Askernish, yeah, that's a Tom Morris course. Put together, oh, 1891 I think. You know, "Old Tom" Morris, one of the greatest golf-course designers of all time?' I must have looked baffled, because she laughed, put her hand on my knee and said. 'Hey, shape up, guy, this is the 1990s, and women play golf too! Not to mention have fathers who're obsessive golf nuts, know the history backwards. You know about Tom Morris?'

I admitted that I'd heard the name, but little else. 'Didn't he design St Andrews?'

'No, he didn't. Christ boy, where you been? St Andrews was used for golf long before Old Tom came on the scene in the, let's see now, 1850s or so. But he was the first professional at St Andrews and he did sort out one or two of the holes. He did design courses, though, all over the place. Like even in the States, he laid out the Westward Ho! club in 1864. You ever heard of Tom Bendelow? He was another Scot crossed the Pond to build golf courses, about 600 of them. They said the only qualification he had for it was his Scottish accent. Mind you,' she glugged a fair proportion of the Becks, and grimaced. 'Jesus, I could do with some Rolling Rock or Miller Lite. Anyway, most of golf-course design is just tees and greens. A good set of sand dunes'll design its own links.'

She was called Sharon Sharp, and her father, it emerged, Donald Sharp, had been a successful architect in North Carolina (hence the accent) with an addiction to both golf and being a professional Scotsman. 'He's lately passed on, though. Always loved the Uists, where his great-grandpop came from he kept telling us, me and my brother Kevin. Kev's got three kids and sells computer software out of Michigan, and that's why it fell to me to come over here to square things away, set things to rest.' She smiled. 'Get you a drink?'

By the time we had both decided we wanted to have sex with each other, and were drunk enough to admit the fact – the wagon I'd intended being on having long ago passed me by and left me lying spreadeagled beside my sprackled good intentions – it was drizzle-blue-half-dark, 8.30 p.m. and we were pullng into Castlebay, Barra. Sharon removed my hand from her thigh, and said, somewhat incoherently, that she wanted to go on deck to watch Barra approaching. Well, I'd certainly decided I wanted to have sex with her, but for a man that's hardly a difficult conclusion to reach when you've been sitting next to an attractive woman and getting slowly plastered. I was too old, though, to become demanding and insistent: if she wasn't into it, fine. If not, I could always stand on deck and think of great Partick Thistle sides of the 1950s. I pondered the possibility of renting a cabin for the two-hour crossing to Lochboisdale, but somehow it seemed so . . . premeditated, and slightly sordid: the leering dangle of the keys, the raised eyebrow, the guess-what-if-you-fancy-a-bit-of-privacy . . . no. We wandered outside into the wetness in time for the spectacular sight of Kismul's Castle, floodlit, appearing on the right . . . the starboard bow, I supposed. Then, through the gloom, the ring of hotels and houses which was Castlebay. Sharon squeezed against me, and I put one leather-jacketed arm around her, hoping no Barra dwellers would steal my leather jeans, stowed, with my rucksack, in the luggage racks next to the cafeteria.

'Whisky Galore,' she said, and for a moment I thought she was recollecting the large Taliskers she'd started knocking back with her Becks. Then I looked again, and we were in the same movie. Castlebay was where they filmed the famous Ealing comedy, even though the real SS Politician, with its cargo of whisky, was wrecked nearer Eriskay. So many liberties with the truth: a Catholic island, where the Sabbath would have no impact to speak of, and yet Sabbatarianism was a crucial plot-trigger in the movie; and the cheeriness of the whole filmed escapade, when in actual fact men had spent time in jail and disgrace over their part in the removal of whisky from the wrecked boat. Still, it was a wonderful film, and as the village, its lights soft-focussed through the rain and fog, drew closer, it was like sailing into a fantasy. Whereupon Sharon was sick. Not, thank God, over me. Oh, romance!

I helped her back inside as cars and lorries rumbled off the *Lord of the Isles*. She apologised profusely, if in somewhat fragmented form, as we sat in the now-closed bar, with a few drunk or sleeping lorry drivers slumped in various corners. 'Jesus, that Becks . . . I'm so, so sorry, that was just so . . . gross.' She shook her head. I wondered about the cabin that I'd considered hiring for a drunken binge of passion. I felt slightly woozy, but not bad considering the large quantity of Talisker I'd consumed. Maybe it would be better if we both lay down for the couple of hours it would take to reach Lochboisdale. The purser was sympathetic, and within a few minutes I was leading Sharon to a cramped two-berth cabin. She was profusely grateful, and smiled weakly at me as she shut the door in my face, just as I was preparing to enter. I stared at the closed door for a few seconds, and then trudged back to the bar. When we finally docked at Lochboisdale, just after 10.30, Sharon didn't appear. The boat would be spending the night in Uist, so before I went down to the car deck to untie my bike I asked the purser to check if she was all right. He knocked at the door of the cabin. There was no reply. Opening it with his pass key, he peered inside with some obvious trepidation. So did I. It was empty.

The tiny tourist office at Lochboisdale was open, and a friendly woman there found me a bed-and-breakfast 'near the golf, oh yes, just walking distance. Well, nearly.' The clear directions and map she gave me couldn't prevent a half-hour of helpless wandering around the township of Kilphedder, passing the welcoming lights of the Borrodale Hotel at least four times, and watching crofthouse curtains flick open as suspicious eyes peered out at this intruding hell's angel searching for Gaelic maidens to deflower . . . at last, Mrs Davidson's guest-house, Tigh Beag (pronounced Shi Vaik, the tourist lady had told me: 'It means a wee one, as in a dram'), appeared out of the gloom, clearly marked with a large sign which I had failed to notice on my four previous runs past it. It was clean, comfortable, large and modern; I was dangerously drunk, the first time I'd ridden the Kawa pissed, so I was glad to tumble off the blue bastard without injury. Mrs Davidson didn't seem to notice, was brusquely welcoming, and within a minute or so of falling, leatherless on the bed, I was fast asleep.

I awoke to the smell of frying bacon and blazing sunlight; there was no choice about breakfast, and heaven help those of the Jewish or Islamic persuasion. Porridge or cornflakes, bacon, sausages, eggs, fried bread, tomatoes, bannocks, butter, tea, toast, marmalade. A mild hangover (brain cortex reduced to a tingling jelly, but not so shrunken it was bouncing about my skull like a pinball) had taken a severe battering by the time I'd finished, and, pleasantly stuffed, I asked Mrs Davidson about the golf course. Was it necessary to book a tee time? She looked at me strangely, then began to laugh.

'Ach, no teas at Askernish. No, not even running water, if that clubhouse is anything to go by. All rack and ruin it is, fallen into disrepair. I don't know if there is even a club still, but you don't have to worry about even paying. Just walk on. There's no one there but the sheep. Would you like some more toast?' Bloated though I was, I accepted, as Mrs Davidson listened to some incomprehensible Gaelic radio programme in which English words like 'television' and 'viewfinder' kept popping up in the midst of the guttural Celtic flow. Suddenly, she turned to me. 'Yes, yes, I remember now. The man at the bank, he was very keen on the golf, and took to do with the course, made sure it was looked after. He lived out there next to the course. And, of course, Canon MacQueen, you'll have heard of Canon MacQueen? He's at Barra, now. He was very keen on it, too. But now, I don't think many take to do with it.'

An edgy wind from the west couldn't spoil a perfect spring day as I revved the Kawasaki north along the main A865, a surprisingly fast, wide road for at least as long as it took to get to Askernish. Walking distance, indeed. It was about three miles. Depended on how much of an enthusiast you were for footsore golf. A sign said RAON GOILF, AISGERNIS, and turning left down a road which quickly became a sandy track, I came upon a wooden board, neatly painted, which gave the translation: ASKERNISH GOLF CLUB. Ahead, I could see mountainous sand dunes, and the roar of the Atlantic breakers on an unseen beach came clearly over the ripple of the wind through the marram grass. The flat, grassy stretch of land leading to the dunes was what they call in Gaeldom machair, the usually very fertile remnant of the sea's retreat, guarded from salt and destruction by the soaring dunes. The machair at Askernish was massive, an enormous table of green, dappled with little lumps and, to the south, a kind of weird jungle of hummocks and hills, ancient, mountainous dunes. Even without much knowledge of golf architecture, indeed any, I could see that this was classic linksland, an absolute gift to any golf-course designer. It had the air of a St Andrews or a Troon, only on a far grander, more rugged scale. I stopped the bike

85

at a gate where another neat notice said ASKERNISH GOLF CLUB. GOLF FEES, 18 HOLES: LADIES, £2.50; GENTS, £3.50; JUNIORS £2.00; PER DAY, £5.00. An arrow indicated the first tee. Pinned to the notice with a drawing-pin, and flapping in the breeze, were some score-cards, and fastened to a pole was a box marked 'fees'. Next to the notice was an ancient structure in wood and green, rusty corrugated iron, whose angles had given up the battle to maintain 90 degrees and was now listing into a parallelogram. One door lay on the ground, amid a litter of mud and sheep shit; the other was hanging off. Inside the filthy exterior lay an old sink, a vintage lawn-mower and some pieces of wood. This, it appeared, was the club-house.

I wedged some wood under the bike's side stand to steady it on the soft ground, unstrapped the clubs and wandered around the back of the wrecked clubhouse, looking for somewhere to leave my helmet, gloves, boots and leathers. Sitting on a green-roller which looked solidified by years of disuse, I changed into golf shoes and felt that quickening, that sense of excitement as the prospect of a fresh, innocent round of golf opens up in front of you. This would be the day I hit a hole in one. This would be the round where every-thing clicked into place, where the muscles would simply do their job without being forced into some strained position, without com-plaint. I could hear larks singing, and feel the first breath of summer warmth from the northern sun. And I was utterly alone, apart from the sheep, beneath an immense sky, in this huge expanse of linksland. Designed by Old Tom Morris, eh? By the looks of things, he'd probably had little to do but plant a few sticks here and there and call them holes, a few markers elsewhere and call them tees. Only one person had designed Askernish, and that was God, who was, on this evidence, a golfer.

This was an alien landscape, where thoughts of Belinda, and even Paul and Patti, did not belong. I walked in the direction of the first tee, which was marked 350 yards on the rusty tin marker and 347 on the score-card. According to a plan on the back of the card, the first hole had its own green, but apart from that 17 widely spaced tees shared nine other flags. Weird. The first was a par four. It dog-legged off towards the dunes and the sea, the fairway wide and bunkerless, but with dozens of sheep pimpling the view. I drew out my driver, unwrapped a Dunlop 65, placed it on a new wooden tee and faced the ball. Link grip, hands dry, legs not too wide, bend-ing slightly at the knees, flexing for power, slow backswing, relaxed, left arm as straight as possible, round, let the club head fall, head down and . . . shit The club hit the ground before the ball, topped the Dunlop and sent it spinning viciously down the fairway for about 30 feet. The old, black poison began to surge through my veins from that great reservoir of golfing self-hatred somewhere inside. Perhaps there was some secret organ which was stimulated by bad golf shots into releasing a toxic enzyme, a chemical brain-trigger which led to this sudden, overwhelming feeling of worthlessness which had taken the place of expectation and well being. Golf. Christ, how I hated this game . . .

But the three iron I hit from the fairway, full of angst and ire as it was, proved a beezer, straight, true and almost fatal to a sheep which had to scamper out of the way as the ball bounced towards it. I was still about 125 yards from the hole, but I was confident again, and felt that a seven iron would see me on the green, if not in the hole. What a manic game golf is, up and down, depression to exultation in the space of seconds. No wonder it has the highest participant death rate of any sport, with all those retired, be-Pringled, overweight, over-cholesteroled gents sending their pulses and stress factors racing as they veer from bad to good shots and back again. Add the necessity of actually walking, with or without a powered caddy car, and it's no wonder heart-attacks claim hundreds of golfers a year. And there are the other hazards too, such as death by ball-strike, lightning, whin-fire and drowning, not to mention stroke, asthma and other strain-induced illnesses. I hit an appalling shot away to the right-hand side of the green, leaving a painful chest-thump of rage which made me at once panic. At my age, a heart-attack? Well, possibly. Unfit, slightly overweight, liver soaked in mood-changing liquids for years.

I heaved the rattle of clubs on to my shoulder and strode onwards, trying to swallow the frustration of inability, let the annoyance fade. After all, the skylarks were singing, the sun was shining, I was alone on one of the most beautiful linksland golf courses it was possible to imagine. Death? So what. It would solve quite a lot of problems, actually, and leave Belinda raging. Although perhaps not, as she was still the beneficiary of my insurance policies. Well, the kids would get the cash. I stopped, gazed up at the shifting streams of wispy cloud against the Rangers blue of the sky. My heart was no longer palpitating. Maybe I should just hold an iron up to the sky and wait for a million volts of electricity to zap me, courtesy of God. After all, I was on what appeared to be His personal golf course. But I put such fancies out my mind and went to look for my ball.

I was on the green, if you could call it that, in four, but it was hardly worth putting. The surface was only vaguely discernible from the fairway, and covered in sheep droppings, some of them as big as my golf ball. Nevertheless, I chose a relatively shitless line and went for it, eventually sinking the ball after it had initially come to rest against a gigantic turd. Call it six then.

I turned to look for the second tee. No clues. High on a dune perched what looked like a tee, so I huffed and puffed my way up there, only to find a complete lack of anything to indicate which hole I was on, or which direction to go in. Several ragged flags fluttered in the distance, and on the great flat table of machair, any one of them could have been the target. The map on the score-card didn't help. Behind me, an enormous series of valleys, mountain ranges and plateau in grass-covered dunes stretched out, with what looked like clear, if overgrown remnants of tees and greens lurking. It was as if half the golf course, and by far the most interesting, hilly part, had been abandoned completely. The rest of it looked as if it would soon be going the same way. While to the west the Atlantic surge thundered in on a perfect silvery beach. It was all a bit like a golfing heaven run to seed; maybe God preferred it that way.

I chose a flag out to the north-east, about 200 yards away, and was just setting myself up with the trusty, and slightly rusty, thanks to high-pressure motorcycle rain, three iron when I heard a shout behind me. It came from the jungly, abandoned part of the course. High on a dune about 100 yards away stood a tall, female figure, loose peanut-butter-coloured hair flicking in the wind. She was beckoning. I sighed, put the three back in my element-battered nylon bag, and hoisted it on to my shoulder. Then I began walking down the slope of the dune I was on, into the deep valley which lay between Sharon and me. I could see she was slithering down to meet me. As I descended, the sheltering effect of the sand hills made the wind die away until a curious silence fell; there were no sheep on this rougher, harder ground with its sharp, long grass, and even the larks seemed to be tweetering much, much further away. Gradually, the sound of the Atlantic diminished too. Then all I could hear was the clank of the clubs, my breathing, and, as Sharon drew closer, the movement of her body and clothes, feet on grass, and her breathing, deep and juddery.

'Hey, here you are, and here I am . . .' I looked at her face. It was streaked with tears, and in one hand she was clutching a strange object, a kind of old-fashioned biscuit-tin thing, made of what might have been silver, or perhaps polished pewter. She coughed, shook her head fiercely. 'Gosh, I'm so, so sorry about last night on the ship?' That questioning American lilt. 'So gross, I can't believe . . . anyway, you found Old Tom's handiwork, I see.'

'Yes. It's in shocking condition, though. I can't really work out where to go, what holes to play.'

'Well, from what my father told me, they left the best half of the course to the tender mercies of the sheep and the wind in the 1930s,' she grimaced. 'I mean, don't you think this is golfing paradise, or could be? Isn't it just magnificent? Dad always said this was the most perfect natural golfing terrain in the world, classic links . . . now it's just nine, or is it ten holes? . . . and I suppose they use alternate tees on the same greens to make it up to 18 . . . Jesus, not that you could tell . . .' She was sobbing and laughing, trying to hide the emotion, embarrassed by it. 'Yeah, dad was here, his one big trip back, oh, ten years ago, back to the home of his ancestors. Couldn't find a single Sharp, but that didn't put him off. I think the course must have been better then, but it was his dream, his memory, his glory, this place. Which is why I'm here, with this . . .' and she brandished the pewter tea-caddy biscuit tin. I said nothing. She looked at me. 'Ashes, you dope. His ashes. Last will and testament, scatter his ashes over Askernish, take out a life membership for the family, except I can't find anybody to talk to about membership. They say the club's defunct, and I've just been up on those dunes pouring out Daddy's remains on a course which is just gonna die like he did, all worn out and abandoned . . .'

'But surely you didn't abandon him, after all you're . . .'

She snorted. 'Oh yeah, me and my big flashy brother Kevin were there at the end, called to the bedside, but were we there for him when he was sitting dreaming about this place? Did we come with him when he flew over here on his own to find his past, his family? No, we were too busy being successful and independent. Maybe if Mom hadn't . . .'

I laid the clubs on the ground, which was green and soft. Here in the sheltered bowl created by the dunes her sobs seemed curiously muted and echoless. Her face, close to, was freckled and seemed almost translucent; a blue vein throbbed in her temple. One of her hands, bony but very strong, gripped mine, and pulled me towards her. I put one hand behind her head, feeling the thick weight of that amazing American hair, and kissed her. She'd had kippers for breakfast, it occurred to me, then used Gold Spot breath freshener, but it didn't matter. Nor did the fumbling ignorance with which I discovered her expensive canvas fatigue trousers buttoned at the side. She was very practical, Sharon. And she carried condoms, too – Mates peppermint flavour. All this time without sex, all this pathetic sublimation into swings and clubs and, Freud save us, bunkers and holes, and what happens? I lose my temporary, late-developing virginity on a golf course.

We remained in that still, grassy bowl for about an hour, huddled, half-clothed, the empty urn rolled away to one side next to my golf clubs. Then she said, suddenly, 'Come on. Let me try a coupla balls. Golf balls, that is, shooter.' And she giggled. The tear stains had dried dirty on that pale face, with its ingrained laughter lines and innate toughness.

'How about if we leave that old urn here? I think that's what Daddy woulda wanted, and there maybe a smidgin or so of him left inside . . .'

I raised an eyebrow, then took the pitching wedge out of my golf bag. 'I've dug some holes in bunkers with this in the past. A slightly deeper one shouldn't be too much trouble.'

And in the middle of the dune-bowl we buried what had once contained Mr Sharp's last mortal remains, while his ashes merged and melded with the sand of the shore and fell among the marram grass of Askernish's abandoned holes. Mr Sharp, golf obsessed, Askernish possessed, had eventually become part of the bunkerless, half-abandoned course he adored. The fact that his daughter had lately been screwing enthusiastically on said holy sward seemed not to have annoyed his ghost. Indeed, when we finally climbed out of the dune-bowl, back up on to what may or may not have been the second tee, the wind had dropped. Sharon's Dad smiled down as she picked out a seven iron and hit a tremendous shot towards the nearest of the visible flags. I took the same club and hit a reasonable, lifting ball which landed some 30 yards behind hers. Her swing was loose, casual and incredibly natural, not that geriatric American woman's swing inculcated by bored country-club-gigolo pros you see sometimes on television. 'Pretty good shot,' she said.

I gave her one of those looks you sometimes hear described as old fashioned. 'Come on, Sharon. So your dad played a lot of golf. You obviously haven't been short of practice, have you.'

'Well . . . no. Actually, I get quite a lot of practice . . .' she gave me an arch little sideways grin . . . 'at golf, too. But then, you do in the United States Navy. I'm in the service's team, the women's team naturally. May even take a tilt at the circuit when I get my pay-off. But then, if I enlist for another ten years I could end up an admiral instead of just a commander.'

'You're a naval commander?' I was understandably incredulous. Having sex with a naval commander was a fairly rare occurrence for me.

'Yeah, computer-services division. We create the virtual-reality games for the hard-ons to play, let the big boys practise their killing abilities; killskills, it's called, you know the stuff. Mostly aviation, but some submarine manoeuvres as well. I've had some indirect approaches from Microsoft and Sega as well, sounding me out for an out-of-uniform career. But who knows?'

I let her win the hole, which wasn't hard. A taxi had dropped her and her strange burden at Askernish earlier ('the only one I've ever been in with a sheepdog in the back seat'), so she squeezed on to the pillion of the bike, and, hair flying helmetless and illegal behind her, we shot down the road in fear of policemen to Daliburgh. Not a cop car appeared, but it has to be said that her hair was a mess by the time we stopped. 'Fantasy stuff, boy, pure fantasy *Top Gun* shit!' she muttered breathlessly. 'Fortunately, I've got a brush with me.'

A lunch in the Borrodale Hotel's immensely friendly lounge bar – all mammoth chips, deep-fried haddock and Beamish Stout ('definitely no Becks') – elicited the information from a waitress that there was still an Askernish golf club, and that if we went to the Hydro Electric offices in Lochboisdale and asked for a lineman called Alan MacDonald ('you'll have heard of his father? No? Oh well, Ronald is famous! He's always on the television, the man who was first onboard the *Politician* for the whisky . . .') Ronald MacDonald. Sharon couldn't help but wonder aloud if there was any relationship with the hamburger chain's clown, but I quashed this ridiculous notion – the burger McDonalds were clearly Irish, from the lack of an 'a' in their Mac.

Alan turned out to be club secretary, a laid-back sort of character aged, maybe, 25. He confirmed that there were only a dozen or so members of Askernish Golf Club now, but that he had high hopes for a future helped by council grants and a touch more local enthusiasm. He nodded politely when both Sharon and I enthused about the course, about how, with some money spent on it, and the sheep muttonised, it could become one of the world's great links, an attraction for tourists throughout the world. 'Ah well, the sheep.' He shook his head. 'It's croft land, you see, owned by the crofters, and we don't have any right to stop them grazing their own sheep, you see. It limits what we can do, too. That's why there are no bunkers. We're not allowed to dig them.' I wondered about Mrs Sharp's buried urn, and the digging done for that, but said nothing.

Alan had no idea what a life membership for Sharon and her brother would cost. 'It's £35 a year at the moment for local people,' he said, 'and probably less for visitors.'

'What's that, about $50?' Sharon sat calculating for a moment. 'Supposing I gave you a money order for, oh, $2,000? Would that give the Sharp family life membership? Or maybe we could sponsor a trophy? But Alan shrugged that off. There was already a whole cupboard full of trophies, silverware going right back to 1891, and few to play for them. But yes, $2,000 would be enough for a family life membership.

It turned out that Sharon was staying at the Pollachar Inn, a wonderful building right down at the southern tip of Uist, looking out towards Barra. 'I found it in this guide thing, called *Scotland the best!*' she told me. 'Said it was untouched by the twentieth century. Unfortunately, I got here the day after it reopened, like . . . refurbished from top to bottom. It's still good, though, but I just wish I'd seen it before they got the stripped pine in . . .'

We arrived, still aboard the Kawa, her hair once more a tangle of wind and weather, her face burnished, glowing. Despite some rather unfortunate work with the Black and Decker and the B&Q catalogue, the bar was fun, with a great old fireplace, and we were well looked after by a sociable young barman called Donald MacNeill, whose parents had owned the place until the death of his father, whereupon it had been sold to a local builder and comprehensively upgraded. 'It used to be great,' said Donald cautiously. He was in a difficult position, I suppose, working as an employee in what had been the family business. The food was average pub gear, although the salmon steaks tasted good, if undoubtedly farmed, and the Australian Cabernet Sauvignon – both Sharon and I agreed that red wine was much more a salmony kinda groove – reasonable, if chilled.

We skipped the sweet, and any more alcohol, settling for coffee and sex in the room. During both the coffee and the sex I found myself with a stupid tune runnng through my head, nagging and impossible to erase. 'In the Navy' by the Village People. Well, you don't get to play golf and doctors and nurses with a naval commander every day, do you? Certainly not a near-professional-golfer, computer-whizz naval commander who happens to be female. That is, I would say, fairly unusual, especially in the Pollachar Inn, South Uist.

I kissed Sharon goodnight at about 3.00 a.m., tasting no kippers this time. We held each other; said nothing. I scribbled my phone number and address on a piece of paper. She did not reciprocate. Then I went back to Mrs Davidson's, trying to keep the engine note at a decent level, rumbling through the half-twilight to the house, which still had its hallway lit, and was unlocked. So this was the Hebrides. I quite liked it, I decided.

The Rules are those adopted by the Royal and Ancient Golf Club of St. Andrews, with the following:

LOCAL RULES

1. Fenced Greens. A ball which strikes a post or wire may be replaced without penalty. If fence interferes with stroke on green, or is in line of play to green, the ball may be moved, but not nearer the hole.
2. Rabbit holes and scrapes. Rule 32.
3. Bunker on 7th. A player may choose to lift and drop outside the bunker but not nearer the hole at a one stroke penalty.
4. Tracks. Def. 14. A free drop is allowed if ball lies in sheep or tyre tracks.
5. Pond on 3rd fairway. Rule 33. Def. 14c. If hoofmark interferes with the ball, a free drop is allowed, but not nearer the hole.
6. On the second nine holes right of way must be given to those at a later stage in the course of a round.

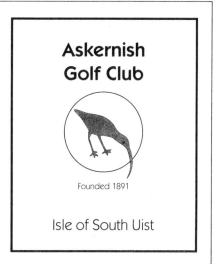

Askernish Golf Club

Founded 1891

Isle of South Uist

Over the Years, the Clubhouse Has Been Blown Away

Alan MacDonald, secretary, Askernish Golf Club

It goes back to 1891, when it was founded by Tom Morris. I don't know a lot about the history. I suppose it's possible that he just happened to be over here on holiday, and advised the local gentry on how to set out the course. I don't know. This year we have 15 members, who each pay £35 per year. Most of them are younger people, and although that seems like a small number, there are actually about 40 to 50 people who play. They don't seem to be interested in joining, though. It can be difficult, although over the years we have had a few grants from people. We have plans drawn up for a new clubhouse; over the years the old one has been blown away by the weather. This year we are putting in a green-fees box for visitors. We did that two years ago and made £700 in four months during the summer. It is a fantastic natural course, and it could be potentially one of the greatest courses in the country. It was an 18-hole course until the 1930s, until part of it fell into disuse, and it could all be opened up. We'd like to see that happening, if there was the money. It could be fantastic. But with 15 members a year you can't do much, can you?

Seven or eight years ago, we used to have the army coming down from Benbecula, and about 40 of them were members. They've since built their own course, but it's nowhere near as good as here. But if the army withdraws, as they're saying they might, their course might not go on, and perhaps the members in Benbecula might come back here

It is a bit difficult to find your way around. Our signs aren't very good, It's a wide open space, and you need to know your way, or be with someone who does. The sheep are not a big problem. The course itself, the land is owned by crofters, not the club. For six months of the year, between October and May it's used for grazing. But it only takes three or four weeks to clear up and then it's playable again.

It's quite a hard course. The greens are small, there's not many bunkers, but the fairways are narrow. Because it's croft land, we can't cut a lot of grass and we can't dig bunkers. In many ways it's a return to traditional links golf, as it was played on the traditional Scottish courses. It's a par 67 – of the 18 holes, played that way there are six par threes, one par five and the rest are par fours. I'm a 12 handicapper and the best score I ever had was 75. We had a centenary open in 1991. Who won that? Well . . . actually, I did.

We welcome visitors. Nick Faldo played the course not so long ago, when he was making a tour of the Western Isles, but I've no idea what he scored. We welcome visitors. They can get score-cards either in the local hotels and some of the guest-houses, or sometimes there have been score-cards attached to the noticeboard on the course. But with the weather we have, they've been blown away.

CHAPTER FIVE

Outside Agency

I LEFT Mrs Davidson's and headed north into a species of rain which the Gaels probably have a word for but which conjured up to me English terms such as saturation, sopping, mist-like, swimming-pool, what's-that-running-down-my-back, what-am-I-sitting-in and, in Scots, drookit. Riding a motorcycle in the rain is not just unpleasant; it's patently moronic. Your visor steams up, so you wipe it with your soggy gloves, smearing it with grease. You open your visor, and are immediately deluged with high-speed, stinging wetness, all going into your eyes, nose and mouth. Your boots gradually fill up with water. Your waterproofs don't work. Your leathers become slick and squeaky and clammy, and to cap it all the road becomes treacherous and slithery. Not to mention the effects of approaching cars and lorries, slipstreaming you into near-oblivion with a mixture of mud, water and abuse. At least on a pushbike you're not going as fast, and you're exercising enough to keep out some of the cold. But then, you can't carry golf clubs on a pushbike.

Like a stage set being struck, the murky rain lifted and in seconds a grey and black sky was giving way to patches of pale blue and an abashed sun. I had already passed several roadside shrines, of the kind you see in France, Spain, Italy and South America, doubtless marking the sites of road crashes where either miraculous recoveries had later been staged or loved ones had shuffled off this Ford Cosworth mortal coil. From what I could see, the standard of driving in Uibhist a Deas, South Uist to you and me, was somewhere between Death Race 2000, the average stock-car meet and a motorised community suicide pact. The single-track roads veered suddenly into half-finished, two-lane blacktops, then just as quickly back into car tracks last surfaced in the middle ages, while huge trucks piled high with harvested seaweed surfed straight towards you all too frequently, and not a passing place in sight.

Suddenly, soaring above me to the right was a hill festooned with ugly, prefabricated look-out posts, giant aerials and radar devices, and, bizarrely, a huge statue of a woman, arms outstretched. I presumed this was the Madonna. The Catholic nature of South Uist had been inescapable from the first, not just in the roadside shrines but in the massive, blockhouse churches and the constant whiff of rural Republic of Ireland laid-backness. Discernible nowhere was the vicious Presbyterian guilt'n'whipping I'd been told to expect in the Hebrides.

I knew about the army's presence, of course. The rocket range extended from Benbecula over to remote St Kilda, the island stuck like a target handily in the middle of the Atlantic, and down to South Uist, where they tracked the giant willies as they shot up, up and away to explode harmlessly and drop to earth in bits. Sharon had told me she'd seen a notice on the Askernish beach which read WARNING: DO NOT TOUCH ANYTHING. IT MAY EXPLODE AND KILL YOU. I bet that had given a few visiting golfers a scare. Is that really my Wilson Proflite ex-lake ball lying there on that jellyfish, or is it a piece of high explosive from a missile, disguised as a golf ball to try and fool, say, some harmless golf-mad, Third World tribe? Good sales point, golf-ball-shaped missile-innards . . .

Suddenly I was trundling across a rock-shielded causeway, and a sign saying BEINN NA FAOGHLA was indicating I should learn Gaelic. Benbecula, home, Mrs Davidson had told me, of the only British armed forces NAAFI store open to the public. And Balivanich Airport, from where, if I felt so inclined, I could put an end to this stupid, wet rollicking around on a motorbike and go home. The flat would be waiting for me, clean and tidy. Then I could go to work, re-engage with real life, instruct a lawyer to instruct a hit-man to kill Belinda . . . I pulled into the airport carpark, in a jumble of horrible, undesigned, half-fabricated buildings, tilted the bike on to its side stand and switched off the engine. Pulling off my helmet, inevitably tweaking my ears painfully and leaving my hair, such as is left of it, unpleasantly sweated on to my scalp, I scanned the small departure-lounge-cum-café-cum-check-in-area for Sharon. She'd said she was leaving by air from Glasgow, and thence back to America, having done her filial duty. I presumed this did not include having sexual congress with me, unless her father's will had contained some bizarre sub-clauses.

She wasn't there. I asked the uniformed girl at the British Airways check-in desk what time the flight to Glasgow left, and she pointed wordlessly towards the tarmac. It was like being in a foreign country, but then, maybe she didn't speak good English. Through one of the windows I could see a straggly line of people approaching one of those twin-prop excuses for aeroplanes British Airways insist are safe, modern and efficient. At the back was Sharon, tall and still wearing that LL Bean Ms America El Salvador outfit. There had been no promises, that night at the Pollachar. There had been no arrangement to see her off at the airport, but it had seemed . . . a good idea. Male pathos. The tug of something – affection, lust, loneliness, a desperate hoping for love – had brought me there, in contradiction of the casual coolness I'd affected the night before. Both of us had been casual and cool, in fact, but I had assumed she meant it. Never sleep with a naval officer if you're looking for a long-term relationship. A man in every port. Besides, she could play golf better than I could. Anyway, I'd missed saying goodbye, and she wasn't looking back. I watched her climb the steps into the aeroplane, and she didn't even turn once before disappearing into the tubular innards of the craft. But she was that sort of woman. I walked out of the airport, put on my helmet and geared myself up for more golf. I didn't feel like it.

The army headquarters in Balivanich has, mounted on its concrete gate-posts, two highly polished missiles, their gleaming gold tips positively shrieking for immediate psychoanalysis of all who enter therein. I parked the bike and wandered into the guardhouse, being all but ignored by the bored-looking staff. The telephone was being used, loudly and volubly, by a smallish man in a body-warmer, clearly a union official of some kind. 'I'm the convener here,' he was saying, 'and if I say they're out, they're all out. You tell the Brigadier to stop eating his pot noodle and take some notice. Working practices are being breached here.' From what I could gather from some intensive eavesdropping, divisions had arisen among the female civilian catering and cleaning staff, between non-union local islanders, presumably grumbling Gaels, and incomers. The non-union locals were receiving better treatment, apparently, and 'they're racialist here, you know!' The union man was English.

When he had finished and stalked importantly out, I asked one of the corporals on duty where I could find the golf course. No one had challenged me about my business, and the only weapons in sight were the polished missiles on the gate-posts. I could have been an IRA bomber on reconnaissance patrol, but I got the impression that such an event would have been a welcome intrusion into a life of awesome monotony. The golf course was about a mile up the road, said the soldier. I couldn't miss it. Just look for the rugby posts. The rugby posts? I left, and accelerated out of the grimy, grim, new-townish sprawl of Balivanich, with its decaying army houses, car showroom with a single used Skoda on display, and general atmosphere of valium-dulled tedium. The scenery didn't even compensate. Yes, the beach, smelly with rotting kelp, wasn't far away, but the landscape was flat and waterlogged. It was clearly the posting from – or to – hell.

The golf course fitted. I saw a few flags dotting ground which was flat, featureless and the size, it seemed of two rugby pitches. Sure enough, as I'd been informed, H-shaped rugby posts appeared next to the main airport runway on my left, and a sign indicating that Benbecula Golf Club welcomed visitors. I turned off on to what had clearly once been a runway. The cracked concrete apron had a small steel blockhouse in the middle of it, and as I approached, I saw that this was the clubhouse.

Compared to Askernish, the Benbecula clubhouse was like Lytham or Muirfield or the Gleneagles Hotel. It had lockers, a bench, terse, military notices of training nights, development plans for the course, lists of duties for members to perform. A door led to a lounge area, but it was locked. No one seemed to be around. Suddenly I was filled with a kind of weary anger. What was the point of being here, in this neat, tidy, dowdily armyesque pitch-and-putt course with pretensions to a grandeur it seemed not to deserve?

When was the next flight back to Glasgow? Maybe I could catch up with Sharon if . . . but I knew there were no more flights that day. And besides, what would I do with the bike?

The day remained uncertainly bright, with a sluggish wind coming in from the west. Unwillingly, I climbed out of my motor-cycle boots, which were still sodden, my leather breeks and my jacket, leaving me more or less dry in a fleece jacket and jeans. On went the golf shoes, and there I was: Faldoised, or as near as dammit. There were score-cards, cheaply duplicated, in a pile by the now-expected honesty box. I picked one up, and scanned the local rules. There were one or two fairly bizarre ones, including the thoroughly surreal Rule Three: 'All tarmac roads staked by red markers are deemed a lateral water hazard'. Also it was useful to learn that out of bounds extended not just to all boundary fences, but to 'Navigation Aid Compound and concrete road at entrance'. Whatever a Navigation Aid Compound was. I put a score-card in my pocket and ignored the requests for £3. I felt tired, heavily post-coital, perhaps, and generally not in the mood for golf. Still. I went outside, crunching golfily across the old tarmac, unstrapped my clubs and began searching for the first tee.

The hole was called Blue Job, was 284 yards long, a par four, and I had no idea where the green was. The whole course was con-centrated on such a small area, and was so utterly flat that flags popped up in almost every conceivable corner. The remains of a runway stretched in front of me, before a choice of three flags appeared, all more or less 284 yards away. I picked out my driver, and after a few practice swings, hit a daisy-cutting, topped shot fairly hard into the concrete. It rocketed off a kerb and into the air, before bouncing again on the old runway, about 40 feet up this time, and spinning on and on towards the hole. It was unconven-tional, I had to admit. But not ineffective.

Of course, when I reached the green (in three) I discovered this was not the first green at all, but the fifth. Well, actually I had gone slightly awry with my second shot, a five iron, and in the end just attacked the nearest green. Still, I two putted for a very creditable five and managed to discover the sixth tee without too much diffi-culty. At least here it was fairly obvious where I ought to be going, as a defined fairway led alongside the fence which marked the boundary with the main airport runway. Stern, official notices warned that the runway was strictly out of bounds. I wondered if anyone had ever successfully downed an aeroplane with a golf ball. Maybe an explosive ball . . . Interesting form of undercover terror-ism. The only trouble would be preventing the ball exploding on contact with the club head . . . Three hundred and sixty-five yards, par four. The wind had strengthened, and was now blowing directly towards me, plus there was no concrete this time to help me on my way, but still. I hauled out the driver and battered a long, high and spectacularly sliced shot across the airport fence. I had been wrong. I was concrete-bound. I saw the ball bounce on the runway, hugely high into the air, and then off to the grass on the other side. Oops. I took another ball out my bag, swung (sloooowwwwly back, eye on the ball), and did exactly the same thing again.

I slumped on to my haunches, feeling angry and slightly weepy. It was all Belinda's fault. I launched the driver like a dart at the tin tee-marker, extracting a satisfying clunk from Belinda's symbolic head. I only had one ball left, and I was determined not to lose it. The next thing I knew, I was up and running for the boundary fence. I was like a mad thing, possessed by some crazed spirit, determined to break out of this prissy, prison-like course, with its 18 stupidly named tees incomprehensibly targeting nine greens on an area the size of a bowling green.

I vaulted the fence into long, jagged marram grass, stopped and looked aloft. Nothing but that watery sun, the restless blue-and-white and puffy grey sky, that bored wind. 'I HATE THIS GAME!' Who was shouting? 'I HATE THIS BLOODY GAME AND EVERY BLOODY THING ABOUT IT! I HATE NICK FALDO AND HIS ARROGANT WOOLLEN WEAR! I HATE COLIN MONT-GOMERIE AND HIS REFUSAL TO LOSE WEIGHT! I HATE TONY JACKLIN FOR FAILING! I HATE SANDY LYLE FOR BEING SO BORING! I HATE BERNHARD LANGER FOR BEING SO GERMAN, SO HANDSOME AND WHAT'S MORE A BORN-AGAIN CHRISTIAN! I HATE KEN BROWN FOR GIVING UP! I HATE THE ROYAL AND ANCIENT GOLF CLUB OF MASONIC MARTINET MILITARY-MINDED, TORY-VOTING, AUSTIN-MAESTRO-CLUBMAN-DIESEL DRIVERS FOR EXISTING! I DETEST THE HONOURABLE COMPANY OF VERY RICH EDINBURGH GOLFERS! I HATE JACK NICKLAUS FOR BEING NICE! I HATE SAM TORRANCE FOR JUST NOT BEING QUITE GOOD ENOUGH! I HATE CYLINDRICAL PUTTERS AND TITA-NIUM-SHAFTED CLUBS! I HATE PROFESSIONAL GOLF TEACHERS! I HATE GOLF SHOPS AND HIDEOUS HOMO-EROTIC GOLF MAGAZINES! I HATE SEVVY BALLESTEROS FOR NOT BEING BRILLIANT ANYMORE! I HATE IAN WOOS-NAM FOR BEING SHORT, PETER ALLIS FOR BEING FAT AND INSUFFERABLY SMUG! I HATE ANY GOLFER WHO WEARS PLUS-FOURS! I DEMAND AMPUTATION! I HATE AMERICAN

GOLF COURSES, ALL OF THEM! I HATE BRUCE FORSYTH AND RONNIE CORBETT AND ALL PRO-AM COMPETITIONS! I HATE JIMMY TARBUCK, GEORGE BURNS, SEAN CONNERY AND CLINT EASTWOOD! I HATE ALICE COOPER AND LLOYD COLE AND IGGY POP FOR PLAYING THE GAME WHEN THEY'RE SUPPOSED TO BE REBELLIOUS SEX GODS! I HATE ANYONE WHO GOES ON A GOLFING HOLIDAY TO MAJORCA OR PORTUGAL! I HATE GOLFING TIMESHARES! I HATE JOHN DALY FOR EXISTING IN HIS CURRENT FORM AND ESPECIALLY BECAUSE OF HIS HAIRCUT. I HATE GOLF . . .'

I only realised it was me, that my lungs were giving vent to this tirade of blasphemy, when I halted, out of breath, on the other side of the runway. I hadn't realised that all this information, from years and years and years of televised golf, had lodged in my brain. Yet it had, and now it was haemorrhaging out. I felt light-headed, but supremely alive and confident, as if I'd just done some cocaine. The only time I'd ever snorted coke was at the behest of a very important Pitch customer from America, and while the immediate sensation of control, superiority and pleasure was everything you would accept according to the structures of the Trades Descriptions Act, the fact that I began fitting half an hour later and had to be rushed to hospital was not. One night in hospital, a lecture from a sympathetic young doctor, and I was off hard drugs for ever and a day. Still, I could understand why some golfers used coke. It might come in handy, in a game where confidence is all, if you were equipped to handle it. I was not.

Balls. I had to find my balls. Curiously enough, they lay together, a Slazenger Interlok and Spalding Top Flite XL, both fairly battered but definitely usable, I picked them up in triumph, and was about to run back across the tarmac when I happened to look to my left. Straight (at least it seemed straight to me, though I must have been a bit to his right) into the staring, terrified eyes of Captain Bernard Summers, pilot of a Brogan Airlines Flying Shed, or rather a Short 360 passenger aeroplane owned by Loganair and under contract to British Airways under the rather optimistic label British Airways Express. Not that I knew Captain Summers personally, you understand. He was later to spend ten minutes shouting at me in a colourful but to my mind fairly predictable fashion.

The plane was landing into the wind, which accounted for my not having heard the engines. I threw myself back and down into the grass as the hot, oily buffeting breath of the ugly machine hit me. In actual fact I was at least ten feet away from the wing-tip; but it felt closer. And the pilot must have noticed his underpants changing colour. I felt drunk, now, swaying, but inexpressibly happy. 'I HATE THIS GAME!' I shouted, shaking my fist at the retreating tailplane of the Shed. I could hear the sound of sirens in the distance, and from the terminal building I could see two Land Rovers, two fire engines and an ambulance racing towards me. Oh dear. It seemed they took their out-of-bounds rule seriously at Benbecula.

They were, I surmised, Royal Air Force military policemen. I'd forgotten that the airport was technically under the control of the military, and not the army at that, but the RAF. Perhaps that accounted for the name given to the first hole – Blue Job. They didn't laugh, they didn't smile, they were large and they had sub machine-guns, or semi-automatic rifles or whatever you call them. They were pointed at me, anyway, and I didn't really feel like discussing the exact terminology. I did think of picking up blades of the prickly runwayside grass and peaceably inserting it into one of their dull-metal barrels, singing Dylan's 'Oxford Town' and giving it peace-child-versus-the-National-Guard . . . but it only crossed my mind for a micro-second.

They said nothing. 'I'm just a golfer,' I said, voice unexpectedly quavering. 'I was just sort of . . . looking for my balls . . .' I reached to my pocket for the Slazenger and the Spalding, and was immediately spreadeagled, Starsky-and-Hutch-style against one of the Land Rovers. The body search was rough and thorough. My balls – the golf balls – were taken out and examined minutely. Maybe there was a terrorist bomb in the shape of what Bing Crosby called in song 'that little white pellet'. Or maybe there were bits, secret bits inside some of the rockets being tested for sale to Third World tribal despots in the shape of dimpled Dunlops. I was driven off, still without a word spoken to me, still with the guns pointing at my chest. I looked at the clean-shaven faces, with the brow missing inside gleamingly peaked hats. 'I hate this game,' I told all and sundry. They did not seem impressed.

Nor, it must be said, was Royal Air Force Security Commander Squadron Leader Horace Goodfellow, who had a painfully thin handlebar moustache held in place with copious amounts of wax, and was at least five feet three inches tall. On a hot day he must have looked like a walrus. He at least seemed to accept, after examining my driver's licence, wallet and golf clubs, which had been brought in by some more gun-toting Air Force dudes, that I was just a golfer gone astray.

'Honestly, I don't know what happened,' I said. 'I hit two balls over the fence, really bad slices, and . . . something just snapped. I just couldn't help myself. I ran, shouting and screaming, and I didn't think. I'm sorry. I'm really, really sorry.'

The diminutive squadron leader looked at me coldly. 'I'm a golfer too,' he said. 'I play off nine, and have yet to lose control in the way you describe. Your handicap?'

The word 'Belinda' sprang to my lips, but I swallowed it. 'Ermm, well, I don't . . . I'm not really a handicap . . . just an enthusiastic hacker, actually.'

His cold look became positively refrigerated. 'Well, Mr . . . Palmer.' He sniffed. Clearly my name was close to blasphemy. 'You would have noticed the honesty box in the clubhouse?'

I nodded.

'One assumes . . . that you were intending to pay your green fees on your return to your motorcycle? Does one?' He raised one almost invisible, sandy eyebrow, and the moustache twitched. He couldn't be married, I decided. No wife would put up with that monstrous piece of facial hair unless she had some kind of serious perversion. He gestured with my wallet.

'Please,' I said, 'yes, I was certainly . . . take, oh, take say £20, contribute to the upkeep of the course, very impressed. Oh yes, tremendously so.' He took out a £20 note, the last one in fact, leaving me in desperate need of a cashline machine, and carefully folded it in four.

'Thank you. We have, you know, a junior section, and a development plan which your contribution will be most helpful in contributing towards. And of course you would probably like to join the club?' Of course I would. Out of my Helly Hansen jacket I hauled my chequebook. My last piece of punishment was the dressing-down by Captain Summers, which I won't bore you with. It involved lots of words like 'bastard', 'careless', 'passengers' and 'risk'.

Eventually, they let me go. I turned out to walk back to the golf course for my bike and leathers. No lift. It had begun to rain again, this time in a Victoria Falls deluge. I reached the clubhouse, nearly drowned, depressed and suddenly realising that they hadn't given me my balls back. My leathers were hanging inside the still-deserted clubhouse, wet. I slithered into them, bungeed the clubs on to the bike and left, nearly blind in the rain. I paused at the entrance to the course, and screamed at the top of my voice into the gloom: 'I HATE THIS GAME!' Then I tried to do a wheelie, revving the bike as hard as I could. But I couldn't manage it.

LOCAL RULES

* 1. OUT OF BOUNDS
* (a) Over all boundary fences
* (b) Club house car park
* (c) Navigation Aid compound between 4th and 5th holes
* (d) To the right of white posts on 1st hole
* 2. LIFT AND DROP WITHOUT PENALTY
* (a) Ball on GUR or animal scrapes
* (b) Ball on concrete road at entrance and around the Navigation Aid Compound
* (c) Where any tree or shrub interferes with stance or swing
* (d) Ball plugged on fairway
* (e) Grass piles aft by greenkeeper
* 3. All tarmac roads staked by red markers are deemed a lateral water hazard

BENBECULA STATION

B.S.G.C.

GOLF CLUB

Balls

In 1902 a rubber-cored ball – the Haskell – was made in America by the Goodrich Tyre and Rubber Company of Akron, Ohio. By the mechanical winding of elastic thread or tape, a core was formed which was then covered by gutta-percha. This ball went further when hit properly, and even if miss-hit it still performed better than previous gutta-percha balls. The widespread adoption of this ball did much to stimulate the growth and spread of the game of golf.

Robert Price, *Scotland's Golf Courses*, Aberdeen University Press, 1989

Alvin and Dougie out of Uniform in the Benbecula Clubhouse

DOUGIE: I've seen some near-misses, but no one's ever frightened a pilot yet as far as I'm aware.

ALVIN: Going back to the old days, we used to play down at

Askernish, but it was a long way to go, and a lot of effort – so all the military lads got together to build their own course.

DOUGIE: It was purely voluntary, both military and civilian. The administration was done by the military originally, but we take on as many non-combatants as we can. We're approaching 70 members, and we're now attracting sponsorship from local industry.

ALVIN: It's about half and half military and non-military, I'd say. The chairman is military, because of the politics of it being on military land. But many members are civilians. The vice-captain is a fireman. Whatever happens to the rocket range in the future, the RAF will always be here, and so this course will always stay, even if the RAF are the only people here. Also because we have such a high population of civilians, and that's going from strength to strength. We'd like to extend the course, but we can't, because the land we don't use is actually bog.

DOUGIE: We're limited by budget. Our idea is for the committee to push the fact that it's an island facility, being used by civilians. Then, if the military do leave, the facility is here. The council could take it on. I wouldn't knock Askernish. I wouldn't like to see any golf club go out of business. But if we could remind these people that there is a facility up here . . . OK, we have more members, we're more central, we have easier access, but I wouldn't like to see people be put out of business. Let's develop one or the other and make it a facility for golfers.

ALVIN: It's a par-62 course, nine holes with 18 tees. We only operate four par fours. The rest are par threes. It is slightly small. Actually, it's a very difficult golf course to play. If you go out of bounds at the sixth you're not allowed to go and get the ball because access to the airfield is restricted. So it costs you not only a few shots, but also your golf ball.

DOUGIE: One day a year we've been allowed, with permission, to go over the land, then we've come back and sold the balls to club members. I think it started off as a charitable idea and the money was supposed to go to charity. But we don't do that anymore.

CHAPER SIX

Smoothing Irregularities

I NURSED my wounds and wetness in the slightly uncertain, bus-party luxury of the Dark Island Hotel, a weather-scarred modern building where the welcome was effusively efficient, the water hot, the food served on a massive scale which bespoke an imagination forced to parley with constant local demands for T-bone steaks with curry sauce and chips. And credit cards were acceptable, a boon in my cashless state. The décor was weirdly out of place, I thought, kind of heavy early-80s wine bar. A few military haircuts were in evidence, but I was left unharassed about my ball-hunting escapades. Although one craggily elderly Gael in the lounge bar turned to me, apropos of nothing, and said, liltingly, 'Sometimes, you know, it can be a good thing to miss an aeroplane.' I stared stonily into his mild, rheumy eyes, and did not reply. He picked up his Bacardi and Coke and walked away. I stuck to an unremitting diet of large Highland Parks, defiantly drinking an Orcadian perdition to the hateful Western Isles, as they had suddenly become, to Belinda, to golf, to this ill-advised (by myself) journey, to aeroplanes. Off the wagon. In the midst of all this spiritous or spiritual intake, I downed an acceptable – in my state, turpentine would have been acceptable – claret, a T-bone steak, curry sauce and chips with a side order of onion rings. It wasn't on the menu, of course, but I was going with a drink-fuelled hunch that this was the local fare. It was, as far as I can recall, excellent.

There was enough bulk in the meal to modify the next morning's inevitable hangover – I'd finished up with hot apple pie, ice-cream, coffee and two more large HPs – into something relatively containable.

Indeed, with my leathers crispily dry, my soul felt somewhat revived, or perhaps the zillions of brain cells destroyed by the alcohol had helpfully erased much of the previous day's embarrassment. The weather, however, was diabolical once more, the rain not so much falling as suspended in the air. It was like some kind of filthy, gelatinous fog, capable of saturating even the stoutest piece of treated oilskin in seconds. I stoked my hangover hunger with a gargantuan fried breakfast, zipped the waterproofs over the leathers, and went out to navigate my way north to Lochmaddy and the ferry for Harris.

Lochmaddy is in North Uist. It had initially come as a surprise to me that North Uist is separated from Harris by sea, while Harris isn't an island at all, but has always been land-linked to Lewis, although a barrier of large, glum mountains stand between the two communities. Barra isn't connected to South Uist, though there is a causeway to Benbecula, which is mostly water anyway, and is, in turn, connected to the even smaller, even more watery Grimsay by another causeway. Yet another stone-and-concrete dam then leads to North Uist, but that's it. You have to take a boat to get to the other bit of the Western Isles, the absolutely and thoroughly Protestant bit, where Ian Paisley goes on his holidays because it feels like heaven, or home, or both. Though North Uist is Protestant, they said. Oh really? Who cares, anyway, in this day and age? I'd heard muttered shards of stories in South Uist of powerful priests attempting to create a Catholic state in the southern isles, but no one locally seemed to take such crazed religiosity seriously. South Uist has an almost Andalucian mañana mentality about it, which seemed to become smeared and sullied by Benbecula's rocket-fuelled military incomers as you travelled north.

Once on North Uist, the road narrowed and the landscape became forbidding and alien. I began to hallucinate: I was in an early episode of *Doctor Who*, and terrified lest a Cyberman or Dalek leap from the heather (did Daleks leap?) and exterminate my soaking self. Then I began longing, positively longing for a Dalek or Cyberman to zap me, remove me forever from this hideous land-and-water-and-murk-scape. At last, Lochmaddy appeared, what there was of it. A hotel, a bank, a few houses, a shop and a pier. It was a carbon copy of Lochboisdale, with that same, shuttered feel. Not so much closed as clenched. I was early for the morning boat to Tarbert, Harris's main port, or at least the one Caledonian Macbrayne sailed to, so I parked the bike in a lane at the pier, peeled off my sodden unwaterproofs and leathers, and telephoned Pitch from a strangely unvandalised call box. Bob seemed surprised to hear from me.

'Yes, yes, things are fine, Arnie. No probs. No need to hurry back. Itsuoko have done the deal, or at least we've set the date for signing everything in Japan. We'll need you for that, of course. Fuyaki's insisting the whole thing's done at his golf club after he plays you, he says, to repay you for your hospitality. Probably means he's going to cut your guts out with one of those bloody swords, after what you put him and his retinue through. But that's not for another month. So go on, enjoy yourself.'

I had hoped Bob would frantically demand my immediate return. Deflation set in. Besides, I was now so far into this trip that I might as well continue. There was a ferry back to Uig in Skye from Tarbert, but what the hell, with Harris just across the water, I might as well struggle on northwards. I asked Bob to collect whatever mail Marlon had piled up at my flat during his cleaning frenzies, and forward it to . . . but I couldn't think of a destination. I didn't quite know where I'd be going after Stornoway, in Lewis, which was the end of the Hebridean line. The boat went from there to Ullapool, where there was a hotel-cum-café-cum-art-gallery-cum-folk-club called the Ceilidh Place, owned by actors Robert and Jean Urquhart, and run by an enormous team of young people, most of them from the Antipodes. I'd been there before on a brief, get-away-from-the-kids break with Belinda, an attempt at mending whatever was going wrong between us. It hadn't worked, and while I had loved the

Ceilidh Place, Belinda had hated its admittedly studied, arty informality and the large number of attractive young women who worked there. Or maybe it was the way I kept looking at the attractive young women who worked there that annoyed her. I remembered the sensation acutely: it was a thoughtless, sexless habit which I just could not control. I would find myself following the movements of a waitress, my mind on something else entirely, like the gritty edge one of our prototype amps had at certain volumes on a Erik Satie piano record I loved, or how much I detested *Eastenders*, and why, when an irate Belinda would nudge me and hiss: 'Stop ogling, you dirty . . . bastard!' And the inflection on the word 'bastard' told me she was seriously upset. It worried me, because I'd never been conscious of this before, this sleazy habit. God, maybe I'd been doing it for years, but I swear it was innocent, no mental undressing involved. I became intensely conscious of my gaze's target, and made strenuous efforts to look anywhere but at women. After the split, I stopped worrying about it, and occasionally found myself waking from a daydream looking straight into the irritated eyes of some woman who did not like being watched. And who could blame her?

'The Ceilidh Place, Ullapool, Bob. Forward everything there, and leave any messages that come through for me. Belinda hasn't been trying to get hold of me?' She hadn't. I mumbled a goodbye to Bob, and wondered what had happened to her, since my pathetic phone call, and more importantly, to Paul and Patti. If she really had contacted the CSA about me. Then I thought, for God's sake, who cares about the CSA? What can they do? At least there would be some system, some structure around my support for my kids, and maybe access would be . . . and suddenly I had to speak to them, to Paul and Patti. I dialled the number. The answering machine bleeped, then Belinda's metallically rendered tones: 'I can't come to the telephone just now, but I may be in, so please leave a message.' One of those security-conscious, don't-assume-the-house-is-empty-jerk, anyway-maybe-I-just-don't-want-to-talk-to-you announcements.

I trooped through the air-suspended water to the bank, where I finally managed to acquire some papery green stuff, and then to the tourist office, where the young girl in charge looked nervously at me. I suppose I did have the air of a soggy Charles Manson. I didn't linger, but pushed on to the shop, which had not very much of everything, including copies of a poetry book by one Angus Peter Campbell called *The Greatest Gift*, *Popular Mechanics*, the *West Highland Free Press*, some apples, frozen mince, dog food, cat food, mousetraps, paraffin, cigarettes and whisky. All, in other words, the essentials. I eyed the fags. I was conscious of steam coming off my clothing, and it was one of those cigarette moments. To hell with it. I bought 20 Benson and Hedges and some matches, wrapped them in a plastic bag and shoved them deep inside my slimy clothing.

As I walked back to the pier, I could hear the bray of the ferry's siren, announcing her arrival. About a dozen cars and lorries had joined the bike, which glistened in the rain. My rucksack, bless its remarkably expensive waterproof qualities, remained bungeed in place, as did the clubs. No casual thieves on North Uist. I waited astride the bike for permission to go aboard, where, doubtless, taciturn seamen would rope the bike to stanchions and there would be chips. I had the impression that Lochmaddy hadn't quite discovered the chip. I reached for the plastic bag containing the cigarettes, and with red, tingling-cold fingers, pulled out a fag, what Dennis Potter had called 'the tube of delight'. The rain had stopped. I struck a match and inhaled the flame through the B&H behind cupped hands. Heat hit my face, then my mouth and lungs. No coughing. It was as if I had never stopped smoking. I was conscious only of relief. Sometimes a cigarette is your only friend. Four, five deep draws . . . then the fear, the guilt the worry: that's it then, enough to get you cancer . . . I stubbed out the fag, crumpled up the pack with the matches and threw the wasted lung-rot into the nearest bin.

Next morning I found myself in bliss. A warm sun shone from a cloudless blue sky as I gazed out at the flawless silvery gold of Scarista beach, and I had just hit a wondrous, a truly miraculous drive on to the green of the first hole of the Harris Golf Club's stunning course at Scaristamhor. I stood on the edge of the green, marvelling at the fact that this shot, which had felt physically no different to hundreds of other, disastrous attempts, had overcome the problems of a blind approach over a large lump in the 203-yard fairway to land 25 feet from the hole. And the view . . . My map indicated that the hill in the distance was Toe Head, but that beach was to die for, there with the rumpled stretch of undeveloped dunes behind it, perfect golf-course territory. But I decided this nine-hole treasure would do, on a gorgeous Saturday morning with no one playing but myself.

I had picked up a score-card on the way out of the Drinnishader Hotel, which at first glance has been preserved as a museum to 1950s hotel-keeping, complete with irascibly jolly, rather self-important mine host, apparently terrified, white-bloused waitresses, a single coin box for guests, lounge-bar décor from a range of periods, beginning in the 1930s and ending in 1959, and a

111

range of food quite stunning in its blandness, served in a cavernous dining-room redolent of a wartime London club. This is what happens when you let locals loose on tourism, I pondered. Where were the incomers, the English settlers with properly cooked vegetables, French recipes, polenta, brown rice, local mussels, home-made muesli and low-fat milk? Where were they when you needed them? Nevertheless, a small selection of malts behind the bar took me, via Clynelish and Bunnahaibhean, into a mellow acceptance of the place, with its effortlessly threadbare Gaelic atmosphere. A quarter of a million pounds would bring it up to scratch, I reasoned. Talk in the bar was of the quarry, the quarry, and yet again, the quarry. This was the result of a proposal by Redland Aggregates to remove, over a few decades, an entire hill on the south-east coast of Harris, creating an artificial sea-loch, providing some local employment and, claimed the environmentalists, destroying the unique atmosphere of Harris, possibly poisoning the sea, and vandalising what was definitely one of God's listed landmarks. In the bar of the Drinnishader Hotel, I eavesdropped on fat men who talked diffidently of the Sabbath, and how it might be broken by ballast-unloading, although the benefits would be huge, all those jobs for the young men . . . and I wondered about the jobs, the dirty, grinding, boring, unskilled jobs, and the mess, the huge clouds of filth, and the money to be made from all the incomers, money for shopkeepers and bar-owners and hoteliers, and the changes those incomers would bring. I went to bed in my narrow, single room, and dreamed of giant trucks encrusted in pound notes.

So I had a 15-foot putt for a birdie at the first, and as the waves crashed against the nearby shore, rocky for half the length of the course, massively sandy for the rest, I of course missed it. But I holed the tricky three-footer I left myself, and felt good. A par. What a wonderful game! A couple of cars had drawn up next to the first tee, and as I readied myself for second hole, I noticed two figures strolling towards the first, ready to play. At a distance, I could tell from the bulging bags and fluorescent couture that they were taking their golf seriously, even if no one else was. The second was a 217-yard skite which I comprehensively blew, sending my admittedly powerful drive hooking off to the left in a gigantic curve which ended on the road, the main A859, shooting enormously into the air and landing with a a sticky permanence in the grass verge. I sighed, but nothing could destroy my buoyant mood. A lift, drop and good recovery shot would see me on course for a five. I strode off to search for the ball.

By the time I'd found it, lifted and dropped, played a dreadful five iron into a stiffening, but not unpleasant westerly breeze, and three-putted, I'd taken a not unreasonable six, but found that the fluorescent Real Golfers behind me were watching my antics intently, as they were now on the second tee and obviously confident of reaching the green in one. I lifted my hand in salute and waved them through, taking a seat on the sandy grass to watch them play. Their tee shots were all but identical, high, straight and within five feet of the pin. When they drew closer, I noticed that the eye-mauling golf-wear clad two very similar figures. They were male, tall, thin and sunburned in that ingrained way which tells of years in a hot climate. Their ages could have been anything between 35 and 50; one wore a baseball cap, the other a tartan bunnet. Neither smiled as they approached the green. Not a word was spoken as each sank their birdie putts and, without filling in a scorecard, moved towards the third tee without so much as a glance at me. I wasn't having that.

'Morning,' I said, 'feel free to play through.'

They halted. One of the pair, distinguished by his sandy moustache, a relatively restrained one compared to Squadron Leader Goodfellow, nodded towards me, still unsmiling. 'Why, thank you, sir. We appreciate that.' The accent was American, Southern, Tennessee Williamsish. I was being stalked through the Western Isles by them it seemed, y'awll-have-a-nice-day Americans. However, I had no desire for sexual congress with either of these two. Where was Sharon now? Probably back in a crisp white uniform, computerising in New England, or striding long-leggedly down a golf course, her hair streaming in the wind, her . . . oh, stop it. They moved on, laid down their bags and, motionless, stared down the long, undulating fairway of the 282-yard third. They clearly had no intention of asking me to accompany them on their round or indeed having any further conversation with me.

'On holiday?' I ventured. 'Fine day for it.'

The moustacheless one turned to me and stared in silence for a second, then said, deliberately, in a Bostonian drawl, 'It is a fine day, sir, and truthfully we are not on holiday. We are engaged in a golf match, though, so if you'll excuse us?'

He picked a three wood out of his bag, placed his ball, and with a fluid, compact swing, despatched it as far as I could hope to drive with a force-eight gale behind me. And with God on my side. I shrugged, and let the other one hit a similar shot without interruption. Rude bastards. But my curiosity was aroused. Americans? In Harris, and not on holiday? Why did they have to be honest? If they'd lied and said they were vacationing, I wouldn't have been curious at all. I mean, two Americans, golfing, a fine day in the Western Isles? But they could have been Mormons or maniac Free Presbyterians on a battery-recharging prayer-and-golf-and-study trip, or CIA men looking for a suitably secret location for training agents to destabilise some fledgling democracy. Or perhaps the quarry? But Redland was British, surely? I let them play on, and after they had swiftly dealt with the third hole, continued a round which, if not exactly up to the nirvana of its beginning, had enough satisfying shots, lucky pars and bearable bogeys to restore my faith in the game. The eighth, an exquisite par three, took you from a high tee to a green right on the edge of the Atlantic, at the corner where the sand dunes of Scarista changed to rocky inlets and coves. I scored a four, after a wonderful three iron was, typically, let down by crap pitching and worse putting. Well, I say a wonderful three iron. It was nearly on the green. The ninth smiled nastily, a par-four, 361-yard monstrosity with the sea inches to your left the whole way in, which gave you the option of punching straight across a nasty cliff-edged inlet on to the fairway beyond, or playing safe up into some light rough on a rising slope to the left. Recklessly, I went for the whack across water, and lost my first ball of the game, down into the heaving surf. I didn't care, though. I was having a good time, if it hadn't been for those damned Americans. I played another ball to safety, and completed the hole in seven. Pretty creditable, if you ask me.

By the time I reached the tiny, locked clubhouse, the Americans and their cars had vanished. I was feeling footsore and starving, and as it was nearly lunchtime I decided to try the nearby Scarista House Hotel, much-fêted in the guidebooks. It was a few hundred yards away from the golf course, and in its cool, beautifully renovated interior, I was provided with superb crab pâté sandwiches on homemade brown bread, a selection of cakes, and a pot of the best coffee I'd tasted since leaving Glasgow. All served in a library sporting some seriously literary mind fodder. I was impressed. I asked if they had two Americans staying there, but the owner, who by his accent was most certainly not a local, said no, only English, Scots and Germans. And he was sorry, but they were full up, or he would have gladly taken my booking. Oh well.

I rode into the golden afternoon through Leverburgh, where soap magnate Lord Leverhulme unsuccessfuly tried to found a fishing dynasty to supply his Macfisheries shops, and then down to Rodel, on the southerly tip of Harris, where the twelfth-century St Clement's Chapel looked visitable, if you were into that sort of thing. The rest of the place looked as if it was waiting for the end of the world to happen next week. Just a mile or two north-east, hell had already arrived.

The east coast of Harris is unbelievable, literally like the backside of some chilly hades, a moonscape of truly sinister appearance. It is all rock, an ancient, grey, fungal stuff which looks diseased. It is truly awe-inspiring, and capable of evoking religious impulses or fear in almost anyone, I would say. It made me feel small and afraid, and fully in support of those men who wanted to rip the rock out to build roads in England and Germany, who wished to set their gigantic mark on this inhuman place, to render it tamed. On a motorbike, I felt like a speck, like a midge crawling along a cliff face. I had an inkling of that effect people sometimes get on the long, straight roads of Australia – hypnotised under those huge skies, they drive off into the desert and are lost forever, made ever smaller by the landscape until they vanish. At Lingerabay, I felt as if I was being crushed by the omnipresent rock, was caught in a time-delayed avalanche or landslide, and was tempted just to run for the sea, and escape . . .

But I kept going, and arrived back at last in Tarbert. It is called the Golden Road, that horrifying tarmac track up from Rodel, because it cost so much to build. I would pay a fortune never to have to travel it again.

As I coasted down the hill towards the doomy, cliff-shadowed harbour of Tarbert, a bizarre sight met me. There in the assembly area for the ferry were my two Americans, their two cars – now obviously hired Ford Sierras – parked side by side, with a large banner hung on two poles poking out of the two vehicles. In white letters on red, it read: CALLING YOU HOME. I pulled up and switched off the Kawasaki's engine. In front of their banner, which had been professionally printed, my rude golfing non-partners, now attired in matching pale-blue suits and sober ties, were standing. One had an accordion, which was playing that unmistakable hymn tune, so reminiscent of drunken Glasgow Saturdays, when drunks would sing it along with the Salvation Army bands, whisky or gin-scented tears running down their faces . . . The other had a Bible the size of an *Encyclopedia Britannica* volume, and was clearly preparing to preach. As I drew closer, I could see a small public-address system had been set up, and both men were wearing lapel microphones. One or two curious onlookers watched from behind the men, from the street which wound its way up the side of the hill which towered over the pier. An elderly couple stood near me as the mustachioed American, hatless and now revealed as wearing an appalling, reddy-brown wig, began to speak.

'BROTHERS AND SISTERS,' he declaimed, his voice tinnily amplified and echoing off the stone and concrete around him, 'BROTHER HIRAM AND MYSELF, BROTHER JARED, HAVE COME TO YOUR FAIR ISLAND IN THE NAME OF THE LORD JESUS CHRIST AND THE SECOND CHURCH OF THE REDEEMER'S CALL TO THE HOMEWARD BOUND, JUSTICE FORK, NORTH CAROLINA, IN THE UNITED STATES OF AMERICA. WE COME NOT AT OUR OWN BEHEST, OR THAT OF OUR ELDERS AND LEADERS, BUT AT THAT CALL, THE SOLE AND GENUINE CALL, OF OUR LORD HIMSELF.' Here Brother Jared Moustache paused and looked around at his audience. While there were others gathering above and behind him, and children clambering down to the war memorial to observe the spectacle, the only people he could see were me and the elderly couple, who had the bronzed, pastel-attired look of English tourists. 'SOME OF YOU,' and here he looked directly at me, 'SOME OF YOU MAY HAVE SEEN US TODAY ON THE GOLF COURSE, YOUR GOD-GIVEN AND DIVINELY LOVELY GOLF COURSE OVER THERE AT SCRRRRISTAH. WELL, WE AT REDEEMER'S CALL TO THE HOMEWARD BOUND BELIEVE IN THE GREAT, THE DIVINE ALLEGORY OF THE GAME SOME CALL THE GLORIOUS GAME. WELL, WE BELIEVE THAT IS AN APT DESCRIPTION, BROTHERS AND SISTERS, BECAUSE THERE ARE SO MANY PARALLELS BETWEEN THE TRUE HOMEWARD GOSPEL AND THE SEARCH FOR GOLFING SUCCESS. AND WE HAVE EVOLVED A MEANS OF PRAYING, OF WORSHIP, IN THE FORM OF GOLFING TECHNIQUE, BROTHERS AND SISTERS. IN THE EXAMINATION OF THE HOLE, COMES THE EXAMINATION, THE SEARCHING OF THE SOUL. AM I WORTHY, LORD, WORTHY TO TEST MYSELF AGAINST THIS FAIRWAY, THIS DIVINE STRETCH OF GRASS AND SAND? AND IF THE ANSWER COMES, OH YES, CHILD, YOU SURELY ARE WOR-THY, THEN IN THE CHOICE OF THE CLUB COMES CON-NECTION WITH THE DIVINE INTELLIGENCE. OH YES, FOR ONLY AS WE THROW OURSELVES ON GOD'S MERCY WILL THE IDEAL CHOICE OF CLUB BE REVEALED TO US IN OUR HEARTS. IN OUR SECRET SOULS. NOT OF OUR OWN CHOOSING BE THE IMPLEMENT, BUT THE LORD'S. FOR ONLY HE WILL KNOW OUR DEEPEST, TRUEST THOUGHTS AND FEELINGS AND PHYSICAL NEEDS AND YEARNINGS, AND PLACE IN OUR HANDS THE TRUE IRON, THE TRUE WOOD, THE TRUE METAL WOOD, BROTHERS AND SIS-

TERS. AND THEN, IN THE STRIKE, OH THE UPLIFTING OF THE SPIRIT! THE ECSTASY OF GRACE, OF BEING IN THE VERY HANDS OF GOD! CAN ANYTHING MATCH THAT GLORY? WHY YES!' His voice, which had been soaring up to that point, fell to a dramatic, tinkly whisper. 'Ours is the only church built within its own, spiritually designed parkland golf course, with holes, oh ye of Harris, you chosen, spiritually aware people of God, holes named on Biblical and godly themes. There is Calvary, of course, with its three crosses overlooking the green. And lo, it is a hard hole, harder than Gethsemane, both par fives. But at Resurrection, a 145-yard par three with no bunkers' – his voice began to rise, quickly – 'GLORY, GLORY AND EASE AND LIFE ETERNAL, A LIFE OF SOARING ON THE WINGS OF THE EAGLE, THE BIRDIE, BEYOND THE PAR, IS REVEALED TO THE CHOSEN, THE ELECT! COME! COME NOW AND JOIN US! MYSELF AND BROTHER HIRAM HAVE COME AMONG YOU, SENT BY THE LORD, AND HAVE RENTED A COTTAGE, A CLUBHOUSE OF THE SOUL IN YOUR MIDST! BE WEL-COME TO OUR NEW TABERNACLE OF PRAYER IN THE SWING, IN THE CHIP, IN THE PUTT, THAT MOST HOLY OF PRAYERFUL EXPRESSIONS IN PHYSICAL MOTION. OH COME, YE WHO ARE WEARY AND HEAVY LADEN, YE OF HARRIS WHERE GOD IS ALREADY AT WORK AND WHERE THE WAY OF THE LOW HANDICAP IS OPEN TO THOSE WHO WILL BELIEVE AND FOLLOW!'

I gaped. We all gaped. None of the children jeered, which would certainly have happened in any other, less hell-fearing part of the country. The gulls squawked as Brother Hiram began playing 'Just As I Am', the old Billy Graham appeal hymn, softly on his accordion. Brother Jared began to whisper, eerily, like some kind of surreal religious rapper: 'Oh yes, come now, come here and accept a leaflet which could alter your entire way of life, and hopes for death. Could take you into an open-air lifestyle of spiritual depth and philosophical truth. Could deliver you forever from the mere toil of existence and other lesser sporting activities. Come. Oh, please come . . .' As if hypnotised, the elderly couple moved towards Jared, but I forced myself to turn to the Kawasaki. I pulled on my helmet, started the bike, and revved it as hard as I could, great bitter roars of sound washing away the deranged religion which still lay like a drug in the air.

It was hardly any distance to the Drinnishader Hotel, where my narrow bed and odd fish course, lurking unexpectedly in the middle of the set dinner, awaited me. I resolved to get drunk, again. Perhaps I had imagined Brother Hiram and Brother Jared. But no, all talk in the lounge bar was of the pair, the Church of the Redeemer's Call to the Homeward Bound, and rumours that they were millionaires and planned not only a new golf course, but a massive church building which would become a world centre for this golfing religion. 'I hear they've been rejected out of hand by both the Royal and Ancient and the town of St Andrews,' said one local with whisky blossoms bulging on his throbbing nose. 'They've rented a cottage out at Bigotraigh, near to that Jehoshaphat MacLeod, you know the one that talks about Catholics and homosexuals on the telly. Indeed, Jehoshaphat might join their church. It would be very handy for him . . .' Mine Host nodded, wisely. Whisky Blossoms continued: 'Ach well, maybe we could have the godly golfers instead of the quarry. If these Americans were to build something which brought in the tourists, well then, that would be fine. And not so dusty. Besides . . .' he sipped first at a half pint of heavy beer, then at a large dram, 'I wouldn't mind improving my game a litle bit. I want to beat that bastard MacTavish in the monthly medal. And if God can help me, I'm all for it.' Then an awful thought struck him, and he slammed his whisky glass down on the bar, very nearly spilling at least one drop of the contents. 'You . . . you don't think . . . you don't think they could be . . . Romans . . . do you?' A general negative murmur rose from those around the bar. The Americans may have been daft, mad, dangerous or worse, but they weren't Catholics. At least that was something in Tarbert. I took a last large Tormore to bed. Tomorrow I would head for Lewis. It was Sunday, and Lewis would be shut. But Harris was making me feel uneasy. What I hadn't wanted to admit to myself was that Brothers Hiram and Jared had almost brought me weeping to their feet, screaming, take me! Take me! For as I'd listened to Jared preach, I had thought, well, why not? Give it all up, everything, for golf and religion, a stunning, brilliant, perfect combination of body and soul. I could be like Bernhard Langer! Retain my hair! Live here, in this dreadful, awesome, monastic place, and become absorbed in God and the rocks and the sea and the search for the perfect worshipful swing . . . And then I thought, no. There's more to life than golf. And God. There must be.

HARRIS GOLF CLUB
SCARISTA
ISLE OF HARRIS

Secretary: J G Mitchell
0859 82 214

'Perseverance'

Member's Name & Number

MEMBERSHIP CARD
19

Name . . . .

Member No . . . .

Please show this to officials
if requested

Play the Game

Because in general we approach the arts and entertainment from the outside, because we go to art, we regard it as external to the main part of our life. We go to the theatre, to the cinema, the opera, the ballet; to museums; to sports fields (for a part of all great games is as much art as theatre or ballet). Even our reading is outside the main occupations of our day; and even the art that is piped into our homes we feel comes from outside. This holding at a distance of art, this constant spectatoring, is thoroughly evil.

John Fowles, *The Aristos*

It Looks Like Grass But it Isn't

Willie Fulton, *vice-captain, Harris Golf Club*

I am vice-captain, for my sins. The course is absolutely beautful, and I'm just wondering to myself what the courses on the mainland are like at this moment, early on a Saturday morning. I mean, here we are, you and I standing here, overlooking the Atlantic with the sea coming in and we're on our own, Many a golfer would give his eye teeth for this I'm sure. I'd give up the game if I had to queue from the early hours of the morning, as they do in some places.

Way back in the 1930s this was an 18-hole course, but it fell into disuse, and about seven years ago it was reconstituted. It's run by local stalwarts with the co-operation of the crofters who own the land. It's basically croft land – we couldn't exist without the help of the crofters. There are times when we can't play, because we're at the behest of the crofters. During the month of May lambing takes place and the course is closed, but mainly we have a very good relationship with the crofters.

I'm the current club champion. Whether I would be if I was playing in Bishopbriggs or Clydebank is very debatable. I only took up the game as a challenge about four or five years ago, though as a youth in Glasgow I knocked about as boys do. I've no ambition to take on the likes of Ben Crenshaw, but a couple of years ago Nick Faldo played this course, and I know I've scored only six or seven more than he did. He left a signed five-pound note after his round. Nobody met him, but he left this fiver, and now every year we have the Faldo Fiver Competition, and the winner gets to keep the fiver for a year.

The tees here are a bit on the small side, and the whole course does require precision play. We're hoping to do a bit of development on the course, some improvements, but it's run mainly by volunteers, so there's no money pouring in. The annual membership is a bit prohibitive, perhaps, at £30 a year.

Just now, we're seeing Harris at its most spectacular, though there could be changes if the superquarry goes ahead. The quarry development is ongoing. I've not given any major thought to it. My personal feeling is that the scale worries me, particularly when you look out on a day like this, at all the beauty before you. Sometimes I really do worry about it. I feel very privileged standing here today. We're looking at the vast expanse of Scarista beach, and it's absolutely gorgeous. On the left there's Toe Head, and you can catch the Uists in the background.

The course drains very very quickly – it looks like grass, but it isn't. There's sand underneath, and in some ways it's like one gigantic bunker. The terrain is difficult enough, but I remember a couple of years ago we had a crow which appeared on the scene. It lurked around and above us as we were playing our shots and flew off occasionally with our balls. We were going to get a shotgun, but that crow was far too clever for us. We heard some time later that someone had found the nest. There were over 100 golf balls in it, but unfortunately they were all so well pecked they were unusable. That was the story of the crow which chewed our balls off. Yes indeed.

I Come From Over the Border

Calum MacRitchie

I come from over the border in Lewis, so I've got a 90-mile round-trip to play golf down here. There is a parkland course in Stornoway but it was very wet yesterday and it was closed because of the rain. Here the land dries out in about ten minutes – it's much more interesting to play down here, because you can play real golf, whereas in Stornoway today you would probably have to play on tee-pegs. That's the reason. Stornoway is confined within a woodland. Although there are some impressive views at the top, it's not as majestic as this. You can come down here almost any time to play your nine or 18 holes without waiting. Probably we are the only people in the neighbourhood who don't have sheep, and the sheep get first priority in the morning. Once they have been settled and bedded down for the day, then golf finds a space.

This sheep fank next to the first tee commands greater respect than does the Royal and Ancient when you're walking down the 18th at St Andrews. Because we play golf on grazing land and from next Monday the course will be closed for a month because of the lambs, we have to live in harmony with the crofting people. They had to fight hard to acquire these rights and we don't want to infringe them in any way.

CHAPTER SEVEN

Agreement to Waive Rules Prohibited

THE Sabbath, and despite glorious sunshine, a dour fog of holy indolence seemed to have settled on the Hebrides. At the Tarbert Hotel, breakfast was served as if it were communion, rather than fishy bacon and runny eggs. I settled my bill and headed into the morning; even the gulls seemed reluctant to break the silence of the psalms, but I let the Kawasaki's four cylinders roar blasphemously out through the Marshall four-into-one exhaust, a rebellious hymn to individual liberty. The Blue Bomber ruled.

The 35-mile run into Stornoway took me spiralling up through mountains which frowned disapproval, bare, brutal, forbidding peaks which matched exactly my perception of the local brand of self-hating God-fearingness. Every so often grim, blockhouse churches would appear, glumly gaping their doors as service time approached, and I would find myself overtaking shiny, snail-paced cars, loaded with fur-collared coats, holy hats and handbags, and being driven by some bent old man as if God was about to bombard him with flaming sheep for daring to use the car on a Sunday. The fragrant aroma of burning peat, usually the hallmark of a still Western Isles morning, and a smell which had pursued me all the way from Uist, was missing. Clearly, it was a case of burning in hell if you dared to burn peat on the Sabbath. Above Arivruiaich, the landscape grew higher, plateau-like, a kind of monotonously inhuman mixture of bog and water, with a faltering road treading lightly over the top of it all. The bike beneath me rumbled and spat. A few other bikers, presumably pagans out to escape Stornoway's theocracy, zoomed past going towards Tarbert, all with the customary bikers' salute, a flip of the left hand to indicate unity in the brotherhood or sorority of *Wild One* fantasists, would-be Brandos, emotionally stunted middle-aged adolescents or people with small willies. I felt grateful for those tiny waves, as, beneath God's unfriendly gaze, I reached Stornoway unscathed by lightning bolts.

First came the big bungalows, suburban, timber-framed kit houses run to fat. Then there were trees, as I dipped down through this insular suburbia, out of the pebble-dashed rancherias with BMWs and Audis and Mondeos in the gravel drives, and I was among grey, scowly houses with grey slate roofs, and even under a warm sun and blue sky, the windows glinted like the blank stares of a convention for the blind. As I approached the town centre, parkland on the right opened up as a securely shut, utterly deserted golf course, hilly, tree-studded and impressive-looking. Further in towards Stornoway's guiltily beating heart, cars by the dozen rolled slowly up and down, filled with clearly irreligious young people, smoking, touching, shouting through open windows, occasionally smoking their back tyres with a *Dukes of Hazzard* screech and howling away in a display of good-humoured aggression. The churches were in, for by this time it was nearly noon, so these were the lost souls of Stornoway, parading their God-defying evil in an innocent, motorised, sexual, public way, which nevertheless saw them safely cocooned inside their metal shells. I was stunned. I had expected to find a town patrolled by the Church Police, the Thought Monitors, chasing anyone displaying any unnecessary flesh or even a smile into the darkened, curtained privacy of their own homes, securing the streets for a gloomy Jesus. But here was a kind of Mediterranean parade, twisted, slightly paranoid, yes, but there, in defiance and exuberant celebration of a damned life beyond godliness.

But behind the closed doors of Stornoway the Sabbath still held sway. I needed to find some accommodation, and after trying two smallish hotels in the centre of town and two nearby guest-houses, I was wondering how Lewis expected to have any kind of tourist industry at all if it ceased and desisted on the seventh day. Doors had opened a crack, and reluctant, suspicious faces had peered out at me. 'We do not take guests on a Sunday.' You don't what? Good God, what is this all about? What about the tradition of Western Isles hospitality, about Christian fellowship, for God's sake? In the end, an apologetic, slightly embarrassed woman at the quaintly named Bridlington Guest-house directed me to Bermudan House, a tall Victorian terraced house with peeling paint which had a small bed-and-breakfast sign in a grimy downstairs window. I rang. Nothing. I rang again. Somewhere, the sound of shuffling feet, and the door was flung open by a tall woman in her late thirties, wearing a dressing-gown of supreme frilliness and a blotchy, morning-after-the-night-before expression coupled with a lopsided grin. Her hair had once been gelled and spiked, but now it was in dark disarray. It was 12.15, which I would have thought pretty sinfully late on a Stornoway Sunday not be dressed.

'Hello,' she said, stifling a yawn. 'What can I do for you?'

'Eh, I was told by the lady at the Bridlington that you might have a single room for one night . . . sorry to have got you up.'

She laughed. 'Och, no, no bother.' The accent was pure Fife, Kirkcaldy or maybe Dunfermline. 'I should have been up ages ago, but I was out last night, and God, we didn't get in until about three.' She yawned again, prodigiously, revealing a drink-and-fag-furred set of tonsils. I was fascinated, and my eyes locked on to the back of her throat like a dentist's. The morning light played around her mouth like God's searchlight. The prospect of a kiss flitted though my mind, something from the deepest, dankest horror-movie section of the sub-conscious. 'Aye, yes, come in, no bother. I'll give you room 15, up on the second floor, private facilities, like. Is, emm, £23 a night all right?' I nodded, and followed her in, my leathers squeaking. The subconscious, that old unreconstructed macho male bullshit repository, was flickering fantasies now: maybe she's got a thing about leather trousers; maybe she'll turn round and make a grab for you. But she didn't, thank God, though she did reveal that her name was Ina and that her husband was working offshore. But, fantasies aside, I had the impression that this was said in a sort of matter-of-fact, non-flirtatious sort of way. Then again, maybe not. She gave me my room key. My leather trousers squeaked. She seemed oblivious. Just as well, perhaps.

I carted my rucksack into the room, which was clean but basic, with framed postcards of Stornoway harbour on the wall and four single beds. I hoped the £23 bought me exclusive use. The idea of finding three hulking German hikers sharing my space did not appeal. I changed into less bikerish gear and wandered downstairs, meeting Meg, now dressed in those hideous floral leggings women seem to be addicted to, and an expensive hand-knitted mohair jumper. Her hair had been gelled, her face made-up and she looked wonderful. 'I'm just going out to get something to eat,' I said. 'Is there anywhere open?'

Ina laughed, revealing those tonsils again, now relatively pink and exuding the distinct flavour of Euthymol toothpaste. I like Euthymol toothpaste. Maybe a kiss wouldn't be a bad idea, though I was so hungry it wasn't too overwhelming a prospect. Kissing during extreme starvation can result in nasty tongue-chewing incidents which are very hard to explain, especially if it's your own tongue. 'Well, there's the Indian restaurant, it's open at lunchtimes now, despite being cursed by the Elect of Macleod, and the Seaforth, its got a sort of Italian café place, it's open. That's where you have to go to get milk or sweeties or lemonade on a Sunday, by the way, in this godforsaken place. Or rather, no' godforsaken. And if you fancy a drink there's the County, back entrance, you can sneak in there, right beside the Free Church, but watch out for the Elect of Macleod there as well. They're mostly harmless, just shout at you a wee bit, but it can be disconcerting.' I looked at her. The Elect of Macleod?

'Och yes, you know that man, that man, the holy one, at least he's always saying he's holy, always on the telly? Lives in Harris?'

My mind flashed back to Hiram and Jared, the Church of the Redeemer's Call to the Homeward Bound, the cracks in the Tarbert Hotel about Jehoshaphat Macleod, the world's only Calvinist television evangelist, welcoming them to Bigotraigh. I had seen him on the TV once or twice, but had only heard about one particularly inflammatory programme about Catholics, at the behest of an astonished Bob. 'I don't know what he's trying to do,' he told me the next day, 'but he seems to be aiming for the Pastor Jack Glass audience, and also just to provoke outrage by shoving dangerous shite in people's faces.' Bob, a good son of the confessional, didn't lightly use words like 'shite', so it had clearly provoked a fierce reaction in him. When I heard what had been said, I understood why he'd been so angry.

But Ina was continuing. 'Aye, well, anyway there's a group of young men in Stornoway, real born-again Presbies, know what I mean? Here they call it "getting the Cuiram"', or something, it means like converted, from a life of fun, going all funny? Well, anyway, about six of them, all big fans of your man Macleod, formed this society called the Elect of Macleod. They all wear black suits with floral waistcoats, black silk ties and white shirts, and they've formed what the call the Sabbath Patrol.' Oh? 'That's right, the Sabbath Patrol. They're quite polite, really. Just sort of approach sunbathers or anyone playing football and quietly inform them that they're breaking God's law. Happened to me last Sunday, in fact, down there by the bowling green. Nobody knows if Jehoshaphat Macleod himself agrees with it, of course, but they had one of the Elect on local radio, and he was saying they believe that this guy has been sent by God as a kind of sign of the Last Days before Christ comes again, and that in imitation of him they are fulfilling the prophecies of both Christ and St Paul. They have little cards, sort of leaflets, giving Bible references for what they're doing. There's stuff about the . . . what is it? Priesthood of all believers, and about the shamefulness of men loving men, too. Though they haven't picketed the chapel yet, as far as I know. They supposedly hack through the bushes up by the golf course, up in Lady Lever Park, looking for adulterers and any boys giving each other blow jobs, but that's only a story, I think. They curse you if you swear, so they say. They didn't curse me, just told me God loved me and hated the sin I was committing. I suppose my boobs were showing a bit too much, but well, if you've got it, flaunt it, that's what I always say! Anyway, the Seaforth's your best bet for lunch. Have to go now. Bye!'

She slammed the door behind her, leaving me in a state of numbness. I'd had an inkling that Stornoway was a little deranged, but this? The Elect of Macleod, indeed! I had been contemplating taking a three iron out with me and surreptitiously attempting a few sinful shots on Stornoway golf course, but the existence of a real live church security force was, to say the least, somewhat off-putting.

I gathered my wits in the perfectly pleasant and Italian restaurant attached to the Seaforth Hotel, La Terazza, feeling distinctly sympathetic to all things Roman, eating lasagne and drowning it with a couple of the biggest glasses of Chianti I've ever experienced outside my own kitchen. Sitting in the window as the clock crept towards 1.00 p.m., I was able to witness the emptying of the churches, the gradual outpouring of beautifully attired people from Stornoway's many kirks. The women and girls all had complex headgear and long, floral, discreetly feminine dresses. It was a bit like Ascot in the early 1950s. The older men wore homburgs and black suits, and were very reminiscent of elderly attenders at some of Glasgow's synagogues, while the younger ones had mail-order Next or Freemans double-breasted suits, complete with snazzy Jeremy Paxman ties. Even the children were formally dressed. As I sipped my Chianti and the sun shone down, it was like being abroad, somewhere utterly alien, lost in its own social, theological and probably political time-warp. Albania sprang to mind.

I paid the bill and walked back along towards the golf course, determined at least to have a look at what was, until the following morning at least, forbidden fruit. I still hadn't decided whether to stay and play the course, or take the morning ferry to Ullapool and shake the dust of the Western Isles off my boots and tyres. I passed a children's playpark, and sure enough, the swings were chained together in an attempt to prevent children besmirching the Sabbath with the sound of enjoyment. But the roundabout and slide had been left untouched. I suppose the powers that be could have sprinkled them with broken glass and superglue, but perhaps even the God of Stornoway couldn't sanction that. Anyway there were children, and some casually dressed, clearly evil parents messing about on the chute and the roundabout. It was hot, and I noticed a bare-chested man slumped against a park shelter, sipping from a tin of Carlsberg Special. Further along, to my astonishment, a bounce game of football was in progress. Where were the Elect of Macleod? Maybe Ina had been winding me up.

But sure enough, through the playpark gate came two figures, their dark suits counterpointed by waistcoats which could have graced a brace of Mississippi gamblers. They bore gigantic, floppy black Bibles and carried handkerchiefs wound around their left hands, presumably as some kind of religious statement. At a canter, the light of missionary zeal in their eyes, the two young men, one tall and thin, the other puffingly fat, came up to the parents who were slouched near the chute, and spoke to them quietly, although I could see they were out of breath. I was too far away to hear what they said, but the tall one reached into his pocket and presented the couple concerned, who were attempting to ignore this interruption completely, with small cards or leaflets. It was all true. I watched, fascinated, as the two Elect of Macleods, or Elects, made their way at the same ungainly jog to the nearby footballers, running one by one, and fairly skilfully, up to each player in turn and trying – mostly failing – to present one of their leaflets to them. The astonishing thing was the lack of reaction the two Elects evoked. On any other Scottish football field, real or imagined, they would have been felled summarily by righteous boots or fists. In Stornoway, fear of the almighty was so strong, and guilt about Sabbath-breaking so ill-hidden, that they were treated with a kind of contemptuous respect.

Outside the clubhouse of Stornoway Golf Club, a lone car, doubtless abandoned the previous night by some tipsy golfing drouth for the safety of a taxi, lay stranded in the middle of the carpark. A strong smell of stale beer was everywhere, a kind of airborne hangover. Golf and drink are almost as closely associated as pool or snooker and alcohol. In some ways, golf is just snooker played out of doors, a sedentary, physically undemanding sport which attracts potential heart-attack victims, gives them clubhouses in which to smoke and drink to their heart's discontent, then sends them out to spoil a good walk with emotional stress and strain, the upper-body chest-slash of a golf swing, and sudden coronary thrombosis. I breathed deeply of what remained from Stornoway Golf Club's Saturday night. I could have done with a drink.

One of the several, mostly inaccurate golf-course directories I'd picked up in tourist offices and hotels from Southend onwards had indicated that the Lady Lever Park course at Stornoway, 5,178 yards and a par 66, possessed what was 'reputedly the most difficult par-five hole in Europe'. I found this extremely hard to believe, but it was difficult, indeed nearly impossible to work out where the holes were when I began walking around, or rather up and over the Stornoway course. All the tee-markers had been removed, presumably to prevent secret Sabbath-breaking golf. The flags were mostly still in place, and dozens of dogs, some accompanied by their owners, were publicly defecating on the principle and practice of the Sabbath. But identifying the most difficult hole in Europe was nearly impossible. In truth, the course was sticky, muddy and while not in bad condition, devoid of Harris's awesome, lightsome coastal beauty. It struck me as a dour course, but then maybe that was just my Stornoway Sunday mood. It was certainly big, steep and testing, though, and from the top of the hill the view right across to what seemed to be Skye was impressive. I thought of how busy every single one of Glasgow's courses, of how teeming virtually every course in the United Kingdom would be on this Sunday afternoon, and looked again at the dog-walkers, their presence a sign of how golf-less this course was. Then I saw an amazing sight which put golf completely out of my mind.

They were clearly Elects of Macleod, slightly older than the two I'd seen previously, and operating as a team. They were approaching the dog-walkers, and handing over large white objects, far too big to be the calling cards I'd seen earlier. I went towards the pair, who were soon revealed in all their identikit, dapper glory. One rather spoiled the uniformity by wearing a mustard woollen cardigan rather than a floral silk waistcoat, but perhaps that, too, was a penance of some kind. Each had handkerchiefs wound – and, I noticed, tied – around their left hands. One carried a large, floppy Bible; the other had a pile of what looked very like junior-sized disposable nappies. As I approached, the smaller of the two Elects, the one with the Bible and the acne, called out to me: 'Sir, is that your Rottweiler?' I looked around, and sure enough, a large demon dog was bounding along behind me in a fairly jolly fashion. Both Elects – the other one was about six foot five and balding prematurely – looked nervous, but the acned one continued: 'The sanctity of the Sabbath is paramount, sir, and if that is your dog, may we request your co-operation in attaching one of these' – and he lifted one of the nappies – 'to its posterior, in order to avoid the passing of faecal matter publicly on the Lord's day?' I smiled.

'Can I ask you,' I said, 'if the Sunday ban on passing, err, shall we say, jobbies, extends to human beings?'

'Oh yes,' said the tall balding Elect. 'It has been revealed to the Elect of the Macleod that fasting on the Sabbath in terms of food should be accompanied only by the smoking of untipped cigarettes and the drinking of one's own urine, utilising a specially designed opaque plastic tube which prevents the liquid from ever reaching the atmosphere. The weaker brethren among us wear these items of apparel' – he brandished a Pamper, as I could clearly see they were – 'and dispose of them after the last stroke of midnight has sounded and it is Monday. The rest of us practise what is known as constipatory prayer, a form of meditation we believe to be entirely Biblical and environmentally friendly.'

I looked at them. I decided in an instant to leave Stornoway on the first available boat. 'Fascinating,' I said, 'but the dog is not, in fact, mine. However, I'm sure its owner would not be averse to you attaching the said item of apparel to its posterior on your own initiative, if God is telling you that's right. Because, I have seen the jobbie of a Rottweiler, and it is an offence in the eyes and nose of the Lord, undoubtedly.' They shook their heads in unison.

'No, conviction is a work of grace which we cannot enforce.' The tall one smiled and turned away, his burden of nappies flapping slightly in the breeze. The shorter Elect handed me one of his leaflets, which were printed on card and contained a number of references such as 'ABOMINATIONS: Leviticus 18. 26: Thou shalt not commit any; DOGS: Revelations 22. 15: Without are.' It was all very odd.

The Bermudan House seemed to be completely empty when I returned, but Ina, a large smile in place, burst fully made-up from a door on the ground floor: 'All right at the Seaforth? Hope you got something to eat anyway. I went off to have my fortune told at the Tarot specialist over in Tolsta. Good news on the way, she said, very good.' Was it just me or was that an arch look on her face? Actually, the erotic possibilities of a liaison with Ina were becoming more and more, well, if not attractive, then feasible. But she had disappeared again, behind the door which was marked 'Private'.

I telephoned Belinda's number again. Lots of the bleeps which showed that messages had been left, about 15, which signified that she had been out for a while, days probably. I was worried, so I called Bob's number. Another answering machine, three bleeps indicating recent departure. 'Bob, it's Arnie. Listen, everything still stands with the Ullapool thing, but could you check up on Belinda and the kids, that they're OK? No reply when I phone them, that's all. Cheers, and I'll phone tomorrow. It's, uh, Sunday, and I'm eating sinful Indian tonight in Stornoway. No hi-fi shop, either, by the way, so see if Rob in marketing support has any ideas. It's a mad place but no sense in discriminating against them. Might as well take their money.'

The curry was good, and I sneaked into the back bar of the County for a pint or two of fizzy brown beer afterwards, feeling Bhuna-bloated, and well Parathaed. The boat was horribly early in the morning, so I staggered back to the Bermudan, thankful that I had a room with a private loo. Curried beer is not an ingestion to be taken lightly when the toilet's in some isolated corner of an unknown guest-house. I settled into bed – none of the three other single beds was occupied, thank God – half-hoping that the enigmatic Ina would softly open the door and slide naked in beside me, her smooth thighs rubbing deliciously . . . there were footsteps on the stair outside, slow ones. I listened intently to the creaking, my heart thumping in erotic anticipation. Those smiles, the chatter, the way she had touched my arm . . . the leather trousers had turned her head, I knew. Her husband was away, she'd been at pains to point that out. The footsteps reached the landing I was on, halted. I could hear blood pumping around my arteries. Then a nearby door opened, and through the thin plasterboard walls, I heard distinctly an old man's wheeze, hacking cough and dribbling spit. Then a zip being taken down, and a tiny, short-lived trickle, which was then repeated every few seconds for about ten minutes. Nothing less erotic than this I have ever heard. I hadn't noticed the presence of a toilet near room 12, but there obviously was one. And there was another resident, who by the sound of it had both chest and prostate problems. The zip was eventually raised, and the slow tread – accompanied, I thought, by the aroma of cigarette smoke, thus feeding the certainty that I would be burned to death by the invisible fellow guest's setting his sheets on fire – retreated upwards. I shut my eyes, wondering if one of the Elect of Macleod patented urine-sucking tubes would be of any help to the person I was sharing the Bermudan with. Apart from Ina, of course, who never appeared that night.

The invisible enlarged prostate of the creaking stairs and smokey breath did, though. Once every hour-and-a-half, waking me every time. In the end I got up at 7.00 a.m., packed, and went downstairs to the dining-room, which was, predictably, empty and in darkness. So was the kitchen. I didn't feel like disturbing Meg by banging on the door marked 'Private', so I made myself some coffee, unearthed some cornflakes, and sat alone, crunching the taste of the Sabbath between my teeth, and swallowing hard.

Sic Other Pastimes

Seeing the Sabbath day being the Lord's day, it becomes every Christian to dedicate himself, his household and family to the service and worship of God . . . no inhabitants of the burgh, be it themselves, their children, servants or families, to be seen at any pastimes or games within or without the town on the Sabbath day, sic as golf, archerie, bowls, penny stane, tennis or sic other pastimes . . . and also that their daughters and women servants be not found playing at the ball nor singing of profane songs upon the same day . . .

Proclamation by Edinburgh magistrates, 1592

Talking to Yourself in Stornoway

They really do chain the swings together to stop anybody using them in Stornoway . . . however, there are signs of change . . . there is a mass motorised parade through the streets in dozens of expensive cars . . . it's a beautiful day and despite the fact that it's the Sabbath, everybody's out walking, the place is on holiday, people are playing football next to the chained-up swings. The slide can't be chained up, and it's being used. It looks as if children and adults are taking delight in taking their shirts off and holding up two fingers to the Sabbatarians. Two fingers and a belly button. No breasts, I have to say. Mind you, a couple of hours ago there was an even bigger traffic jam when churches poured out their contents of behatted women and beautifully dressed men and little boys and little girls too. Meanwhile, I am on the only golf course in Britain next to a town with 15,000 inhabitants which on a Sunday is totally and absolutely deserted – apart from dogs, and people like me just walking about.

I'd heard that before the Sabbath all the pins are removed – but that's not true. They take away the tee markers so you don't know where to hit. Assuming God hasn't struck you dead if you have the temerity to try and sully the sanctified Sabbath turf . . . but they can't kill your fantasies, can they? I think if I lived here, which God forbid, I think what I'd do is set up a Sabbatarian fantasy golf league, in which all of us would indulge our willingness to play Sunday golf in the company of famous players . . . you could work out some complicated system of scoring, according to their recent tournament performances . . .

Gaelic. This is supposed to be the heartland of Gaelic, the Western Isles, but on South Uist, where you expect to hear Gaelic nearly all the time, what you actually get is a sort of fractured, half-English, half-Gaelic gobbledegook. Pidgin Gaelic. That seems to be the way ahead, with no one speaking it on its own. Why not, I suppose? In Harris, I hardly heard anyone speaking Gaelic, and here in Stornoway, you could be somewhere like . . . Tain, or Paisley. This golf course . . . is very wet. It must be unplayable whenever there's a downpour. The point is you could be anywhere. There's no view of the sea until you get to the top, and it doesn't seem in the least like an island course. No wonder Calum MacRitchie goes to Harris . . .

I've climbed high up on the slope of the course, on what may or may not be the 12th green . . . I can see the mountains of Skye, see for miles in fact . . . and there's a bizarre contraption here, a metal post with two bells attached to it. It might be to let those waiting on the tee know that you're off the green – on the other hand, perhaps it's an early Lewis tradition, stemming from the time when leprous golfers wandered the course and had to warn unseen players in advance of their approach. Or maybe it's something to do with the Sabbath Patrol . . . you ring the bell if you see anyone swinging a club sinfully, and out of the sky come helicopter patrols which descend on the transgressor, and sweep him or her off to a fate better than death . . .

It must be said that the greens here are the best I've encountered so far on my travels. They're in the best condition. No sheep droppings. No crofters. When I was a kid I used to plunge about in the whin bushes on the Lochgreen municipal course, hiding away inside the bushes, and you'd find the spoor of the golfer there, abandoned balls, tees, tins of beer . . . here in a wooded part of the Stornoway course is an abandoned umbrella, corporately sponsored by CIRS Ltd, whoever that is.

I'm up on the high section of the course now and the views are wonderful. What are those hills? Cuillins, probably. Sea and mountain and sand on three sides, far away, and lots and lots of horrible little and not so little kit houses. One of the curses of the Western Isles, everywhere you go, crofting-subsidy kit houses with ranchero roofs. Do they have architects here? Do they have planning laws?

The thing about golf is, you hit some really good shots, and some really bad ones . . . and I think the difference is mainly in how you feel when you connect with the ball. The problem is, you only know how you feel after you've hit the ball. It's that split second of connection – of course, it's more than that. You're trying to create a pendulum effect, an accurate one: position the golf club at the ball and swing it back, then let it fall again so it hits the ball squarely. But how do you do that? HOW DO YOU DO THAT? The same way, every time, so it always works? I don't know. Practice, yes. Physical practice. And drugs too. The last professional sport without compulsory drug testing. Who do the R&A think they're fooling? Have they seen the eyes on some of these guys when they come off the course? Eh? And you don't have to snort cocaine, you know. There are other ways of taking it. But there's all this talk about the inner game of golf, mental preparation, self-belief, auto-hypnosis, transfer this energy into the ball . . . I don't know. What you have to do is keep your left arm straight, your head down, and try not to embarrass yourself too much in front of whoever else is playing with you. Then again, when you actually do hit the ball perfectly, it is kind of . . . transcendental. It's beyond description, really. There is a sense of – naff though it sounds – of inner peace. It is an inner, Zen type of thing. People look at it from outside, and they see these middle-class bank managers in horrid cashmere and imitation cashmere sweaters waiting to have heart-attacks . . . it's seen as a game of bourgeois ideals and masonic handshakes. Yet that moment when you hit a ball well is so . . . perfect, so wonderful, that you want everyone to share it. Nothing else is as good.

CHAPTER EIGHT

Ball in Lateral Water Hazard

WE'D been at sea for about 45 gut-wrenching, breakfast-detaching minutes, in conditions euphemistically described over the ship's Tannoy when we left Stornoway as 'breezy', when suddenly we weren't going to Ullapool anymore. Instead, an apologetic captain tinnily told us, we were diverting to Uig on Skye, where buses would be available to connect with Inverness, and 'ongoing transportation arrangements' would be made by Caledonian Macbrayne staff. There had, he said, been an accident on the Ullapool pier involving a Russian vessel, one of the so-called klondikers. 'It seems that access to the berth is denied us, so my apologies, but we will be coming alongside in Uig in about an hour-and-a-half's time.' So I was going to Skye after all.

Skye. Where the Cuillins don't so much soar above you as threaten you with imminent destruction from their collapse. Where the locals are dour and unfriendly, and hundreds of anglified, candle-making incomers do their level, horsey-laughing best to make them even more so. Belinda had loved it, and had dragged me there for more summers than I cared to remember, bitten by midges like vampire bats, drinking the soupy tap-water down on the Sleat peninsula, which at least was pretty far away from the bloody Cuillins. The kids had hated it too, especially when it rained, which was 22 hours out of every 24; but then, maybe they just hated me hating it. Anyway, I'd planned to avoid Skye on this trip, erase it, in fact, from existence, and now here I was heading straight – well, not exactly straight, more sort of up and down and round about – towards the place.

I wasn't sick. At times it seemed everybody else on board the MV *Suilven* was throwing up, though, and outside, the wind gusted vomit-flecked around the decks. I lay semi-prone in a reclining seat, eyes shut, trying not to breathe the sour aroma of seasickness. At Uig, I was groggy but not too nauseated, and after the Kawasaki had been untied from its stanchions, it started first time and I roared out of the now-steady ship and on to Skye. Uig, a prettified, suburbanised version of Lochmaddy and Lochboisdale, is not to be lingered in, and I revved up from the coast and over the dreichest section of Skye through Trotternish towards Portree.

I was tempted, as Borve hove into sight, to descend on the Skeabost House Hotel for lunch, as the food is excellent and it has a sort of golf course . . . but no. The kilted semi-grandeur was not for the likes of me, muddled with movement and grimy, with my leathers assuming a patina of road wear. Skeabost had too many memories, too, of what had once passed for romance between Belinda and me, of a weekend back, BC, Before Children, when we had luxuriated in log fires and fine food and malt whiskies of indecent cost, going back to . . . oh, I could remember drinking our dates of birth in single malts, then engaging in rampant, drunken, woozy, daft sex on a four-poster bed. Skeabost, a slightly overdone castellated lodge, had once played host to, of all people, Al Capone, who had bootleg-whisky interests in Skye. Sir Harry Lauder had been shipped in to entertain the party of hoodlums and society pals. The recollections I had of the place were both precious and poisonous; surprisingly tender. The golf course carved out by the place's owners had taken a long time to reach nine holes, and was on a kind of three-quarters scale, as far as I could remember. Maybe it had improved. Maybe I ought to . . . but no. Not even golf could tempt me within the seductive range of that place and its memories. That ancient, mangey snooker table, impossibly worn, with Belinda and me giggling about whether Al Capone had played it, and whether we should jam the door shut and make love on it, and . . .

A gaggle of horrible, pebble-dashed houses. Portree. I was safe. Old familiarities die hard. I parked the bike down on the pier, and wandered, as if by habit, into Harry Dick's, the tiny, dingy, wonderfully atmospheric bar at the Pier Hotel. And as usual, I was ignored as a bloody tourist, but I didn't mind. A pint of sweet black and tan cleared my head of the *Suilven*'s residue, and I left. No music, but then it was Monday. Heads and accordion-playing fingers were probably still sore from the weekend.

I lunched in the Tongadale, more upmarket but still local-centred as Portree bars go, on salmon steak and fluffy potatoes, washed down with a glass of horrible white wine which left a funny, metallic taste in the mouth. An unfortunate combination with salmon, whatever the wine was. It tasted like some hideous blended German gunge, the kind you get in boxed bags. What Skye gives with one hand she throws in your face with the other. I was pondering this as I walked out of the Tongadale and walked straight into Belinda, Paul and Patti.

Jesus Christ . . . Frozen outside of time and space, three, maybe four heartbeats taking forever . . .

'I'm sorry . . . God Almighty! What the hell are you . . . I've been trying to get hold of . . . Patti! Paul! Come here . . .'

They hung back shyly at first, but Patti finally threw herself into my arms, and Paul, bless his male reticence, followed her in towards me and stood close, looking up at me.

'Where've you been, Daddy?' Patti looked at me reprovingly from a distance of about three inches. 'Mummy said you . . .'

'Mummy said you weren't very well, actually,' interjected Belinda, in an understandably brittle voice. Thump. Heartbeat. A year passed. 'How are you, anyway?'

I looked at the woman whose head I had so many times imagined catching a ferocious blow from a driver or sand wedge in full swing. 'I'm fine,' I said, evenly, I thought, given the state of my emotions, which were surging to the surface like the sea against the *Suilven*'s hull.

I looked at Belinda. She looked at me. The children looked at us. Real. This was all real. Super-real, like seeing a home video in Cinerama. Silence. Paul was holding on to my leg. 'These are made of leather, Dad, these trousers. You look like a . . . a biker!'

'I am a biker, Paul. I've been doing a sort of trip on a motor-bike. It's down by the harbour. Would you like to see it?'

'We're on holiday,' said Patti, 'you know, at the cottage in Tarskavaig. Mummy said we had to come into Portree today for provisions. We're having quite a good time. It would be better if you were here, or Victor.' Oh the killing frankness of children. 'You'd be better of course, and anyway Victor's not Mummy's friend any-more. But then you're not Mummy's friend anymore, are you, Daddy?'

A great thick suppurating glob of silence, full of unsayable questions. Then Belinda, bright: 'Let's all go for a cup of tea! Come on Arnold, Paul, Patti . . .'

'But we've just had tea,' said Patti.

'I think that's a good idea,' I told her firmly. 'And your Mum's right. I haven't been well, and I've wanted to see you for ages . . . I'll buy you some chocolate . . .'

Paul shook his head. 'We don't eat chocolate. Too much sugar rots your teeth and your stomach.'

'Oh, come on,' Belinda gritted out through a tooth-clamped smile. 'They'll have some carrot cake or something in the Dryburgh Café. Do let's go.'

Her posh Edinburgh, Morningside roots were showing. How had I met and married such a creature? Physical lust, of course. A party, a dance, a night in her single English-teacher's bed, breakfast, pictures, meal, more dancing, more sex, meeting parents, drives to the coast, holidays . . . love. We were totally in love, headlong and headstrong, obsessed, joyful, quickened by each other. And now? Now it was two beautiful children and a façade of politeness over tea and carrot cake in a Portree café. If we hadn't met? God, I had been expecting something at Ullapool, something in the mail, some letter-bomb from the CSA or her lawyers or something. Now? I sipped my tea and we talked like a family, lightly, inconsequentially, and the children relaxed, until we had caught up with each other; they knew about the golf, I knew about school, and of course this was the holidays and of course they'd been away.

'We were going to go swimming,' said Belinda suddenly. 'Want to come?'

'What? Me? Swimming?'

'No, just come and watch. The kids'll swim and we can talk.' Oh.

I fetched the bike, with its burden of clubs and clothes and accoutrements still intact, and took it up to the swimming-pool at Camanachd Square. Belinda and the children arrived soon after, in the Lancia Delta Integrale HF Turbo which I had once shared with her. A wonderful, wonderful car, all Italian style and fire, which made an Escort RS Turbo look as sick as the proverbial passenger on the *Suilven*. How had I stuck with that awful Sierra? Paul looked at the grimy Kawasaki critically. 'It's quite . . . old, isn't it?' I agreed that it was. 'It's not bad, though,' he anounced at last. 'Better than Mr Arbuthnott next door's scooter, anyway.' I would have to be content with that.

It was civilised. We talked sensibly, like adults, almost honestly. I apologised. She said she was sorry. Kind of. I mean she kind of said she was sorry. She'd known Victor was a lying shit before my stupid, out-of-order telephone call. Yes, she'd been trying to keep the children from me, because she thought I was going to steal them away, steal their hearts, and anyway she was worried about the way I was heading, mentally. 'You seemed to be slipping, Arnold. Just sort of drifting downstream towards some terrible pile-up, and sort of unconsciously, as if you let yourself go and then couldn't be bothered catching the bank and getting yourself on some sort of course . . . hauling yourself out . . . I don't know.'

I admitted that there had been an awful blankness, a kind of creeping, hypnotising lassitude, tension, discontent, which had seemed to grow and grow and grow like a fungus, like a cancer. 'Mid-life crisis, I suppose.'

The kids were splashing and laughing; Paul could swim well now, I noticed.

'We just lost it, Arnold, didn't we?'

'Yeah. On the way. On the way to somewhere, we forgot what we were doing, where we were going, where we were coming from. And what we were carrying.' She grinned, looked suddenly younger, and only then did I realise she had aged, like me. Crow's-feet and lines of tension around the eyes. Puckering at the mouth. A blurring of features. She gestured towards Paul and Patti, who were splashing about in the shallow end, happy and unheeding of the unusual sight in the spectator's stand: both parents together.

'We can't forget them.'

'No. No we can't . . . what about this CSA thing? You're not serious are you? I mean, can't we work out some deal which won't send Pitch or at least my part of it into some kind of economic spiral of doom?'

'Oh yes, that was just a threat. I've never written to them.

Besides, you're probably giving me and the kids more now than they'd require.'

'You bitch,' I said, but she could tell there was no real sting in the epithet. Or maybe there was.

'Well. Look, the Victor thing was . . . just stupid. Pathetic, if you like. But he was nice, you know, under the surface . . . weak, though, like you. Like everybody. Anyway we're over, finished, all burned out. You and me, we're . . . beyond that. Cauterised flesh, minds past hating. I am. I don't know about you. Fed up with it. But maybe we can at least talk . . . for their sake. Nothing . . . I mean, talk. Sort things out, you and me . . . when are you back in Glasgow?'

'Soon. Maybe a week. And yes, I know. The fancying and the loving and the hating . . . that's all over, all that stuff is . . . all shed, like skin. Or amputated. But yes, let's talk. We have to talk.'

I let them leave first, the children red and shiny, their hair still wet from the swim and shower afterwards. I kissed them, tasting the chlorine, and waved through the tears as the Lancia – pronounced Lan-cha, by the way; not a lot of people know that, other than Patti and me – snorted its way out of the carpark, the Italian Stallion. We would meet in Glasgow, I'd told the kids, in a week or ten days. And then we'd be seeing a lot more of each other. It was a dream, a sort of waking vision of what I'd never dared hope for. All the bitterness and anger had suddenly, not vanished, but been put to one side thanks to an accidental meeting in the dismal village of Portree, or Portshrug as Belinda used to call it, back in the old days. The old days. No going back. This was now. I felt numb, but strangely happy and alive to the tips of my fingers, as I climbed on to the bike, started it and headed for Kyleakin and the mainland. Get your motor running, head out on the highway . . . Ahead of me, somewhere, was the Lancia, but I went slowly, not wanting to catch them up. That might be bad luck.

Down, south from Portree, slowly into Cuillin country, those hideous, overhanging peaks, balefully scowling bad guys among mountains, made of magnetic rock which can send compasses haywire, unpredictable and nasty enough for no one to sell local guides, because in Skye if you don't already know how to climb a Cuillin, you're not ready to do so and nobody's going to help you kill yourself. Sligachan, with its climbers' hotel, then, down, shivering, along Loch Sligachan past the Sconser golf club, one I'd never had the slightest inclination to play, shadowed as it is by those awful, awesome mountains. Follow the coast into Broadford, a dumpish scattering of hotels, bed-and-breakfasts and light industry, before the turn-off towards Sleat, where even now a Lancia was being driven none-too-sedately down that single-track road. Sentiment. It hit me hard, and as the A851 turn-off approached, my mouth went dry and I felt an urge just to follow, follow the Lancia, to Tarskavaig and memory, family, home on the boat from Aramadale to Mallaig tomorrow. Forget golf, forget whatever this journey was about. And what was it about? Well, clearly it was about me and . . . well, it was a holiday, and escape, a discovery. Selfishness. Me me me me me me . . . go to them. Go on, go. But it was over, we knew that. Maybe the hating part was over too, the anger and rage and spitting dislike, the surrogate golf-ball violence. But the ashes of our love were cold. And I was past the turn-off.

Nightmare Alley. Past Breakish to Kyleakin had always been horrible, a kind of jerry-built half-Butlins, straggling into the nasty sprawl of Kyleakin. But now! Now it was dirty, really dirty, covered with that grey cement dust which is the hallmark of major building projects, the swirl of crushed stone, the airborne stench of diesel and ripped earth. I soon saw the lorries, the filthy, tractor-wheeled lorries, and then, astonishingly vile, the thing itself. The Skye Bridge, the concrete monstrosity which would be the only tollbridge in Scotland without any free alternative to its use. And a massive toll at that, something like £7.00, they reckoned, by the time it was open. Right across Eilean Ban, with its lighthouse where Gavin Maxwell, he of otters and *Ring of Bright Water* fame, had lived, where otters had lived until this visual blasphemy had begun to take shape. Maxwell's last otter was reputedly buried on the island. There had been, were still, protests, but to no avail. A government determined to have its policy of high-toll road bridges fulfilled before it rolled over and died, had bludgeoned through both the design and the location with such a minimum of consultation that the European Parliament was asking serious questions about the whole thing. Not that anyone could stop the bridge now. And when it was built, Skye would no longer be an island, the huge, 24-hour ferries of Calmac would be sold off, and everything, some said, would be different. Maybe they'd start knocking the tops off some Cuillins to make the place more habitable for sensitive souls like myself. I'd be all for that.

The gigantic, double-ended *Loch Dunvegan* clanked me over to Kyle of Lochalsh in five minutes, with the piles for the new bridge rising like ugly warts from the sea, surrounded by barges and dirty old workboats. That damp, dank stench of concrete was every-where. Kyle itself is another in the West Highlands and Islands long line of ill-planned tips, a railway terminus which has crawled and bloomed along the fissures and cracks which lead up the hill. But my diversion from Ullapool, courtesy of Calmac and a Russian skipper, had given me a chance to at least eat well and, memories and ghosts having been to some extent laid by that astonishing encounter in Portree, play a golf course I truly loved, one I'd escaped to often on our interminable holidays in Sleat, skulking away for nine holes on Scotland's cheapest, most hidden, most surprising golf course.

First, I rode down to the longing-for-steam railway station, where you can park on the island platform and shop for rail souvenirs, or, if you're lucky, eat at the excellent Bladh Mhath seafood restaurant, which tucks itself away into the old waiting-room. Unfortunately, its opening hours are rather unpredictable, and while Belinda and I, and the weans once had a spectacularly terrific meal there, attempts afterwards to repeat the experience had always been met with handwritten notices saying, apologetically: closed, open in the summer, open this evening, open next week. But fortunately, we had found an alternative.

The Highland Design Works is how proper craft and souvenir shops and cafés should be. A brilliant bookshop, in a light, airy, well-designed space, with a superb café serving vegetarian wonders which make you wonder why you ever ate meat in the first place, plus a range of decent, non-kitschy, well-made craft objects to take back and display on your mantelpiece. And it opens at all normal times. It's difficult to find, right enough, high up on the back road out of Kyle to Plockton, in an old school. But it is a truly special place. There I gorged myself on stilton and broccoli soup, vegetarian lasagne and, oh heaven, proper cappuccino coffee, bitter and strong and fluffy and white. The long exile in the tasteless, coffeeless, food-destroying world of the Western Isles was over. Civilisation, even in Kyle of Lochalsh, was alive and well and shiny and chromed and bearing the name Gaggia.

Replete and still tasting that lovely burnt, Mediterranean coffee zing, I wound my way up, up through horrible housing estates until what seemed to be a dead end. I knew it wasn't. Down, now, down through lush grass and overgrown tangled bushes, down into a park, though a gate and . . . Scotland's great secret golf course, wet, unkempt and just as I remembered it during those escapes from the sultry, overly midged familial charms of Sleat. Except for one thing. I switched the engine off and climbed off into what should have been silence, but wasn't.

The chesty chug of diggers, the scrunch and thump of piledrivers, the gravelly roar of bulldozers and excavators . . . the noise was distant, but in the circumstances, overwhelming. I took my clubs off the bike, and walked towards the first tee, where an old, white-painted post box served as not so much an honesty box as a receptacle of cash against menaces. The course was sometimes patrolled by members who would demand of players their name, which was supposed, according to a curt notice, to be written on a piece of paper which you wrapped round your £1.50-per-round fee and then dropped in the box. I banged in a couple of quid, and noticed that a fine drizzle was starting to osmose out of the air. Damn. The disused crofthouse next to the first tee, really a sort of greenkeeper's hut, was locked, so there was nowhere to stow my leathers. I decided to keep them on. Maybe the stiffness would improve my swing. But shock swept all ideas of stance and swing from me when I saw the strange, tunnel-like first hole, and what happened to it. To the side and back of the first green, a mere 170-odd-yard par three, once a particularly lovely hole shooting straight off towards Skye, was now a gaunt, utterly brutal pile of stones, huge and continuous, leading onwards to what I now realised was the bridge itself. Gaping, I saw that this was the approach road, raised on a stony embankment, right on the golf course. It was an obscenity. The stunning view of that first hole, all the grandeur and promise on this tiny course, had been ruined.

I played a three iron, badly, slicing it and playing another shot immediately. It landed on the green. Maybe those leathers were holding my stance straight, keeping my arms accurately positioned. Or maybe not. As I walked down to the green, the rain grew heavier, and the sense of oppression, almost Cuillinesque in its intensity, grew as I approached the horrible grey wall of stones which would eventually support the road to Skye. The noise was louder, too, the diseased groaning of the earth undergoing debasement and rearrangement. I sank a four-foot putt for my first birdie of the entire trip, but with no satisfaction whatsoever. Besides, I'd forgotten about that first drive, and I couldn't be bothered going to look for the ball. I left the clubs by the green and ran up the steep slope to the second tee, to see if the rest of the course was in the same shape I remembered, it sweeping off, away round towards Plockton and with the shadow of the Applecross hills in the background. It was. But the rain was falling more and more heavily, so I beat a retreat back to the bike, as the chug and rattle and scrape of bridge-building continued, and I realised that memories were never preserved, never to be revisited in reality. There was always the menace of change.

The rain never ceased as I made the tortuously long detour

eastwards, inland along Glen Carron and Strath Bran, past the lonely station of Achnasheen to Gorstan. I knew this road, and it had a spectacular loveliness which was not inhuman, like the Cuillin-overwhelmed Portree to Broadford route. But with my visor steamed up and gloves sodden, it was simply a test of stamina. I had put on my waterproofs at Kyle, but the saturation was complete by Achnasheen. The rain stopped at the junction with the main A835, which I now had to follow north-west to Ullapool for about 45 miles, half-back in the direction I'd been coming from. A memory of how road-building in the Highlands was really a matter of following whatever the easiest topographical line was; or, rather, the least impossible one. It was moving towards tea-time, and as the strange, Swiss-looking Aultguish Inn appeared in the shadow of the huge dam which turns Loch Glascarnoch into a kind of giant liquid dynamo for the Hydro Electric people, I was tempted to stop before I was left chilled beyond reheating. But I didn't. Once Braemore Junction appeared I knew there wasn't far to go, and then the long inlet of Loch Broom, a kind of fjord, led inexorably to the flickering lights of Russian factory ships anchored in wait for the herring catches of Scottish boats, and, at last, opening up in welcome below me, Ullapool in the twilight, twinkling and almost too perfect. Fishing boats lay at the harbour, tour buses hulked in the giant carparks, and the seen-better-days hotels sucked in the ageing busees, fed them and bedded them as cheaply as possible. I had been taken here as a sullen teenager, unwilling to accompany my parents on a family holiday, but enjoying it in the end nevertheless. And that time at the Ceilidh Place with Belinda had been . . . Christ, was I just following, in some unconscious way, the ghosts of Belinda and me and our dead romance? No, no, it was an accident that the ferry had landed at Skye. An accident. The cold was getting to me. I just managed to get the Kawa, the Blue Bastard, on to its side-stand, and stumbled into the Ceilidh Place like some shipwreck survivor. Only then did I realise I hadn't booked, and a sudden gnawing panic that I might not get in hit me, along with the smell of fresh coffee and garlic. I was starving.

There was room for me, drying facilities for my wet leathers; there was food, drink, wine, whisky and even a bookshop well up to the impressive standard of the Highland Design Works. Somebody helped me, in a non-servile way, to load in my gear. There were bearable folk singers in the bar. And there was a pile of mail waiting for me, forwarded by the ever-reliable Bob. I couldn't face opening it, though, and besides, the meeting with Belinda in Skye had drawn some of the urgency, maybe some of the sting. I showered, ate, drank, flirted pitiably with some teenage Australian girls, drank some more, contemplated the fact that the folk singers' speakers were connected out of phase, and went to bed with a copy of *Dr Jekyll and Mr Hyde*, picked out of the excellent library, lounge and private residents' bar which the Urquharts keep upstairs, where you write in a book what and how much you've had to drink. Honesty. I love it.

Over a breakfast of spectacular healthiness, and filter coffee of not quite Highland Design Works standard, I opened my mail. A note from Bob. The Itsuoko contract would be signed in Tokyo, in ten days. He had booked the tickets, and my presence was essential, double underlined, capital letters. Fuyaki was indeed organising a small golf tournament in my honour. Oh God. The prices were right, production schedules were fine, and the prototype amps were getting rave hint reviews in the hi-fi press, the result of us giving them to journalists on strict embargo terms, and not asking for them back. So the idea had worked. There was a bald note from Belinda, more than a week old, saying she was taking Paul and Patti away to Skye for a break. She would be in touch. And now we had touched. Most of the rest was crap. I had no idea so few people loved me. So few even noticed my existence. I had to fight down a sense of existential panic at the mound of Visa statements, You Have Won a Major Prize (not) circulars, bank letters, tax letters, religious tracts, political pamphlets and dopy catalogues offering electric letter openers and armpit-hair extractors. There was a postcard from Providence, Rhode Island, which showed a picture of a boring, velvet-greened American golf course and had the scrawled message: 'Keep on sinking it, Big Boy!' It was signed 'Sharon', and it made me feel even worse. Would I ever have sex again? Unless with Belinda, but . . . no. No no no no no.

I sauntered along the Ullapool front, anxious to view the damage which had prevented the *Suilven* from docking and sent me on my past-reclaiming trip through Skye. The rust-scarred klondikers were all, however, well out in Loch Broom, and there was little to see at the pierhead. I asked a dog-walking, deer-stalkered surrogate skipper what had happened, and he said: 'Och, it took them two bloody hours to get that rotten hulk off the pier, but really she had just sort of tangled her propeller, and a diver managed to get it free. Inconvenienced some tourists, though, and a bloody good thing too, the bastards.' He spoke with an English accent. A naturalised incomer, he had learned the Highland habit of biting the hand that feeds.

I knew there was no golf course in Ullapool, so I was free of the curse of the greens. But it was a fine, windless morning, so I decided to walk off some of the previous night's congeners, working my way along the headland Ullapool sits on until I met the River Ullapool, out past the inevitable splurge of pebble-dashed kit houses. Fields stretched out on a kind of raised beach beyond and above the river estuary, and as I looked up, I was shocked to see someone standing on what looked like a golf tee. Someone wearing what looked very like a a sleeveless jumper and . . . surely those were plus-fours? The figure was wielding a club which, oddly, did not catch the watery morning sunlight. I watched him steady himself, swing, and waited for the crack of connection, or the flight of a ball. But there was nothing. No noise save the trickle of river water and the sudden, flinching blast of a ship's whistle. I looked seawards, and there was the *Suilven*, making her early morning run from Stornoway, tiny in Loch Broom. When I turned back to investigate the mysterious golfer, he had disappeared.

I scrambled up the slope to the raised area where the fields began, and found myself standing on what most certainly looked as if it had once been a golf tee, teetering high above the river and with a superb view out to the legendary Altnaharrie Inn, home, they say, of Scotland's most romantic dinner, bed-and-breakfast, on the other side of Loch Broom. Looking down, over the river to the edge of the sea, I noticed a distinct circle in the sheep-mown sea grass, the exact size and shape of a green. If it was, this was one of the most breathtaking holes in Scottish golf. Or rather, it had once been. I looked around for the plus-foured golfer, but there was still no sign of him.

I spent an hour happily prowling around the nearby fields, but there was nothing there to indicate the past presence of a course. The circle on the sea grass had, however, definitely been a green. It had sunk into the surrounding ground like a saucer stamped upon by God, and the turf inside, though overgrown, was of a different quality from that around it. I felt like an explorer suddenly stumbling on a lost Amazon city.

Back at the Ceilidh Place, I checked out, picking up my now stiff-as-hardboard leathers and clambering with difficulty into them. Had there once been a golf course in Ullapool? I asked the receptionist. But she was from New Zealand. 'I think there are plans to start a golf course, though, definitely,' she said. 'There was a notice up here about it, and a meeting . . . yeah, I'm sure of it.' Perhaps I'd seen some would-be Ullapool golfer having a go at what remained of the little village's old course. Perhaps I'd seen a ghost. Somehow, I didn't want to resolve the question. I didn't want to know any more about the mysterious single hole which lay, preserved from who knows what history, surrounded by farmland. And I didn't want to find out that the man in the plus-fours had been a retired school teacher testing out the ground for a possible new nine-holer. I wanted it to have been a ghost, I wanted the wonderful, preserved river hole to be a secret memory of my own. A discovery I could treasure and keep to myself. And I thought, on the whole, I deserved my ghost, my private memory nothing could spoil. If I left Ullapool now, and didn't talk to anyone else about golf the memory would remain intact. So that's what I did.

I was heading for Durness, north, almost as far north as you can get on the British mainland, and home of Scotland's most northerly golf course, a fairly new nine-holer. The road was busy as far as Skiag Bridge, where the A837 spirals west to Lochinver, with its fishmarket and boats. I was going upwards, up across the Kylestrome Bridge, somehow apt in its mountainous context, then to lovely Scourie, with a bay and a hotel and a caravan site which almost makes you want to take up that motorist-delaying, stroke-inducing activity. Motorbikes, even old, and heavily laden ones like my Kawasaki, can overtake with insolent ease in even the tightest of situations, and so had defused the horror of the slug-like caravan for me. But I had suffered plenty in the past, stuck behind some sight-seeing idiot towing a giant mobile home with a Mini. I had once considered marketing a neon message-board for mounting in the rear windows of cars, with flashing messages such as DEATH TO ALL CARAVANNERS and I HOPE YOU JACK-KNIFE, SCUM but it never got beyond the drinking stage.

The road as far as Rhiconich, the Kinlochbervie turn-off, was being upgraded massively and in places completely re-routed across little lochs and moonscape glens, presumably for the benefit of the massive fish lorries which kept rearing towards me like houses caught in a landslide. Then there was a hypnotising, straight run down the side of a hill, with the road visible for miles, across a huge and quite strange, scree-and-moss landscape. Mountains, unfamiliar ones, rose to the west, and then I was running beside the Kyle of Durness, and . . . and was this Durness? There was virtually nothing to it. A scattering of houses, a guest-house, a large tourist-information centre, a shop, a caravan site, a garage, a kind of strange bistro.

The golf course was closed due to sheep. A notice in the unusual hexagonal clubhouse explained that lambing meant the course, built on croftland, had to be closed until the little woolly gods were weaned and golf-ball proof. A pity, because the course, built on a headland, was in a wonderful spot, overlooking a gigantic slew of sand and dunes called Balnakiel Bay. I was tired, though, and while I noticed that the ninth hole involved a truly outrageous shot across a steep-sided rocky geo, I just couldn't be bothered walking round. What the hell was the point? What was the point in golf anyway? I was crap at it, and one golf course was pretty much like . . . ah well, that wasn't true, but anyway, what I needed was food and drink and crisp cotton sheets to sleep in. Bloody sheep; everywhere I went there were sheep. I determined to eat part of one as soon as possible.

Not far from the golf course I found a weird collection of old military buildings, all painted up in an odd collection of colours and with a signpost outside saying: BALNAKIEL CRAFT VILLAGE. Inside, everything appeared to be shut, including the Far North Hotel, which was in what looked like the former camp mess. I parked the bike and followed various signs marked PRINTMAKER until I found a brightly painted hut, bearing a GALLERY OPEN sign. Inside was a display of screenprints which generally dealt with landscapes and birds and houses and all the accoutrements of local rural life which normally attract artists. But there were two pictures there which left me stunned, wrenched emotionally. One was called *Baby Crawling on a Patterned Carpet*, which took me tumbling back to the days when Patti was new, when everything was new, except Belinda and I, and things between us were just starting to fray, like the carpet in the print, while the newness, the absolute, unforgiving responsibility of innocence crawled all over everything, joyfully, so you had to respond. The other, larger print which hit me in the solar plexus was called CHILDREN SLEEPING. The otherness of those faces, so often seen by parents as they gaze at the strangers in their house, their offspring, was perfectly caught: two young children in one bed. They were painful pieces of art, but clearly I had to have them.

The artist was a slight, bespectacled woman called Ishbel Macdonald. Yes, she could have the two prints delivered. Yes, this had been a military camp, but it had never been used. 'This used to be the camp hospital,' she said. 'It was an early warning station which turned out not to be needed.' There were woodcarvers and potters and candlemakers and wine-brewers in residence, she added. Had been since the 1960s. Once, the camp had been owned by the local council, and artists and craftworkers were offered the units for peppercorn rents. Now most of the huts had been sold off, and some were even being used as holiday homes, which was sad. Hippiedom had turned into the hard facts, the brutal demands of Thatcherism here, you could tell. Yes, she could suggest somewhere to stay. The Port-na-Con Guest House, over at Loch Erribol.

Splendid food. I wrote her a cheque for the two prints, a very small cheque, I thought, for the quality of the work, and left. As I rode out of the camp, I noticed that one of huts, newly painted, bore the sign MASONIC HALL.

Lesley and Ken Black welcomed me heartily into their converted net store at Port-na-Con, with its own pier, its own otters and its resident motorcycle mechanic (their son), who informed me that my forks were sagging suspiciously. The food was extraordinary, cooked up by Lesley, a former senior accountant with the London Borough of Brent, and served by diver and scallop farmer Ken. Both of them, they told me chattily, were keen on sailing, and had longed to escape the horrors of Central London. They couldn't have got further away, or proved more successfully how good English incomers are at providing superb service facilities that local people just don't seem to have the imagination to come up with. I ate some wonderful lamb marinaded in Laphroaig whisky; another sheep dead, another blade of grass saved. I drank some Australian Cabernet Sauvignon. I took *Dr Jekyll and Mr Hyde* to bed and scared myself into a dreamless sleep. Neither ghosts nor memories disturbed it.

LOCAL RULES

1. Loch Lanlish is a lateral water hazard defined by red stakes.
2. The area between the 9th/18th tees and a line defined by white stakes in front of the last green is out of bounds.
3. The ponds on holes 6 and 15 are water hazards.
4. A ball lying on a sheep track or tractor track may be lifted and dropped, not nearer the hole, without penalty.
5. Rocks, boulders and marker posts should be treated as Immovable Obstructions. A ball lying within one club length may be lifted and dropped, not nearer the hole, without penalty, in accordance with Rule 24-2.
6. Ground Under Repair. Indicated by G.U.R. signs and white markings. A ball lying within such a marked area may be lifted, cleaned and dropped, not nearer the hole at the nearest point of relief, without penalty.

ETIQUETTE

1. No one should move, talk or stand close to or directly behind the ball or hole when a player is addressing the ball or making a stroke.
2. No player should play until the players in front are out of range.
3. When playing the 6th and 15th holes do not disturb anglers fishing on Loch Lanlish.
4. PLEASE: Replace divots, repair pitch marks on greens, rake bunkers and let faster matches through.

Abbey Press, Abingdon, Oxon OX14 3JW   G4742

Durness
Golf Club

---

score card

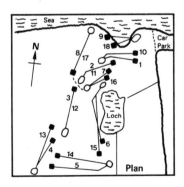

Mary Queen of Golf

Golf is really a royal and ancient game. The enemies of Mary Queen of Scots charged her with heartlessness because she played 'goif' soon after Darnley was murdered. She was seen at Seton one day 'richt oppinlie in the fieldis with the palmall and goif'. Charles I was playing golf at Leith when the news of the Irish Rebellion was brought to him. James, Duke of York – afterwards James II and VII – was a great golfer and played what was probably the first Scots-English international at Leith Links. The title of the 'Royal and Ancient' was approved by King William IV in 1834 and this monarch, although not a golfer, presented a gold medal to the club on which the word golf is spelt 'golph', probably due to the error of some London goldsmith.

H.V. Morton, *In Scotland Again,* Methuen

Going Out in Shoals

In the morning when the feeble light grows stronger,
You may see the players going out in shoals
And when night forbids them playing any longer
They tell you how they did the different holes

R.F. Murray, *The City of Golf*

The Race is Improving

That golf has become fashionable in England, and all over the world, and that thousands play now where only scores did 30 years ago, is a testimony that the race is improving. The late Mr Robert Chambers, a champion golfer in his day, told that once when he had been drawn against a dour-looking opponent who seemed disinclined to talk, he thought he would get on friendly terms by making a remark about the fine scenery around the links. The dour chap gruffly replied, 'A' didna come here to look at scenery, a' cam here to play gowff.'

W. Sinclair, *Scottish Life and Humour*

Those Were Different Times

I don't fool myself, though. I might have been revered by the Royal and Ancient members, in some manner – they commissioned my portrait and hung it in the Big Room – but those were different times. I was a servant to the club. When the new captain played himself in, I built his tee and applauded the shot. I was one class and they were another. I didn't socialise with them. I answered their questions about the game. They took care of me in the monies. I had my own club, the New Club, where I was an honorary member. One day I fell down the steps there. People say I mistook the cellar door for the wine closet. Don't know why they say such things, don't know why. I was old, and I fell. Cracked my skull and died. On the day of my funeral, they closed down the links . . .

The ghost of Old Tom Morris, speaking to Michael Bamberger in *To the Linksland* (Mainstream, 1993)

A Lot of Problems with the *Primula scotica*

Francis Keith, designer and captain, Durness Golf Club; Highland Regional councillor; chairman of council planning committee

I began planning the course in 1971, on almost the same ground, when I came out of the forces. There were no objections, but we couldn't get the agreement of the grazings committee, so we had to wait until the political situation changed. Six years ago I laid out a little golf course on my caravan site in the winter months, and that put pressure on the people who had been holding us back.

We had a lot of problems with the *Primula scotica* and the Nature Conservancy Council, now Scottish Natural Heritage, because the area is of botanical renown . . . but we wanted all the attributes of an 18-hole course, so we went for two tees for each green, and achieved quite a bit of variety. The second nine is quite different from the first nine. I mean, anybody can do a Jack Nicklaus kind of exercise, but we had to blend the golf course in with the countryside, not wreck it. And these days the plant life is actually better than it was originally. It was certainly our philosophy that we shouldn't artificially engineer the course, but make it as natural as possible. It's 5,555 yards long, and the course record is 72, with a par of 70. It's stood up well against scratch golfers.

We have 140 members, despite this never having been traditional golfing terrain. We have members in Germany, all over the place. It costs £65 a year for men, and £35 for ladies. As much as a round at Muirfield. We had Jimmy Tarbuck here last year. He wasn't very communicative, and he crashed his car going back to Scourie, so he probably won't be back. Nick Faldo was apparently in Kinlochbervie, but he didn't come here. Magnus Magnusson played the last hole, and lost a ball down into the sea.

There are a lot of sheep at the moment. This is one of our problems. We share the land with the local grazings committee, and it's a very good area for lambing, so for three weeks in spring the course is closed. I don't feel self-conscious about it, though. Royal Dornoch is deprived of its main course for three months every year for maintenance work, and we get plenty of free fertiliser.

It's unfortunate that on the first hole you get from sea level up to 250 feet. After that it theoretically gets easier, but it isn't. There's a blowhole on the cliffs over that crest, a quarter of a mile away. I actually wanted to lay out the course that way but I didn't feel I could disturb the geological features. Over there, across the Kyle of Durness, are the Clomore Cliffs, the highest on the British mainland. They're used for naval bombardment. Sometimes the NATO fleet out at sea will shell the cliffs. Then we have the aerial-bombing range out at Garvie Island. It can get quite noisy. As a concession, they don't do it in the tourist season, from July to August, or during lambing. But it can be absolute bedlam, with the earth shaking. It doesn't do a lot for your putting. There's still the possibility of a superquarry at Loch Erribol, and how people can say it would spoil the quietness when we have a bombing range . . . we're used to 1000-pound bombs here, and anyway it's four or five miles away. A quarry is just a gentle rumble and a whole cliff-face comes down. I had mixed feelings about it, but on balance having seen young people going away to find work made me very sad. We've got plenty of rock here, and one of the things we can do is exploit that. I'm not sure if it's going to happen or not. The consultants said the quality of the rock is not good enough, and then two weeks later the Scottish Office announced that the northern Highland coastline is one of its preferred areas. So there's a little bit of confusion.

The ninth and 18th hole is already a bit of a legend . . . we decided it should be the last hole, right on the edge of the sea, with the geo you have to play over, right over the water . . . they would be fearing it all the way around the course, knowing they would have to play it and having seen it. There's no margin for error. Indeed the Scottish Tourist Board took photographs of this hole to promote golf in Scotland, and pictures of it with the sun rising were put up in every London Tube station. It looked very dramatic. But it didn't say which course it was. It didn't say that the hole was at Durness. Or that it was only £5 a round.

Cause for Concern

Lesley and Ken Black, Port-na-Con Guest House

LESLEY: It's 200 years old. It was the customs house and harbour store, and this used to be the main pier for the entire area. Loch Erribol used to be a major navy base, and if you climb up the hill behind us you can see the names of the ships written up there by the crews.

KEN: I'm planning a scallop farm, which is why I'm dangling a few mussels off the end of the pier. I've taken a lease off the Crown Estate Commissioners, to try and give some employment to that son of ours. The mussels are for environmental-health sampling, though I'm pleased to say that the loch is grade A classification.

LESLEY: It's an idyllic spot. A superquarry would have an impact, certainly. At times here, with the peace and tranquillity, you can hear minor sounds from three or four miles away. Now if they have 24-hour-a-day loading, then that's cause for concern. Hopefully, it is now in the past – though we'll have to see what Mr Lang says.

CHAPTER NINE

Hole Made by Burrowing Animal

I LEFT Port-na-Con on my sagging forks, the Kawasaki having been given a once-over by the Blacks' son, who pronounced it as a reasonable investment for renovation as a Jap classic. 'Needs properly painted, new exhaust, engine strip, seems to be using some oil, yeah?' I agreed. 'Hmmm . . . swinging-arm bushes are on the point of giving up – all that heavy gear. New chain. Front brake pads a bit iffy. Should get you home, though . . .' Oh well. It started first time, as always, and the engine ran, stutter and grumble free. Maybe a

157

little smoke. I counted my blessings and set off up the hill from Port-na-Con. At the junction with the A838 I turned right, heading back towards Durness. I'd passed signs for something called Smoo Cave, and as I'd never heard of it, I was keen to check it out. Underground caverns were not part of my usual daily routine.

A winding path and well-maintained stairs led down a cliff-face to a shingle inlet, a kind of crack in the rock. It was only once you reached the bottom that the phenomenal scale of Smoo Cave itself became apparent. I stopped, awestruck and gazed at this cathedral-sized hole in the living rock. The idea of actually going inside seemed . . . more than somewhat dangerous. There was some deep, primitive fear which rooted me to the spot. I noticed that hundreds of previous visitors had spelled out their names in white limestone pebbles on some of the grassy slopes of the inlet which led to the cave. A display of bravado in the face of this deep, dark hole in our collective psyche? I picked up my reluctant feet and went forward. Inside, it was muddy and dim, and after about 30 yards a wooden platform allowed a view of the inner cave, which could be entered only by boat. Indeed, some enterprising speleologist had moored a rubber boat next to the viewing area, and a notice offered guided tours of the inner cave. I was already having trouble swallowing whatever base instinct of horror the place had tapped in me, and beat a hasty retreat, out into the fresh air, and up, up the steps, up the cliff sides to a place where the sky seemed to be all around you, in you, underneath you. There is something in me which does not love a gigantic hole in the ground, be it natural or man-made.

The run from Durness to Tongue takes you along the very top of the Scottish mainland, an ignored and truly haunting rock-bracken-and-seascape where old industries – limestone quarrying, limekilns, stone-masonry, fishing – have left their scars and little lasting bene-fit. Ken Black had told me to watch out for infamous former Tory minister Alan Clark's collection of military vehicles parked on the opposite side of Loch Erribol from the guest-house, and sure enough, there they were peeking out above the walled courtyard of the Clark estate. From Loch Maovally over the Strath of Melness to the bridge which crosses the Kyle of Tongue is one of the eeriest roads I have ever been on. Particularly on a motorbike, the way the tarmac, the impermanent way, seems to float between blank moor-land and the vast sky shrinks you, diminishes your soul until you feel insignificant, worthless. Fortunately, the descent to the spread-ing sandbanks of the Kyle restores some semblance of scale, and Tongue itself is a jumbled, twisted old village, some up the hill, some down, which manages to squirm out of appearing welcoming.

After Durness, where the lambing had deprived me of a game I really did not want, I felt that Britain's most northerly 18-hole course, at Reay, really ought to be tested against a player of my immense stature and skill . . . or at least, to give the journey some semblance of structure, I had better unstrap the clubs and bash a ball around. The afternoon was lengthening by the time I arrived at Reay, a precisely nice, almost English-looking village with lots of whitewash and 'character': conscious characterfulness. The course itself looked stunning, a classic, compact links with lots of hilly dunes, a sandy bay, and the appearance of graceful, well-looked-after old age. I slowed, but didn't stop. I needed to get to Scrabster to check out the ferries to Orkney. I was determined that, this once in my life, I would get to all three main Scottish island groups, and maybe in the northern, supposedly Viking isles, I would find some decent golf and make some decisions about what happened next . . . where I went, who with, doing what. Because after I reached Shetland, which I fully intended to, there was nowhere else to run, no more courses to play or to avoid playing, no more greens or fairways or tees. After that it was time to leave the links and start living, handicap or no handicap.

Just past Reay the science-fiction horrorscape of the Dounreay nuclear plant appeared, with its sinister white sphere, the barbed-wire and armed policemen. No wonder they built this poisonous little toy for tunnel-visioned scientists here, far, far away from the centres of population and in a county with such high unemployment that virtually no one would be likely to complain about health risks, lest the place closed down and the jobs disappeared. I shivered as I passed the place, wondering if even now Caithness was hopelessly polluted by radiation which the government had simply failed to tell anyone about. As the grey clutter of Thurso appeared, I slid off to the left, down into the depressing port of Scrabster, which has the appearance of an industrial estate half-built into a cliff and half-fallen off the top of one. Yes, said the woman from P&O, I could get to Orkney tomorrow. Yes, there was a morning sailing. Yes, I could go on to Shetland the following day, if I wanted, picking up the Aberdeen ferry *St Sunniva* as she stopped off in Stromness. I booked the tickets.

Thurso looked as though Dounreay had already Chernobyled itself and dumped its load of toxicity all over the place. Bleak wasn't in it. Decayed, downtrodden, a one-company town where the industry was dull, dangerous and going nowhere. On the seafront, great shelves of rock slid out shallowly to sea, and enormous breakers came tumbling in. Weirdly, bright, wet-suited figures seemed to be riding them, coming in to the hard rock of the non-beach as if they were going to smash themselves to smithereens. I noticed a sewage-outfall pipe piercing the white foam. Of course, this was Scotland's Surf City, the place where wave-obsessed teenagers of all ages come to test their balance in the teeth of freezing breakers, Thurso's untreated ordure, radiation and a noticeable lack of sandy beaches to land on. Cornwall seemed a much better bet to me. Maybe these were lost souls who had been told this was Cornwall. After all, both Caithness and Cornwall begin with the same letter.

I booked into the Pentland Hotel, another establishment with the appearance and aroma of the 1950s, had a reasonable bar meal and then headed back out to Reay. It was a quintessentially northern evening of silvery, low-horizon light, where everything seemed touched with an aura, even the *Quatermass and the Pit* nastiness of Dounreay's dome.

I parked the bike among a gaggle of mixed cars, ranging from a Lada to a BMW, unbungeed the clubs and shoes and walked towards the clubhouse, acutely aware that this was a proper golf club, with people around, and that I looked like something a particularly large cat might have dragged in. The green Wilson golf bag was mud-stained and weather-worn, while the leather jeans had gone a bit grey with their frequent soakings. I had probably gone a bit grey about the gills too. I couldn't speak for my hair, which I tried not to examine too carefully for fear of discovering hitherto uncharted areas of scalp. Inside, a pleasant bar was just beginning to buzz with conversation and tongues loosened by exercise and a first pint or gin. It was £10 a day and would I like a drink before playing, said the clearly voluntary barman. I could tell that from his expensive White Shark jumper, one step beyond Pringle courtesy of Greg Norman's own clothing company. Yes. Over a pint of heavy I learned that the club was used as the local pub by all and sundry, that the keynote was informality, that everyone was welcome, from pro-nuclear Dounreay workers to local protesters against the plant, 'even though it was really Dounreay which saved the course in the 1960s', said the barman. There was something northern, unpretentious and welcoming about the place, I had to admit. I changed into my best golfing gear – jeans, Helly Hansen fleece, my trusty Stylo shoes – and prepared to embarrass myself.

But it was a magical evening, or perhaps there was radiation in the air, or something. The low sun glittered, the sweep of golden sand lazily received a much less frenzied sea than the one I'd watched in Thurso, and I played the best golf of my trip so far. Not that the course was easy. But it did not have Dunaverty's scouring wind, or Askernish's wild emptiness, or Carradale's cowpats. or, for that matter, Durness's sheep. I stood on the dog-leg sixth tee, Braid's Choice, wondering what someone like me could hope to do with a par-five, 492-yard monster like this. Then I looked out to the little harbour which adjoined the course, a harbour which appeared to have little function at all, but presumably had once had something to do with the local flagstone industry. Everywhere you look in Caithness there are flagstones, used as roofing, as fencing, even as paving. Now the harbour looked run down and deserted, but chromed by the dying white sun on this wonderful night, it had an air of magic. And so did the par I managed to achieve at that hole.

In the end, I scored a straight 80: forty out, forty in, no disgrace to anyone and a matter of tremendous pride to me. I was overjoyed by my finishing par three at the 18th, Clachan, and most frustrated by a nervous, stupid putt at the glorious ninth, Chapel, a 174-yard dune-side stormer of a hole, on which a cracking tee-shot left me four feet from the hole for a birdie. I missed it, of course.

It was getting on for 9.30 when I trooped, footsore and weary but at ease, happy, back into the clubhouse. What was it that had changed? Maybe my brain and body had conspired together to weed out, in the gap since my last awkward swing of the club in Kyle of Lochalsh, some of the gremlins of muscle-use and movement which had been rendering me so unbelievably incompetent at the game. Also, I'd stopped thinking about it, stopped caring, if you like. Suddenly, it had become just a game, something which didn't really matter all that much, and was there for enjoyment. I didn't have to prove myself, or somehow show myself that I could master this complex series of moves and rules and landscapes. I could just relax and have fun. Yes, empty my mind, act intuitively, meditate on the perfection of land, sea, light and air . . . all those hippy things too. But mostly just have fun.

I was sorry I hadn't booked into a bed-and-breakfast in Reay, because the crack in the bar was excellent. I allowed myself one more pint of heavy, spinning it out while sitting on a bar stool and smiling stupidly at everybody. Strangers came up and said hello. A big Caithness farmer who looked like he wrestled Charolais bulls to the ground single-handedly talked of his past involvement in motorcycle racing, how he'd done the Isle of Man TT twice, the last time breaking a leg in four places. 'Gave it up after that,' he said, laconically. 'Four places is enough for any man's leg to get broke, I think.' I had to agree. I was, I admitted to myself, getting too old for this motorcycling business. The cold, the wet . . . I could afford a car. Maybe something Italian. But practical too. A Lancia Delta HF

Turbo, maybe. I'd always liked the machine, and they were cheap, possible classics, now Lancia had stopped importing into the UK. Would it look a bit naff, Belinda having retained what had formerly been ours? No. It was the ultimate rallying machine, the magazines said. And a hatchback, too. With seats for the kids. Practical.

The light dimmed slowly outside, and my pint sank to nothing too quickly. I got up to get changed; the farmer said goodbye to me, shook my hand; the barman handed me a membership application form, told me to come back anytime. What did I do, anyway? I hesitated. 'I'm . . . involved in a company which makes hi-fi . . .' He looked interested. He was about 45, this cashmered barman, with a sunlamp or recently tropical tan and too much hair for me to really like him.

'Really . . . manufacturing, eh? Ever thought of moving your operation north? Skilled workforce as Dounreay runs down, you know, cheap, even free factory space, and man . . .' he swept the clubhouse and the world beyond with an open palm, 'what sporting facilities! Friendly folk! What an environment to bring the kids up in, eh?'

Unfortunately, it was then that the word 'leukaemia' popped into my mind, and the much-publicised association, possibly, maybe, with the nuclear industry. And pictures I'd seen of waste dumps at Dounreay, waste dumps which looked like something you might have expected in Russia in the 1950s . . . I looked at the smiling face, out through the windows at the gorgeous golf course, scene of my triumph, at the dark blue of the sea, and then I smiled too.

'Yes. What an environment. Listen, it's been tremendous. A great course, and you've all been really kind. Thanks . . . thanks for everything.' I shook a couple of proffered hands and left for the locker-room, slowly climbed into my leathers, and walked out to the carpark, busier now than before. In the darkening northern twilight I was truly reluctant to leave. I strapped on the clubs, climbed on to the bike, and as I stood on the footpegs I was just high enough to glimpse a dark shadow over to the east, something man-made, just visible above the blackening farmland against the indigo sky. A life here, among these friendly people, with all the tax breaks and economic aid a desperate community could give? And contributing to the people and the place, bringing life . . . A new life? A half-life? In a million years, Dounreay would still be lurking, doom-laden. Shadowing the sea and the land with its fading, poisonous cargo which had once held so much hope for the future. I pushed the Kawasaki's starter, slid the Blue Beast round on a revved back wheel and headed for Thurso, and bed.

It had been a good day, starting with that deep instinctive embrace of the natural and unknown at Sutherland's Smoo Cave, ending with fear of the violent science unleashed by man in that bland white terrifying building on the shores of Caithness. Unknown to unknown. And tomorrow I was leaving Scotland. I laughed to myself as the engine thrummed through the cold dew and Dounreay fell away behind me, replaced by cattle and hedges and old, abandoned cars. Leaving Scotland? Hardly. Orkney and Shetland were just other counties, after all. Weren't they?

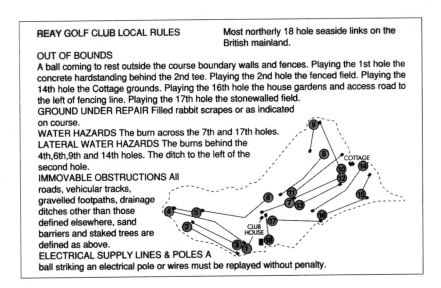

REAY GOLF CLUB LOCAL RULES   Most northerly 18 hole seaside links on the British mainland.

OUT OF BOUNDS
A ball coming to rest outside the course boundary walls and fences. Playing the 1st hole the concrete hardstanding behind the 2nd tee. Playing the 2nd hole the fenced field. Playing the 14th hole the Cottage grounds. Playing the 16th hole the house gardens and access road to the left of fencing line. Playing the 17th hole the stonewalled field.
GROUND UNDER REPAIR Filled rabbit scrapes or as indicated on course.
WATER HAZARDS The burn across the 7th and 17th holes.
LATERAL WATER HAZARDS The burns behind the 4th,6th,9th and 14th holes. The ditch to the left of the second hole.
IMMOVABLE OBSTRUCTIONS All roads, vehicular tracks, gravelled footpaths, drainage ditches other than those defined elsewhere, sand barriers and staked trees are defined as above.
ELECTRICAL SUPPLY LINES & POLES A ball striking an electrical pole or wires must be replayed without penalty.

Watch Out for Killer Whales

Neil McDonald, captain, Reay Golf Club

I hope this is an enjoyable course to play – we have a large number of visitors, and we're certainly seeing it on a super night tonight. The main factor here is the wind. It's usually blowing extremely hard, but tonight it's perfect. Light, and quite quiet.

It's an 18-hole course, Britain's most northerly 18-hole mainland course, par 69, 71 for the ladies. It's a hard 18 holes, demanding, with difficult rough and small greens. It originated with the Pilkington family, the glass people, who set the course up in 1893.

They owned the whole estate and Sandside was their summer residence. They brought a number of professionals up to advise on the layout and to teach the locals and themselves.

I'm a member at both Reay and Royal Dornoch. I hope there's no clash of loyalty, but I do enjoy Reay best of all. They're both unique in their own way. Historically Dornoch is a very famous course. Reay is typical of what a lot of golf courses must have been like in the past, so to compare the two is really not fair. It's like comparing a Morris Minor and a Rolls Royce.

The sun is setting on a blue sea and an azure sky – it's just ideal tonight. We're looking out to Sandside Harbour, and if we look around we can see the Sandside Estate House at the end of the course there. Beyond that the yellow building is HMS *Vulcan*, and Dounreay itself is hidden by the high part of the course. If it hadn't been for Dounreay, this course wouldn't exist. In the late 1930s the course had run down, and after wartime had virtually closed. It wasn't until Dounreay started that the course began to get going again. The Dounreay social club put money in to get the course back in shape, first with 12, then 14, then 18 holes. The majority of the members are Dounreay workers, though there are a number from Sutherland. It's a good mix, I'd have to say. Call it nuclear-powered golf if you want.

In some ways this is the embodiment of Scottish links golf – of the days when people just got out their scythes and cut out the greens. The course is really mother nature's design. A large part of it is a Site of Special Scientific Interest – the dune system up to the burn and along, and a number of other parts of the course have the *Primula scotica* growing on it. The rocky shelf on the inlet at the ninth hole had an unusual visitor recently. Some salmon fishers in the bay spotted an object in the sea, and when they got closer it turned out to be a killer whale. They brought it ashore, and I believe it was one of the first killer whales to be landed in Scotland since the end of the last century. Funnily enough, I believe there's now a new golf club called Killer Whale.

The beach here is absolutely beautiful, but the only access to it is across the golf course, so it's always very quiet. There's absolutely no risk of radiation. Some of the salmon fishing here is the best in Scotland.

If God Were a Golfer: Dounreay, the Divine Solution

If God were a golfer, He could take a celestial sand wedge and, with one heavenly swing, send into hyperspace that gigantic, sinister white sphere, that mutant Dunlop 65, which symbolises a nuclear Dounreay.

A sizeable divine divot could also excise from the Caithness bogscape the reprocessing plant, HMS *Vulcan* next door, with its rumoured missiles and redundant Polaris engines, and the suppurating pits of radioactive waste which surround the perimeter fence, its armed guards and slavering dogs. Ridding nearby Thurso of its leukaemia cluster, damaged genes and unemployment crisis might take more than a few holy hacks: the nuclear industry's invisible and visible effects can't be erased at a stroke. Not even by a gowfing God.

The godly Cecil Parkinson, however, set the ball rolling towards the bunkering of Dounreay when, as energy minister, he announced that the Prototype Fast Reactor, the plant's pride and joy, would have to close, having cost zillions, produced hardly any reliable electricity, and – although he didn't exactly say this – been rendered redundant by the peace dividend. Because fast reactors, producing as they do more plutonium than goes into them, are basically bomb factories. As plutonium and all the other components of the Baghdad Bitsa Briefcase Bomb are now readily available from your local neighbourhood iron and warmongers, the PFR had to go. And today it does. Switches will be thrown by balding men in white coats, probably huge, cast-iron switches of the type seen in 1950s science-fiction movies; because the inside of Dounreay, begun in the '50s, is B-movie kitsch run to seed. Then, with an emphysemic wheeze and a gurgle of liquid sodium coolant, the dream of cheap power from Caithness will end.

And the nightmare will begin. Because what do you do with a redundant nuclear plant? Lumps of metal and concrete, buckets of chemicals which will be radioactive killers for thousands of years? Of course, you could do what the British nuclear industry has been doing for decades, and simply dump the whole lot in the sea. Dounreay has already sought permission to increase its radioactive discharges into the Pentland Firth by up to 1,300 per cent, as decommissioning work on the reactor begins.

It will last up to a century. But the radiation will be there a great deal longer. And what are they doing with the reactor core?

Reprocessing it into bomb-friendly plutonium. Oh, they say, but it can be used in other fast reactors. Except there aren't any, other than in Japan, where they're eating tuna and plutonium sandwiches they've got so much of the stuff.

Talk to the scientists at Dounreay about that, express your fears, worry about the threat, the leukaemia, genetic damage . . . in my experience, the reaction is withering contempt. The arrogance of the people who operate Dounreay is breathtaking, leading them eventually to humiliation at their own hands, when the shambolic waste-pits were opened to the inspection of Highland Regional Councillors and journalists, and damning photographs commissioned by Dounreay given to the press. Over nearly eight years of covering events at the Caithness plant, I have been patronised, bullied, ignored and treated with indifference or complete unconcern. That when asking about things like radiation leaks, missing uranium leukaemia in workers' children, the possibility of NIREX building an enormous underground waste dump, the flying in and out of Wick of fuel rods, the allegedly unsafe transport of nuclear material and, once, the Atomic Energy Authority's use of a clairvoyant to try and find a piece of lost radioactive material. Scientists, don't you just love them? And they wonder why they're regarded with suspicion.

One minute they're denying any conceivable connection between cancer and nuclear plants, the next they put their faith, quite literally, in black magic. The reaction was almost always: 'Go away, sonny, we know best. We're SCIENTISTS!'

I have met a senior Dounreay employee who carried in his briefcase a lump of uranium. 'Feel that,' he would say, handing the heavy slab of grey metal to some unsuspecting soul. 'Warm, isn't it?' Our skins were enough to stop any harmful radiation, he reassured us. It was then I knew the nuclear industry had something bonkers at its core.

Worried workers? We got loads. The trade unions at Dounreay are so pro-nuclear it's a wonder they don't wear uranium medallions. They laugh off the risks, and understandably perhaps fear that their jobs will be flushed out to sea along with the threatening radioactivity which caused this dirty little plant to be built far, far from important people.

Redundancies from the traditionally high-paying bomb factory are inevitable, and efforts to attract industry continue apace. High-profile investments have taken on far fewer local people than was hoped.

Meanwhile, the pigeons and starlings still flutter around inside that great white *Edge of Darkness* golf ball, that globular symbol of threatening technology. In fact, the sphere has been empty and unused for years, and is a metaphor for the Dounreay's central problem: it's frightening, dangerous, redundant. And getting rid of it is going to be incredibly troublesome.

The boffins, backs-to-the-wall, are, however, fighting a rear-guard action: the cynical lurch towards windpower seems to have stalled. Lunatic notions of launching rockets clearly came from the same joker who invited the medium in to hold a seance for the missing piece of nukerock. But reprocessing, the really dirty end of the nuclear industry, is being marketed like Kirby vacuum cleaners, door-to-governmental door across the world.

Of course, God really is a golfer. But the application of His Holy Niblick to Dounreay seems unlikely. Instead, we must keep pressurising the nuclear boffins to be honest with themselves, and us, keeping their score-cards scrupulously accurate. Instead of, like some human players of the greatest Scottish game, simply putting their faith in a good lie.

The Scotsman, 30 March 1994

CHAPTER TEN

Ball Moving in Water

I FELL in love with Stromness as soon as I saw the place, this cluttered, huddled waterfall of houses, tumbling down to a water's edge where dozens of old stone piers reached outwards, and admonished the sea for coming just a wee bit too close. The *St Ola* had wallowed and bucked her way across from Scrabster, nestling inshore for all aboard to see the surprisngly small rock pinnacle, or stack, called the Old Man of Hoy; then braying officiously as she steamed, it seemed, right slap bang into the centre of Stromness. I couldn't help noticing the golf course, because the ship turned left, or to port or whatever, close in around the headland it was built on as the mischievous whirlpools of Hoy Sound were left behind for the calmer waters of Hamnavoe. In fact, I was fairly sure the wake from the *St Ola* had washed over on to one or two of the fairways, but I couldn't be sure.

From the sea, Stromness had what every port I'd seen in the Western Isles lacked: it embraced the sea, ticked it off a bit, sure, but was at ease with its shoreline existence. In the Hebrides, sullen trees turned remorselessly away from the ocean, houses turned their backs, communities glanced sidelong and surly at the ships and their passengers and crews coming into the pier. No, tell a lie, Barra had been different, with Castlebay's sparkling hug evincing an offer of welcome. But with Stromness, the houses either fell higgledy-piggledy down into the sea or seemed to grow out gradually from the seabed. Either way, it was like a village formed by and for the sea, like the rocks further on down the shore.

Riding the bike out from the bowels of the ferry, I stopped a few yards along the waterfront at the tourist office, and went in to inquire about accommodation. The accent was somewhat unearthly, sing-song but not exclusive and harsh, like Gaelic English. There is a sardonic grin behind that Hebridean drawl, a secret wind-up. The Orcadian lilt has an innocence, a full-frontal smile in it. I found myself grinning inanely back at the girl in the tourist office as she booked me into a guest-house called Thira, in part of the village known as Innertown which was, confusingly, 'round the back and over the other side'. The little map she handed me was clear, though, and so I turned the bike and navigated my way up over the hill called Brinkie's Brae, round behind the main part of Stromness itself and then back into its high southern edge, where I found a massive modern house with a view across to Hoy which could only be described as stunning. Someone was mowing the lawn as I burbled into the carpark, a massive lawn at that and one which clearly needed the attentions of the John Deere mini-tractor which was hauling a giant lawnmower attachment behind it. A small figure in a large, paint-spattered boiler suit climbed off the tractor as I switched off the Kawa's engine and dismounted. This was Alison Shearer, owner of Thira and, it seemed, an incredibly busy one-woman operation. That same sing-song accent smiled me into a house which was sumptuously, but not overwhelmingly furnished, and by far the best room I'd rented on the entire trip, with Power Shower and a view to die for of Hoy's rounded summits. All for £25 a night, too. 'Have to go,' said Alison. 'I'm working in the oatcake factory this morning. Will you be in for dinner? No licence but bring your own wine.' I shook my head. I had one day in Orkney and time was going to be a problem if I was to get to Kirkwall, the capital, where there was another golf course and the much-vaunted St Magnus's Cathedral, which the guidebooks dictated you simply could not miss, was possibly the most striking piece of ecclesiastical architecture in Scotland (yawn yawn). The weather was a turbulent mixture of heat and wind, with marbled clouds clearly visible from the Thira windows rolling in from the just-visible Scottish mainland like something out of *Close Encounters*. Nevertheless, I risked taking off my leather jeans and heading off back into Stromness city centre with an unaccustomed breeze blowing through my denims.

I trundled slowly through the almost medieval untidiness of Stromness, bewitched by the combination of twisting, flagged roadway, uneven houses of all shapes and sizes, the glimpses of the sea through narrow closes, the stairs spiralling up the slope of Brinkie's Brae (who was Brinkie, I wondered?). The main street wasn't really a street at all; more a collision of small squares, old gardens, parks and unaccountable spaces. It was all very much as you would imagine a Norwegian hamlet. This was the home of George Mackay Brown, poet and novelist and great literary love of Belinda's life. She had kept on at me for a trip here, but I'd always resisted, much as I'd refused to entertain the idea of reading any of Mackay Brown's stories. The Mackay Brown fetish had erupted just at the time when things were beginning to crumble away between us, and I had made a point of having nothing to do with any of Belinda's enthusiasms. On principle. Except once I'd happened to see a film on telly of a Mackay Brown story, a film by, God, I think it was Bill Forsyth, *Local Hero* Bill Forsyth, about an old man whose unknown granddaughter returns as a ghost to look after him in his illness after she's already dead, but he doesn't know that . . . a bit whimsical, I thought, but strangely moving as well, in a kind of mawkish way. Anyway, this was George Mackay Brown's home, and I could see how the age of it, the sense of history, the rocky rootedness of the community, would suit a writer. It was also just unbelievably attractive. Perhaps too much so for the good of its native gene-pool, if the number of clearly incomerish arty types I saw parading copies of the *Guardian* was anything to go by.

Victoria Street became Graham Place, merged into Dundas Street and Alfred Street, and then I broke clear of the sheltering overhang of the houses and into South End, where the shore was open on my left, grass and rock leading down to the busy bay of Hamnavoe. The *St Ola* had been replete with information about

Orkney, and one leaflet had partly revealed some of the reasons for Stromness's open-armed atmosphere. It had always been a cosmopolitan place, a base for both the whaling fleets and the Hudson's Bay Company, which in the 1790s had Orcadians making up three quarters of its workforce in Canada. Captain Cook's ships called there, the herring fishery expanded, Scapa Flow became a gigantic naval base and Stromness its main supply centre. No wonder it was a village at home to the sea and seafarers, and used to extending a welcome. I followed the road round to the Point of Ness, with its boatyard and camp-site, and there was the golf course, well-kept on the jutting peninsula, but hilly enough to prove testing to the coronary arteries of high-cholesterol players. Hoy frowned down across the Sound, and to the north, grey tumbledown Stromness merged with the rocky shore to meet the sea.

The golf club had its own sports centre, extensive clubhouse and was busy. I paid my £10 to the bar steward and was told I could have as many rounds for that as I wanted, access to showers, games hall, squash courts and the clubhouse too. The welcome was cordial but not overwhelming, and a couple of ham rolls and a pint of local Raven Ale later, I was ready to do battle with the course. The heat had beaten the wind and cloud, and blue sky was now slowly rolling from the south. It was another good day for golf. But, as it turned out, not for me and golf.

In front of me on the first tee was a middle-aged man unusual in the golfing milieu for the fact that he was not wearing anything manufactured by Pringle, Lyle and Scott or any of the other cashmere marketeers. He had on one of the classic Prince of Wales sleeveless Shetland jumpers, the ones with complex geometrical patterns supposed to have been handed down from Spanish sailors wrecked on Fair Isle, which lies between Shetland and Orkney, when one of the Armada's galleons foundered. Add to that a pair of venerable jeans, weather-lashed face peeping from long, grey hair and a hippyesque beard, and a denim shirt which had been washed almost to extinction, and the studless Reebok trainers on his feet came as no surprise. He was as thin as a rake and carrying a threadbare bag with at most eight clubs in it, some of the heads looking brown with rust and age. He spoke with a strong Cornish burr, after a few seconds of hesitant mutual mumbling about the weather: 'Fancy playing along?' he asked. 'Can't promise you much of a game, but I've been around the place before, if you haven't . . .' I said I'd be delighted to play with him, and immediately regretted it as he hit an excellent, apparently casual, economical drive up the rising dog-leg fairway of the first, called Lookout. I went for a three iron to the turn, hit reasonably but not getting into the air enough. Things felt strained, stretching, tight, compared to that wondrous round at Reay. I could feel my mind drifting, too, on to matters of reality, of life. This was all coming to an end, this escape, and I had the return to work, and family and city to consider.

I realised I'd been as much at fault as Belinda in the process of losing contact with the children. It was so much easier to cut yourself off, to secretly sigh with relief and blame your foul ex-partner for vicious plotting against you. Yet she was to blame, too, despite the sudden pricking of her bubble of joy, the hideous Victor, her willingness to co-operate. Revenge, mental and emotional violence, had certainly been threatened and in part visited on me using the kids. But in the end, they were the ones who counted. I had to, we had to, work something out for their sake. If she would let me. Because I knew Belinda. I knew her moods could swing. Wildly. Like my golf shots, in fact.

My playing partner's name was Bill Eastwood, and as it became evident that his paltry selection of ancient clubs and unconventional attire disguised a casual genius for the game (he parred the first four holes while I struggled along, bogey, bogey, double bogey and . . . best forgotten) he filled me in on the basics of why he was in Orkney. 'I capitalised on the equity in my flat in London, right on the peak of the boom, '85 I think it was. Got a house, land, and enough cash for a cushion in the bank, all out of the one bloody house in Primrose Hill I'd had for 30 years. So now I've got a boat, a few lobster creels, some pigs, a few sheep. No goats. Locals think goats are bad luck, only for the poor and the touched, that's what they say.' Shrug. 'I don't know. No goats, anyway.' What had he done in London? 'Oh, this and that. Worked for a security firm, mostly.' Oh yes? Installing burglar alarms and stuff? 'Yeah. Stuff like that.'

On the tenth hole, Battery, what might have been a straightforward par three down to the sea is rendered extraordinary by the presence of a complete underground naval arsenal from the First World War in the rough to the left of the fairway. Bill had warned me off, but things were going seriously awry by this time, and my fluffed five iron found its way down into the trench which led to the concrete cavern. I could hear the ball pinging around inside the echoing chamber before it either came to rest or disintegrated. Bill raised an eyebrow. 'They used to say you had to play balls which went down there, some of the old-timers, if they were in a bad mood with you. Sometimes they would try and wind me up, you know white settlers, all that. Natural hazard, no out of bounds, play the ball as it lies . . . but I'll let you take a drop.' No smile, just a sort of flicker on the upper lip. I wondered about that upper lip, with the lopsided moustache not quite matching the straggly beard. It was white and puckered and definitely lacking redness, as if it had been repaired or replaced at some time. Odd. I walked down, down into the eeriness of the old arsenal, where guns had once been trained on the entrance to Scapa Flow, and just where a gap led left into some truly inky and foul-smelling blackness, I found my rather bruised ball. Valuing my own head's safety from ricochets, I lifted and dropped. Bill had played on and parred. I scored a six.

The 13th hole had, Bill pointed out, been designed so that the lumps and bumps you saw against the Skyline – its name – matched the outline of Hoy across the Sound. 'Great place, Hoy. Interesting community, a mixture. Got to watch it on Orkney, some of the islands are nearly all white settlers, all bloody English. Craftshops bloody galore.' I gently, I thought, pointed out that he, too, was English. That eyebrow hooked upwards once more. 'Aye, and you know what the Orcadians say? They say they're going south to Scotland, as if it's another country. And some of the bloody Scots, bloody Glaswegians, Dundonians, come up here and they're the worst white settlers of the bloody lot. Besides' – and the white half-lip flicked – 'I'm Cornish. Last of a dying Celtic race, that's me.' He birdied the hole, a slightly generous 266-yard par four. I got a good bogey. Well, I thought it was good. The magic of Reay had vanished, and besides, I was tired, with the prospect of a round at Kirkwall, anticipated in my Caithness euphoria, now becoming less and less appealing. 'You don't want to bother with Kirkwall,' said Bill. 'The Orkney Golf Club, they call it, and it's got some clubhouse, I'll tell you . . . but Stromness is the best, most natural sort of course . . . more like the real thing . . .' I was ready to be convinced, but I still wanted to get into Kirkwall, I said, because my boat left the next day at noon and I felt I really ought to see the cathedral. 'Yeah. You ought,' stated Bill, flatly. 'If you haven't seen it once, you ought. Then you'll want to see it again, mind. You will. There's nowhere else like it, you see. It's not just the house of God. It's the only church I've ever seen where you can sense other, older gods lurking around as well. Yes, you ought to see it.'

My game deteriorated as we neared the end of the course, the 17th, Meadow, undoing me comprehensively on its 333-yard par four, a most ungenerous par four, I might add. Bill, at the end of the round, had scored par. With eight, no seven clubs, and wearing trainers. 'Thanks for the round,' he said. You played well, I told him. In fact, brilliantly well. 'Ah. Yes. Suppose so. In fact, by a good three strikes that's the best I've ever played, so . . . yes.' There was an awkward hiatus as we prepared never to see each other again, as casual playing partners so often do. Then the eyebrow went up. 'A drink, maybe, later on?' I agreed. Why not? 'Right, well . . . the Flattie, that's the little bar in the Stromness Hotel, can't miss it . . . nine o'clock?' Sure.

It had taken us nearly four hours to get round the Stromness course, so as I revved the bike towards Kirkwall through incredibly lush farmland I let the Kawasaki's four cylinders run up the rev range until I was sitting at nearly 90, shorn of the rucksack's drag. But I could detect a reluctance in the ageing engine, and realised the bike, too, was getting sick of this middle-aged, adolescent fling around Scotland. I let the speed drop. The Blue Bastard seemed to want to put its feet up too.

Kirkwall – or, rather, the Orkney – Golf Club appeared on my right just as Kirkwall itself, much more sedate and ordered looking than Stromness, came into view, sitting plumply around a harbour which had none of the serious, bustling shambolic air of Orkney's main port. A large, modern clubhouse was surrounded by parked cars, and the mainly featureless course seemed to bear out Bill's advice that I shouldn't bother with it. But in the lowering sun, something red glowed above the houses of Kirkwall, and I found my attention wandering towards the square tower which could only be St Magnus Cathedral.

The town was quietening as I threaded my way through its streets, which were pleasant and characterful but not as lovable as Stromness's. Shops were closing, people drifting back out to their bloody kit houses (just like in Stornoway, I'd passed a rash of them on my way in) and further out to the hinterland, the little crofts and farms amid the fertility of the countryside. But the catheral was still open. It literally glowed red from the outside, worn and red and golden in its ancient sandstone, massive but somehow friendly, father-ly, not haughty and prissy, like Chartres, or just too big to handle, like Westminster, or still burned and dead from its reformation sacking, like Glasgow. I've never seen a building which looked more alive.

To get inside you have to physically open an enormous Hammer House of Horror door, and struggling with the round iron handle I felt nervous. After all, as Bill had said, this was so old; so much a Viking cathedral, it had more than one supreme being to hold. Inside were all kinds of ancient divinity. Maybe.

Inside was something, that was certain. I was utterly alone, and the cathedral was warm, well-heated for the tourists it most certain-ly deserved. Or pilgrims. It deserved pilgrims, for it was overwhelmingly filled with something other-worldly, and yet it was also . . . human, even in its massive, soaring scale. The stone was rough and worn and ancient, and apparently weathered despite being out of the wind and the northern rain. And it was tactile – the huge, rough pillars inviting not just touch, but a caress; a hug. Suddenly, all the physical ceremonies associated with orthodox and Catholic Christianity made sense, the kneeling, bowing, crossing yourself, the casting yourself down on the stone flags . . . this church beckoned the worshipper, and even the reluctant visitor, not to observe and cluck with interest at the stained glass – though that, too, was extraordinary – but to join hands with this living building and worship . . . something. I picked up a guidebook at the bookstall, and sat in one of the small, rush-seated chairs to read it. The story of St Magnus and the building of this gigantic memorial rocked me. For this was a cathedral which commemorated treachery, guilt, deceit and politics as well as celebrated the divine. First, in 1117, the shamelessly political, treacherous murder of the holy, ethereal Earl Magnus on Egilsay by his cousin, Hakon – or, rather, by Hakon's reluctant cook, Lifolf – had paid dividends. Hakon ruled well, afterwards, bringing peace where before, when he had shared the earldom with Magnus, there had been strife and tension. He begged forgiveness in pilgrimages to Rome and Jerusalem. After he died, his son Paul was eventually defeated by Magnus's nephew Rognvald, who had vowed to build in memorial to his uncle a church, 'that there be not a more magnificent in the land'. Work began in 1137. And here it was. And here I was.

I left, feeling overwhelmed, yet strangely peaceful, not from any encounter with God, nothing as banal as that, but with the building. Call it magic, call it the Divine, or as Bill had said, various divinities, but the place had a power it was impossible to deny. I bought some fish and chips and wandered around the harbour, dodging grease-hungry gulls, and gradually I began to wonder if you could equate the peace inculcated by the cathedral with the calmness, the joy you get when you hit a perfect golf shot . . . yes, yes, I know. Ridiculous. Yet it's a very similar feeling. The difference is that walking into a cathedral involves none of the pain, embarrassment and heartbreak that golf does. There is no competition, no sneering observers, no handicap system, no prohibitive entrance requirement or fee. You just walk in off the street and . . . it's there! You don't need golf. Unfortunately, not everyone can live in Orkney. And for some of us, the only cathedral we have access to has to be carried around with us on our backs in a bag . . . of course! Bunyan was a golfer! He knew that in golf is our burden, our spiritual . . .

no. For him, the burden was sin, and golf is not a sin. I much prefer to think of that bag of steel-shafted clubs and the burden of expectations and hopes as a cathedral, or at least a church. And you don't even need the golf bag. For some of us, the only cathedral we have ready access to is inside our head. Golf can give some of us entry, briefly, or shut us out. So can music, painting, theatre, literature. Not drink. Certainly not drugs or drink. Oh no, not at all.

I was dying for a drink.

Leatherless, the drive back to Stromness was cool, not to say cold. It's often said that men who ride motorcycles have small willies, and are merely trying to compensate for this lack. Well, all I can say is that motorcycling in cold weather will, I am certain, make most willies virtually vanish; they telescope into themselves in an effort to find some warmth. Perhaps some form of knitted willie-warmer would help in such situations, a kind of woolly condom especially for bikers and other cold-weather sporting types, such as skiers. Or cyclists. At least on a motorbike you have a wide, soft saddle to sit on, and you don't chafe your inner thighs with that constant pedalling movement. I had read that cycling, pedal-cycling that is, could stimulate the prostate, and that certain Arabic countries banned female cycling altogether because the sexually induced swooning related to the activity had caused several serious motor accidents. But now, apparently, it has been shown that too-rigid saddles can damage the prostate, even reduce penile sensitivity! Who knows? Pedal-cycling has a certain magic about it, like that elusive perfect golf swing and shot. Can there be anything to touch that whirring, ratchet-chattering downhill run, paid for by a sweating, muscle-shredding climb? A motorbike is thrilling, yes, but colder, because on a pushbike you work to make it go, and that keeps you warm. And my particular motorbike was coming to the point where extensive and expensive surgery was evidently needed. The exhaust was smoking, and above about 60 mph in top gear a kind of grinding, stuttering set in. And even I was conscious of the way the forks had sagged even more since Port-na-Con, leaving the steering sloppy and spongy.

Back at Thira, a packed dining-room was full of smells even my fish-supper-sated stomach reacted positively to. But it would have been sheer greed, and besides, Alison looked rather too busy to entertain one further guest for a late dinner. So I showered and changed, then sauntered down the long hill into Stromness, walking along the shore, past the now-deserted golf course, and the long, low flakes of rock running out to sea which the *St Ola* guidebook had called the Tender Tables, used by generations of Stromnessians for their amorous liaisons.

The Flattie was a small, dark very local pub with a rowing-boat hanging from the ceiling, full-size and somewhat rickety-looking. I ordered a large Highland Park 12-year-old whisky, the local dram, and after some thought a pint of Raven ale with it. When in Orkney, get drunk in the local fashion, I thought, although I did notice that most of the punters in the bar seemed to be drinking Bacardi and Coke. At about quarter past nine a Cornish-accented voice beside me said, 'Get you anything?' I bought Bill a pint of Raven – 'good English ale, brewed by a teetotaller down at Quoyloo; not bad, eh?' – and waited for him to say something else. He didn't.

Truth to tell, it wasn't a very talkative night. We spent an hour reviewing the golf match, each of us being generous to each other, although to be honest his game had been beyond generosity. At one point I asked him what his handicap was, and he raised that eyebrow skywards and replied: 'My golf clubs', as if it was a newly minted joke. I pushed it, drunk, demanding to know what he played off, but he refused to go beyond the wilfully stupid word play. 'Trainers, I know they aren't the right thing, but well, playing off anything else just doesn't feel comfortable to me.'

We moved to the Royal Hotel, another uncompromisingly Orcadian pub, this one with a resident country-and-western duo, male and female, called Ronnie and Elaine, who were, I thought, not bad at all, especially when Elaine picked up the fiddle and began to play some local reels. Soon the place was not so much jumping as lurching, while Bill and I sat and drank what were by now halfs-and-halfs, occasionally exchanging monosyllabic grunts. Then, suddenly, late on, beyond knowing what the time was, Bill looked at me and said: 'You need to stop making golf so important, you know. Golf is nothing. Golf is just a bloody set of muscle movements. When you think about it, nothing could be dafter than a grown man chasing a tiny white ball round a field with some sticks. Anyone can learn the movements. In the end, your brain will take the programme on board, and your muscles'll move the right way, time and time again, and you'll be bored to distraction. Who cares if you're not always going to hit the ball like bloody Nick Faldo? Even he has his off days, you know. If you enjoy it, enjoy the space, the view, the exercise, the walk, the weather, conversation, whatever. Golf is just a means to an end. It's an excuse for a walk, not a good walk ruined, as that old Irishman said. It makes a walk fun, but you mustn't, can't, take it seriously.'

'It's all very well for you to say that,' I spluttered. 'You must be a scratch golfer, you bastard. At some point in your life, you took it bloody seriously, or else you couldn't put on a throwaway display like you did this afternoon, could you? And you must be in your fifties too . . .'

Bill puffed some air out through narrowed lips, blowing up his cheeks like Billy Bunter's. 'I'm just trying to give you the benefit of my own experience, Arnold. I wasted a lot of time on golf. Too much. It was my only solace at one point, when I was younger, my only interest outside work, and sometimes it was useful in work as well. I got good at it; I got very good at it, but I'll tell you, it's only now I'm really enjoying it. And I was lying, by the way, this afternoon. About that being the best round I've ever played at Stromness. I've done it in 62, actually, and I'm only telling you because I'm drunk. It's a long time since I've been this drunk, in fact. Not since Beirut in . . .' but his expression changed, and his scorched, dead upper lip clamped like a vice over his lower one. I let it lie. I dimly remembered him saying he had been involved in security. It was beginning to dawn on me, clarity in the midst of imposed fuzziness, that this might have involved something a bit more interesting than burglar alarms, when someone cannoned into me, one of the dancing lurchers or lurching dancers. My drink went flying. I was too surprised to do anything; the large, flushed young man who had hit me had hit his head on the bar, not hard, but badly enough to anger him. Needless to say, he decided not to take it out on himself, but on me, and drunkenly grabbed me by what would have been the throat had I not been wearing one of those light cotton polo-neck shirts. I saw Bill putting his drink down out of potential harm's way, sliding soberly off his bar stool and apparently poking the large young man – who was grunting threateningly in my face – with two extended knuckles, just above the kidneys. As if he'd been hit in the head at close range by a John Daly drive the bulky youth crumpled and fell gasping to the floor. I watched him tumble, satisfyingly and painfully; when I turned to look for Bill, he had vanished.

STROMNESS GOLF CLUB

Men's Section

SCORE CARD

Local Rules

1 All loose stones within a club's length may be lifted and removed. Should a ball be moved in doing so it may be replaced without penalty.

2 A ball plugged in any part of the 2nd, 15th and 17th holes may be lifted and dropped, not nearer the hole, without penalty.

3 A ball lying in a tractor or cutter mark, may be lifted and dropped, not nearer the hole, without penalty.

4 OUT OF BOUNDS:
Outside boundary dikes and fences. Wall along the 7th and 9th holes, out of bounds for each respectively. Wall along right hand side of the 18th out of bounds to the 18th.

PLEASE REPAIR PITCH MARKS AND REPLACE DIVOTS.

As Stiff As You Can

After dinner I went to the golve with Henry Legatt. I found that the only way of playing at the golve is to stand as you do at fencing, with the small sword, bending your legs a little and holding the muscles of your legs and back and arms exceeding bent or fixt or stiff and not at all slackening them in the time you are bringing down the stroak, which you readile doe. The ball must be straight before your breast, a little towards the left foot, and your left foot must stand but a little before the right, or rather it must be even with it, and at a convenient distance from it, and ye must lean most to the right foot, but all the turning about of your body must be only upon your legs, holding them as stiff as you can . . .

Thomas Kincaid, Edinburgh, 1687

I Dinna Like to Carry to the Talkateevous Players

There's a hantle difference in players. There's wild drivers, tearers, jist; and there's folk that'll pit aff time lookin' at their bas, as if they were gaun tae fa' doon and worship them; and there's ithers that'll pit aff time by talkin' and talkin' aboot their play, and explainin' and tellin' ye what's garred them miss, and what's the matter wi' their heid or their inside, and what's made them nervish; and some are awfy fond o' blethers, and canna play a decent game witoot chatterin' a' the way alang. Them's no guid for much. They canna play steady for bletherin'. O' coorse, I carries to ony man, but I dinna like tae carry to the talkateevous players; they pit a man oot, even when he's carryin'; and he canna mind the score.

Bertie Flett, caddy, 1876, Orkney

I'm a Retired Deep-Sea Captain; That's Where the Name Comes From

Captain Bill Sutherland, Stromness Golf Club

I'm not the captain of the club. It might be better to wait if you want him, though I have been captain at one time, years ago. No, I'm a retired deep-sea captain. That's where the name comes from.

The naturalness of this course is lovely, and the sound of the sea from Hoy Sound, and the boats going out and the lighthouses, the islands of Graemsay and Hoy . . . this used to be the farm of Ness, until a few of the people here in Stromness got enough funds to buy them out. Before that there was a nine-hole course at Warbeth, on the Rabbit Ground; that was when it was quite a novelty to play, with the ladies in their long skirts.

We've always been very, very open for everybody. We're

delighted for everybody to come and play. I was brought up in Stromness and we're so lucky to have an 18-hole course. And we've got quite a major building here – when we built the clubhouse we thought it was marvellous, because all we had before was a small locker-room. Now we've got a complex here, with indoor bowls and other things. I don't think any scratch golfer could make a fool of the course, really. It's short but it's very difficult, especially when we get the wind up here. Of course you know that Orkney is well known for its lack of wind.

We have a portrait in the clubhouse of G.S. Robertson, one of the founder members of the club and an ex-provost of Stromness. He was always pottering about around here until the day he died. He always wanted to go round the course in the same number of strokes as his age, and it took him until he was 78 – he was quite delighted. Now Raymie Mowat – he got a 65 when he was 65 years old. That's marvellous.

I'll read this report which we have framed on the wall of the clubhouse, from *The Weekly Scotsman*, 7 May 1932. It says: 'During the war a battery of marines was stationed on the land now forming part of the golf course. Remnant portions of that battery have been utilised as a danger to golfers, and they consist of concrete gun emplacements.' Obviously, you've got to play across these. 'If you land therein it is usually advisable to lift and count, ignominious though it may be. Occasionally, a long-legged youth dares all from a seemingly impossible corner, even from inside the subterranean chamber.' There could be a nasty accident. The gun emplacement trench goes back to where the ammunition was stored, which is an underground magazine, and if your ball eventually goes in there . . . well, I think that's too bad. This chap, 'Gamut' of *The Weekly Scotsman*, goes on to say, 'Stromness is the proud possessor of unique hazards, rugged and stiff, rather symbolical of Orkney', and I agree.

The course is not a links course, it's more or less all green. It drains quite easily, though there is a marshy part of the course on the second hole. To the right is a very low-lying point and at extremely high water and strong westerly winds it can be flooded.

There is a strong rivalry between Stromness and Kirkwall. That happens as soon as you're born – it's inherent in the person. I was actually born in Kirkwall, in a private nursing home, but I feel I'm more Stromness than any Stromnessian. I feel the blood coursing through me!

Oh, there's a deadly rivalry, a case of everything that Stromness can do, Kirkwall can do better or bigger. Of course, you know it's the city of Kirkwall? And the Orkney Golf Club? There's a little bit of dispute – why shouldn't we call it the Kirkwall Golf Club? Kirkwall's only a big field, anyway, an uninteresting course. We're lucky to have it but there's no comparison, and I'm totally unbiased.

There's no restriction on the people that play here. In fact, a lot of people play here that are not allowed to play anywhere else, because on lots of courses you have to have a handicap, signed by the secretary to the club. Here we don't care. We're just happy to get the money off them.

CHAPTER ELEVEN

Play of a Provisional Ball

THE *St Sunniva* was a proper ship, bigger and more liner-like than anything I'd seen so far on my trip. It towered above Stromness, sleek and proud in dark blue and white, a veteran of the Aberdeen-to-Shetland run which, one of P&O's Stromness staff informed me, was the longest ferry crossing within the British Isles. 'And the roughest,' he added, helpfully. 'You're doing it the best way, coming to Orkney first, then hopping onwards, so to speak. More civilised, and more sheltered too.'

There was only one car and my increasingly bedraggled motor-cycle going aboard, and as the sun baked down on a preternaturally still late morning, I throbbed and ached and gave way occasionally to nausea in the wake of the previous night's session. Breakfast at Thira had been a stunning array of good coffee, home-made bread, fried dumpling, proper thick-cut bacon and rich black pudding, and despite my delicate sensibilities I had waded in with gusto. It had all been so delicious that the disappointment of missing the previous night's dinner weighed heavily. Also, I wouldn't have had to get so filthily snottered with the mysterious Bill. But it was too late for gastronomic tears and alcohol-fuelled regret. I packed, paid, col-lapsed on the bed for a last 15-minute snooze which turned into an hour-and-a-half's blessed blackness and mental repair, woke and trundled unsteadily to the dockside through a Stromness warm and gold-grey in the sunshine.

Once on board the *St Sunniva*, I found the boat packed with ageing trippers on a three-day mini-cruise from Aberdeen. Apparently, they would be whisked around Shetland by bus, staying overnight at the dockside in Lerwick, the capital, before being hus-tled back to Aberdeen. There was a truly risible two-piece band on board, playing sub-karaoke pub favourites for the over-fifties, and as we set sail out through Hoy Sound, still racked with an uneasy swell despite the calm weather, I grabbed a large Bloody Mary and took it and my hangover to one of the small lounges, where I attached myself to the Walkman, still surviving despite numerous soakings and constant vibration. I reclined my reclining seat and let the hair of the dog do its canine worst, along with Van Morrison's soul-soothing *Veedon Fleece*. Linden Arden Stole the Highlights, eh?. Makes perfect sense . . .

Once out of Hoy Sound, where clearly there were large under-water spirits who simply did not like ships passing above them, the sea settled and the trip to Lerwick, eight-and-a-half monotonous hours, passed in an increasingly inebriated haze. Tomato juice is supposed to replace the potassium in your body which heavy drink-ing removes, while the vodka just alleviates the lack of numbing alcohol. It works. After a while you don't notice your hands shak-ing. I didn't have too many tapes with me suitable for sloth, but World Party's druggy nostalgia just about fitted the mood. T Bone Burnett's *Little Criminals* was just a tad too disturbing. Must have been too much tomato juice.

Of course, balancing on the bike and then navigating it out of the ship's oily belly was not quite so easy in a state of disgrace, but somehow I managed it, and there was Shetland, or rather a horrible

harbour area in concrete and barbed-wire, with hundreds of oil supply vessels and fishing boats tied up, a massive rust-and-grey floating dry-dock and a modern grain silo of a hotel which wouldn't
have looked out of place in the pre-post-modernist Gorbals. I had
been too occupied with my red drinks and green pallor to take any
notice of the passing bits of Shetland as we steamed into the harbour. As a first taste of the islands, this harbourscape was more than
off-putting; it was so bad it was almost awe-inspiring. I wobbled
along past the horrid hotel towards the centre of town, and it was
quickly apparent that Lerwick was big and busy and very probably
rich. That hallmark of frontier-town casual cash, the private taxi,
was much in evidence; there were restaurants and pubs a plenty, and
gradually, as the old waterfront area of the town approached, I
could see how the place had once had a near-Stromnessian character. As you passed what was clearly the old harbour – like in
Stromness, slap bang in the middle of the place – ancient street
plans and straggly buildings which squatted possessively on the
waterfront re-asserted themselves. Directly facing the town was a
large island with a humpy hill topped by radio masts, and the business of the harbour, even this late in the evening, made it clear that
this was a very serious port indeed. Compared to Lerwick,
Stromness was a beautiful, welcoming, extremely enjoyable toy-
town. Here, clearly, serious money had been, was being and would
be made, out of oil and fish and who knew what else. Heritage had
taken a back seat in the face of hard-headed business opportunism,
and yet there were still signs of older sensibilities. A fleet of weird-
looking sailing craft, up on trailers, double-ended and equipped
with high-tech aluminium gear which looked mind-bogglingly
expensive, bespoke some arcane seaborne competitiveness. An
ersatz Viking longship sat moored in the bay, but one or two elderly,
lovingly yachtified and cared-for fishing boats also bobbed at
anchor. The main pier, which was thronged with yachts, a couple of
enormous fishing boats and some bedraggled tug-like craft, was a
pay-as-you-leave carpark, but with the barriers locked up and the
pay-booth deserted. I groggily manoeuvred the bike in and left it on
the side-stand, complete with clubs and rucksack attached. I just
couldn't be bothered removing them. Besides, this was an island,
wasn't it? Where could a thief take them?

I stuffed my gauntlets inside my helmet and made for a large,
uncompromisingly tough-looking bar called, according to an elabo-
rate, indulgently erotic and thoroughly pretentious mural which
adorned its Drumchapel-bunker frontage, the Thule. The world, if
my dim memories of school Latin were remotely trustworthy. I

opened the worn door on a scene from a Brueghel painting. All the smoke of Hades had collected in that pub, which was large, formica-laden and smelled of fish, sweat, fags and spilled beer. A seething, squirming mass, mainly male, seemed to comprise the oiliest, dirtiest, most toothless, tufty-haired, drink-pickled, smoke-charred, swearing-prone, sweat-oozing group of people I'd seen for a very long time. I felt quite at home, and the jungle of accents – Irish, both kinds, east-coast Scots, all sorts of English, eastern European, Australian, even – signified a seafaring bar of distinction. It was the kind of place where fights are inevitable and even welcome as part of the entertainment. Deep in the smoky murk, the green glow of pool tables beckoned, but staring at me as if I was some form of mutant sewage sludge was a gimlet-eyed barman. I warmed to him. This was the kind of place I liked.

The Thule had an almost Glaswegian vibration, the kind of international, highly dubious, anything's-possible flavour you used to get in the pubs down on the Broomielaw, before the yuppification of the old warehouses wiped them out. I ordered a Maclays 80 shilling beer, a bottle which cost a whopping £2.20, gold-rush prices, and my pleas for it to be served in the bottle so I could pour it myself were silently ignored. It was sloshed into a pint tumbler and that was that. Where I came from, the pint tumbler was the weapon of choice, not the bottle, but I suppose they were trying to deprive their customers of the two-handed-attack option.

I felt at one with this place, invisible but involved. My foot rooted itself to the worn metal bar six inches off the floor, my elbow rested easily in the pool of indeterminate liquid lying on the bar surface. Contentment. Drunkenness. But this was where it had all started, hadn't it? This trip? With a wild, drunken night and a hideous hangover? Admittedly, then I'd been feeding that burning, bitter flame of fear and loss and jealousy and inadequacy ignited by the then-bitch Belinda and the absence of my kids. And by me. My choice, too. Me me me me me me me . . .

'What kind of bike is it du's got?' The question came in something more than an accent, a style of speech which hardened the soft, musical lilting waves of Orkney into great crusty knobbly plains of ringing rock. New York to North Carolina, Cockney to Cornish. Yet with a tune all its own, and with unmodified, unvarnished chips of Norse and German in there too, like 'du'. A half-dialect, maybe once, many years ago, even a kind of language.

'Kawasaki Z650,' I replied. 'Had its day, I think, though.'

'Aye.' He was about 30, with long, greasy hair, a prominent, unshaven chin and a leather jacket which made mine look pristine.

'That thine on the pier by the Sma' Boat Harbour? Sagging forks, wrecked swinging-arm bushes? Golf clubs?' I nodded. 'Aye. Great bikes in their day. Classics, maybe if they're in good nick. Some say.' Clearly, mine was not in good enough condition to warrant classic status. So what did he ride himself?

'Aye. Weel, I'm sorta aff the road at the meenit. Peerie tangle with the coppers, du kens, doing the ton alang frae Cunningsburgh, just maybe . . . fractionally o'er the limit. Drink. Banned, anyway. Five years. Still got the bikes, though, in the barn. Commando, Triton, Gold Star, Bonneville. Bloody caught on a bloody Suzuki warp-drive 250, someone else's, comin' hame frae a party, can you believe that? Anyway, aff deep sea shortly, no' take much bother aboot it.' He didn't smile or grimace during this tale, just spoke in that guttural but melodic twang, a Duane Eddy guitar riff of a voice, inconsistent in its use of dialect words and grammar. Soon this fractured dialect would only be an accent; maybe they'd try to imitate the Gaels and ram it down kids' throats in school, force them to learn it like the Irish had so signally failed to force Irish Gaelic into the mouths of their people. History? Why bother with it. No one takes any notice of it.

The grounded biker was called Lawrence, and I bought him a drink, then he bought me one, and we talked bikes, finding a common enthusiasm for Italian machinery, Ducatis and Moto-Guzzis and Bimotas and Cagivas.

'Music? Fancy hearing some tunes? Lounge?' Lawrence's expression still hadn't altered. I had no idea what kind of music was involved, but by the look of him, heavily earringed, I noticed belatedly, it was probably heavy metal. We drained our glasses and I followed him through the blurred mass of smoke, sweat and bodies to the door. Outside it was cool and everything smelled of burnt, rotting fish. My face crinkled involuntarily, and Lawrence grinned for the first time.

'Heogan,' he said. 'Fish-meal factory. Bressay.' And he pointed across the harbour to the big island I'd seen earlier. I decided Bressay was somewhere to avoid. I was looking around for the entrance to the Thule's lounge bar, when Lawrence headed off up a short rise away from the sea. I followed, and found myself on a narrow, flagged street not unlike the ragged road through Stromness, only wider and less reminiscent of pre-Great Plague London shrunken to fit Hamnavoe.

This was some distance for the Thule's lounge bar to be situated, I thought, unless the idea was to keep sophisticated cocktail drinkers away from the living, breathing *Beggar's Opera* in full

189

swing where we'd come from. We veered up a flagged offshoot to the right and seemed about to climb up an almost perpendicular lane when we stopped, and I noticed a very 1960s sign saying THE LOUNGE. Ah. It was a different pub altogether. We ignored the entrance to the public bar and climbed towards some muffled music up some oddly carpeted stairs, emerging blinking into a wrought-iron and formica bar (what was it with Shetland drinking and veneered-plastic imitation wood?), which had been preserved almost intact from the days when Mary Quant pelmet skirts, Jason King, *The Persuaders, The Avengers,* Babycham and Drybrough's Keg heavy ruled the style of the social scene. But then the full force of the music hit me. And it wasn't even loud.

There were no amplifiers, that was what I noticed first. Not even a Pitch product could have reproduced the dynamic I was hearing, there amid the clank of glasses, the roar of laughter and the abrasive shuffle of conversation. Two fiddles raced, chattered, soared, sang, howled and grumbled to one another while a piano played like a complete rhythm section and a jazz guitar chopped like a trick flick-knife through the remaining spaces, glittering in the reflected glory of the other players. Jesus. It was unlike anything I'd heard before, unearthly almost. In a sort of recess next to the door we'd come in through, a middle-aged woman sat at a battered piano, a girl of about 25 and a distinguished-looking elderly man sent smiles spinning between their fiddles and each other, and a small figure with a shock of grey hair and glasses which seemed to encompass his face sat hunched over a guitar.

And the noise went on, part of the room, not a performance as such but like a jazz session, or musical conversation, by and for the participants primarily but there for anyone who cared to listen, overhear . . . and, I quickly gathered, for anyone who was good enough to join in. Lawrence was over in a corner, lifting a fiddle case, opening it. God Almighty, this guy looked like some kind of rock'n'roll biker hoodlum. He looked like a member of the Ramones. Yet the inclusive smiles of the two fiddle players reached out, embraced him as he pulled up a chair and sat down next to the girl. And then there were three mouthless voices singing, shouting, whispering, in perfect time and harmony and conjunction and . . . friendship. Understanding. Union. I stood, lost in the scene. What were they playing? In some ways, it didn't matter. It was folk, jigs and reels and stately, heart-ripping airs; but it was jazz too, with that scything, flickering guitar; and it was rock, with that rolling Fats Domino piano, the left hand thudding down like a bass drum, thud thud thud thud . . .

'Not bad, eh?' A female voice, not local. Scottish. Glaswegian, in fact. I dragged myself back from the near-hypnotic state this strange music had sent me into.

'Astonishing.' Was I drunk or sober. Both.

'Hmmm. Yes, not bad. You kind of get used to it, when you live here. When you've been here a while. Becomes part of the . . . part of the furniture, I was going to say. But you wouldn't want to equate it with the furniture in here, would you?'

She was Carol Macvittie, 28, an artist ('crap watercolours to sell and really dirty oil paintings to save my soul and upset every-one'), tall, short blonde hair, unbottled, high cheekbones, wrinkles, laughter-lines, call them what you like. Beautiful, in an unconventional Julia Robertsish sort of way, had it not been for a badly broken nose ('it reminds me why I gave up team sports. Hockey is a more violent game than American football or bloody boxing') with green eyes and an Irish tinge to her Glasgow accent. We had one of those conversations only Glaswegians have: Where are you from? Oh, Glasgow, whereabouts? Really? I know someone from there, Jim Kennedy. No? Oh, what about Bill Ingram? Uh huh, still live there. What year did you go to art school? Right, did you know Marie Stevenson? And . . . *which school did you go to?* You don't care, you're far too educated and liberal to worry about it, but still it appears, inevitably, like a sort of genetically coded cancer you can't cut out. Which school did you go to? What religion are you? Do you kick with the left foot or the right? Are you a Billy or a Dan or an Old Tin Can? But we understood that old failing in each other, that bricked-in stupidity, and let it pass. Because by that time we knew it didn't matter.

The pub shut and suddenly we were heading out into the half-night, bound for a party in somewhere called Voe, me having left my helmet and gloves in the Thule and not caring, but remembering about the golf clubs and rucksack still strapped to the bike and knowing that it wouldn't be embarrassing to get Carol to put them in her car – a sensibly adventurous Volkswagen Golf GTI – because there was no question about what was going to happen later, none, I was not going to be staying in a hotel. It wasn't love at first sight, nothing like that, but it was lust and understanding. Whatever happened tomorrow or next week, lust and understanding, and music and painting and books would get us through. Or maybe I was drunk. I was, undoubtedly, really . . . maybe I'd miscalculated. But I was sure, certain of her . . . *in vino veritas* . . . she hated motorbikes, though. I took off my leather jeans and threw them in her boot with the golf clubs. She hated golf, too. But then, you can't have everything. Lust and understanding was enough to be getting on with.

At the party, in a big old house about 20 miles north of Lerwick, right on the edge of a village so beautiful, so Norse it made Stromness look like Cumbernauld, there was more music, and as time went on more and more music. I began to wonder, still weirdly caught between dribbling inebriation and an acute sense of connection, of being benignly on top of everything, clutching a half-empty half-bottle of black Trawler Rum, if the whole of Shetland was inhabited by musicians. They came, blurred bands that had finished sets in pubs or halls, and kept on playing. There was rock, folk, jazz, country, bluegrass, all of it wonderful, all of it played with a kind of delight I'd never ever encountered elsewhere. Maybe it was like this in Ireland. I didn't know.

Somehow, sometime in the middle of the night or early, early morning, I met a golfer. I was in the lucid stage which comes after a long bout of imbibery, or that freak pseudo-sobriety which brings perfect memory of some incident, one conversation, sometimes to terrible, destructive effect. 'Four courses in Shetland,' he said. I could swear he was foaming at the mouth. 'Four, four and once five but now it's only four. Only one of the four worth playing, mind you, one. Skerries, man, tee on one island, green on another, but that was just a joke man. No' real. Lerwick, Dale, so boggy and steep, built on oil money, shouldni have been pit there, man, no way. Asta, that's too wee. Four of them, mind you, no bad. Whalsa', Whalsa's the one, boy, man, four but one, one only, fine, nothing like anything, nowhere nowhere no-how, got to try that Whalsay course . . .' It went on for some time, which is probably why I remember the gist of what he was saying. Unfortunately, I don't remember what happened after that. The tape runs out. Negative recall until I woke up in a single bed, fully clothed, sticky and stinking of fag reek and booze and with the ceiling gently revolving around me. It was a nice ceiling, wood-clad in V-lining, stained a dark, translucent brown. But it was spinning. I shut my eyes and tried to stay absolutely still. My left hand had gone numb. I took off my old Omega Seamaster and let the blood flow back in, and lay with my eyes shut weighing up the options: I badly needed a pee. The ceiling was going round and round, and that was a very bad sign. I would almost certainly be sick if I got up. And I had no idea where the toilet was. But there was a window.

It didn't, however, open. And the moment my feet touched the floor – someone had removed my shoes but not my socks – true to form, I began to feel violently sick. I slumped to the floor, and lay on my back, staring up once more at the ceiling, which was still moving, swirling like it was underwater. My throat felt like it had been blowtorched. I had a brilliant idea. The door. The door was behind my head. I would shuffle my way there on my back, open it and see if any sign of a toilet or a way outside presented itself. Painfully, I arched my back and crabbed along the floor, which was particularly attractive polished pine, with a Mexican rug which bunched up underneath me every time I tried to move. Then the door opened. I groaned. The woman who walked in was wearing a long, plain dressing-gown in cream silk. She was wearing nothing underneath it, though. I could tell that quite easily because she was standing directly above my head.

'Christ,' came Carol's voice (how could I have forgotten about Carol?), 'what's a girl to do? Brings a man home, he's too guttered to go, too addled to act in the way God intended.' She reached out one bare foot and massaged my groin area. This was the principal reason why, in addition to the rippling ceiling, the need to pee and also the requirement, for the sake of politeness, to get off my back and the floor, I discovered I had a hard-on. And when the body above me descended slowly on my prone form, and determined hands plucked at my Wranglers, I realised that everything else was going to have to wait.

The Kingsley Amis recommended hangover cure certainly helped. Something to do with the circulation of blood, I suppose. And the condomless nature of what we'd done only occurred once my brain had started returning to its normal, pre-alcohol-shrinkage size. Too late for tears. Then there was a hot shower, aided and abetted and accompanied by Carol, and effervescent vitamin-C pills, and coffee and toast, and throwing up. After that I felt much better.

I was in Carol's home, a lovingly restored former crofthouse set on its own, a mile from the nearest road and facing due south across one of the Shetland sea-lochs known as voes. This was, she told me, the longest in the islands, Ronas Voe. The house was set on a gentle slope of once-cultivated grassland, known locally as Feal, which steepened suddenly into a wall-like hill of raw red granite. The shore was about a 100 yards away, red and rocky and glittering with the same specks of quartz and mica as the granite behind the house. An outhouse, an old barn, had been whitewashed inside and out and roofed in transparent corrugated plastic to provide her with a studio, and there were the paintings. The watercolours were nothing like as bad as she'd suggested, and the oils nowhere near as offensively avant garde. Quite sexy, though. 'Yes, well. They do all right. I've got an agent in Edinburgh and another in New York, since last month.' Oh.

It was a grey late-morning, with low, steamy clouds coming in from the south-east and a morose sheen on the water. It was that difficult time, the morning after a first night together – or in our case, the near-noon after the morning after the morning – though the night, or rather earlier morning, had possibly been more intimate, with Carol, who it turned out was teetotal 'on political grounds – empowerment, all that crap', womanhandling a bubbling and semi-comatose me into her car and into her spare room, some 17 miles north of the party. Distance in Shetland didn't seem to count for much.

'God,' I groaned, 'what about all your friends? Didn't they slag you off? Didn't they . . . offer to help?'

'Didn't notice, I don't think. Besides, if they had, they wouldn't have bothered. Things here are quite . . . different. A different way of life, more relaxed. Harder, colder but more kind of Mediterranean, I suppose. You'll find out if . . .' she let the word trail away.

If. If I stayed. If I stayed for some time. With her. But no, wait a minute, this was ridiculous. A one-night stand, lust in the dust, oh yeah, lust and understanding, because we did recognise something in each other, communicated . . . but surely, a stranger, rebel mid-life-crisis biker, here today, gone tomorrow – this was just some romantic fantasy for her. She wanted me to go, I decided. She probably had a boyfriend, a husband . . . or else she was lonely and weird.

'Do you want me to stay?'

'Yes. If you want to.'

'Boyfriend?'

'Not since New Year. An arsehole welder at the terminal, thrown out of art school, said he was only learning sculpting techniques with a blowtorch that he could use once he'd saved some cash. There's big money still at the terminal, though it's supposed to be running down. What he was really into was taking my money and shagging barmaids. I threw him out twice, he came back twice, and then at New Year he got off with one of my pals. I told him if he came back this time I'd personally take a blowtorch to his balls.' She looked, for a moment, drawn and vulnerable, in contrast to her earlier tough-talking, streetwise Glaswegianisms. 'I really loved him, of course. Bastard. Women love bastards, you know, and successful professional women like yours untruly love the biggest bastards of them all.' She grinned suddenly. 'How much of a bastard are you?'

I laughed, lightly. 'Oh, pretty bad. Two kids, wife, ex-wife rather. She's a bitch and I'm a bastard. I leave, she stops me seeing the kids, or maybe I don't want to see them . . . and now I do. And maybe she's not so much of a bitch anymore . . . I don't know. Depends what you mean by bastard . . . romantic fantasy?'

'Pardon?'

'Is this . . . am I a romantic fantasy? Rogue biker, one-night stand?'

She laughed, loud and chesty, an uninhibited laugh. A no-side, joyful guffaw. 'I've already said I wanted you to stay. Yeah. Romantic, drunken drooling dickhead stumblebum put-him-to-bed-in-the-spare-room fantasy. Do you always drink so much?'

It hurt, that question. The answer, of course, was yes.

'No. A one-off, just sort of landing here, for the first time . . . you know.' It sounded lame. 'You ever drink?'

'Oh yes, to the edge of the bucket, absolutely when I was at art school and really until Pete . . . the boyfriend . . . was finally dealt with. I drank a bottle of Australian Claret, did the business with him, and that was it. No Pete. No drink. Empowerment. Now I keep a clear head and make sure I know what I'm getting myself into and make sure I can get out of it too.'

'So what did you see in me?'

'Oh, I don't know. Someone lost. Lost in the music at the Lounge, someone big and balding and half-handsome. Someone who wasn't . . . a hanger-on. You've got money, haven't you? Some, at least? You look as if you have, or had or know how to. I'm sick of losers. You may be lost, but you're not a loser.'

It seemed a pretty subtle distinction to me. But I told her I did have a little money, and about Pitch, and how unutterably crap her hi-fi – a Sony remote-controlled mini-system – was. Like nearly every woman I've ever met, she showed not the slightest interest. To her, music was music, and what you played it on simply had to work. She got up and put on a fiddle record, something called 'The Selkie's Song' by a local player called Debbie Scott, and as we gazed out at the wispy cloud, the still water and the raw, red, edgy beauty of Ronas Voe, I had to admit that the music, clean, clear, spring-water, icewater music, was wonderful despite the crap equipment.

So I stayed. There was nothing to drink in the house, so I did-n't drink. We spent three days letting lust loose, understanding increase, something tangled and tangling and out of control grow while we talked and ate and slept and made . . . love? Don't say it, don't think it. I didn't think about golf at all until the morning, the exquisite, crispy-bright morning I stood down at the water's edge, and turned round to walk back to the house . . . and suddenly my palms were clenching involuntarily, because I'd just seen a natural par three, just lying there before my eyes, unplayed, unnoticed by anyone in history save God and me. Something shifted in my synapses, and soon I was stalking around, pacing out distances, and then fetching the ignored, worn green bag and picking out that battered old three iron. I felt light-headed, giggly as I unwrapped a brand new Maxfli Proflite, teed it up, then, without a practice swing, hit a perfect 150-yard three iron . . . on to one of the glittering red rocks, the red which gave its name to Ronas Voe, and the huge peak which staggered up eventually behind the house, Ronas Hill, and the whole area to the north called, funnily enough, North Roe. Red Rocks. The new ball hit the outcrop and flew about 60 feet into the air. I watched it fall, slowly, then cannon off another glinting boulder into the sea. I collapsed, laughing, as Carol emerged from her studio, applauding. 'Jesus,' she said. 'The return of the mutant hero golfer. Arnold Evelyn, I think it's time we got this out of your system. How about if I call you Evelyn?'

I shook my head. 'I don't think so.'

'How about if we go out for lunch and then take a look at the Whalsay course? Go on, live dangerously. You said it was the best on the islands . . .'

'Ach, that was only some drunk talking. And I thought it was pronounced Whalsa', anyway.'

'Listen to the native! Not bad for a soothmoother. And now you're Mr Temperance, I suppose. We'll test that as well, and have lunch at Busta.'

The Busta House Hotel was a test, especially as Carol insisted on a bar lunch. The food was exceptional, the place astonishing, an ancient manor house, supposedly the oldest in Shetland, sumptuously and tastefully converted into a country-house hotel which would have graced any city rural suburb. It was also just down the road from the gigantic Sullom Voe oil terminal, so was the local for many moneyed oilmen and women. There was Raven Ale on draught, a superb selection of malt whiskies ('we'll need to take you to Herrislea House,' said Carol. 'They have a list of whiskies the size of a book. Now that would be a test') and the food was just crying out for . . . something other than mineral water. But I stayed straight. And I paid.

It was a 20-minute drive to the Laxo ferry terminal, where a small roll-on, roll-off vessel took us the four or five miles to the island of Whalsay. The main village, Symbister, had a harbour so big it seemed to swallow up what I could see of the island. Whalsay, Carol informed me, was home to not just Shetland's, but Britain's biggest concentration of massive purser-seiner fishing machines, and the island was both very well off and rather self-conscious, embarrassed by its riches. Strangers were welcomed, cautiously, though it was not the place to cross someone. Apart from anything else, Whalsay men were bigger than other Shetlanders. 'But if you take the time, you'll find they're fine folk,' said Carol. 'Incredibly generous, very hospitable. I spent a week doing some relief teaching here and I put on about a stone in weight.' I noticed that Symbister had one of Shetland's seven high-tech, oil-funded swimming-pool-cum-sports-centres, along with the superbly maintained roads and new schools which seemed ubiquitous throughout the rest of the islands. Whalsay was like the rest of Shetland, only more so: there were more new houses, the place gleamed like a new pin, the scenery was more beautiful, it seemed, and to cap it it all the place was incredibly fertile. And they had the fishing boats and a golf course. It all seemed a bit unfair.

At the village shop I handed over £3 and received a score-card and directions. The course was at Skaw Taing, out on the northwestern tip of the island. We drove and drove, though tiny clumps of immaculate houses, along steep, rolling fields and raw moorland. Then the road ended. A stony airstrip stretched away across the moor, and beside the carpark a small building was marked Skaw Taing Airport. There were also notices in the window about various golf competitions, so it appeared we were in the right place. We sat in the car for a moment, looking out towards the Shetland mainland. The vastness of the sky was dissipated slightly by bustling clouds, white and grey, and the wind would make play difficult, I thought.

'When will you go back to Glasgow?'

Never, I thought. 'Next week,' I said.

'Uh huh.'

There was a silence. My hand lay on the Volkswagen's door handle. A Volkswagen Golf's door handle. It wasn't exactly uncomfortable, that pause. And it wasn't exactly silent, either. Outside I could hear sheep bleating and the ever-present gulls.

'Glasgow, see the kids, see Belinda, lawyers . . . straighten things out. And Japan.'

'Japan?'

'Japan.'

Another pause, which I in the end broke.

'We have a deal, a component-manufacturing deal, with a company called Itsuoko Industries. It's not like, we pay you, you make this, pal. These guys are like the ultimate in component craftsmen, the best. We want them to make a particular set of innards for the new amplifier, and if they won't do it, well . . . offhand, I can't think who will.' I gazed out of the windscreen. Where was this bloody golf course, anyway? 'So Mr Fuyaki, the man who runs Itsuoko Industries, he wants to sign the deal with me, personally, in Tokyo, at a special celebratory golf tournament he's organised. At his club. His own, very exclusive, very expensive club. Apparently he was most impressed with a drunken tour I gave him of Lethamhill Golf Course. Do you know it?'

She laughed. 'Do I know it? I was brought up in Ruchazie. Don't you remember me telling you at the Lounge . . . but you were so snottered you won't remember anything, will you?'

I reached for her hand. Unlike the rest of her, it was stubby, short-fingered, the nails broken and cracked. No extraneous paint, though. She was scrupulous about separating herself from her work, scrubbing off every last vestige of oil or watercolour or gouache, every tentative aroma of turps or linseed oil, fiercely. I always thought of her scrubbing the invisible, omnipresent Pete off her skin, out of her memory, and never quite succeeding. She'd said she really loved him. Love . . .

'Can I come back?'

She looked straight ahead, didn't respond to my touch. 'Nobody's stopping you. You can always count on a spare bed at Feal – and no fucking puns – if you're passing through on your way to some major-league deal. Oh, and by the way, the polar route to Tokyo from London comes right over my house. I'll wave.'

'Uh huh. So I can trust you to sell my motorbike, can I?'

'What?'

'Can you sell my motorbike? It's still in the bloody pier carpark, but I'll rescue it when I'm going to the airport. It's had it, anyway. When I come back I want to get a Ducati, for special occasions. Sunny days. Put the Kawasaki in the local paper, at something like . . . oh, I don't know, £800? But hang on to my leather trousers.'

She turned her head and gazed solemnly at me. 'What about the not-so-much-a-bitch-anymore Belinda? The kids? And how will you run a company like . . . what is it, Pitch, if you come here?'

'Bob's been getting on fine since I've been away, and besides, all this telecottaging stuff, digital telephone lines . . . I can probably set up quite a nice little marketing base in Shetland. Maybe even in your other barn, the one without a roof. If you'll let me. And Belinda the half-a-bitch?' I smiled. 'Lost ball. I'm playing a new one, and you can't ever go back to the old one.'

'Jesus Christ. Golf and love and sex. What about the kids? What are they? Difficult bunker shots or something?'

'I can make that work. She does, too. We all have to. It's just a question of wanting to.'

She opened her door and got out. I followed. 'What do I do with the £800?'

'Put it towards the rent.' I opened the hatchback and howked out that stupid green bag with those stupid clubs in it. We walked to a wire fence, and gazed out on quite the most incredible golfing sight I have ever seen. An ocean of coarse, tufty heather stretched out to a sea-gashed point far in the distance. Flags peppered the skyline, and splashes of well-cultivated green marked putting surfaces. But there were no fairways. Small tees, mostly matted with Astroturf, were clearly marked and obviously well cared for. But the absence of fairways, and the vast acreage of purple, ball-scoffing heather and bog, was far and away the most intimidating prospect I'd ever come across in my short and not notably successful golfing career. But still. Despite the guttering clouds, despite this fearful, ball-crusher of a course, I felt good.

'Shit!' I shouted at Carol. 'Come on, let's have some fun with this motherfucker of a course! Let's hit and hit and swing and swear and scream until every last bloody ball has been lost, and then let's throw these clubs in the sea and make love on the greens!' I was shouting into the wind, grinning, laughing, tears running down my cheeks. 'Do you love me? Because as sure as fuck, as sure as Bernhard Langer's boring, I love you. I love you more than the perfect swing, more than St Magnus Cathedral, better than Stromness, wilder than Askernish, more dirtily than the Carradale fairways. And I hardly know you.'

Carol put one hand through the crook of my right arm. The golf clubs were between us. 'I don't think the Whalsay folk would appreciate sexual congress on their greens,' she said. 'Come on then. Show me what you can do.' An ambiguous remark. We walked towards the first tee.

WHALSAY GOLF CLUB
Skaw Taing

Player . . . .   Competition . . . .

Handicap . . . .   Date . . . .

Marker's Score	Hole	NAME	Yards	Par	Stroke Index	Score	+−0	Marker's Score	Hole	NAME	Yards	Par	Stroke Index	Score	+−0
	1	Da Wick	401	4	10				10	Hamra Neap	381	4	5		
	2	West Nettler	399	4	4				11	Mast	398	4	12		
	3	Da Holms	150	3	17				12	Haa Clett	529	5	1		
	4	East Nettler	311	4	6				13	Da Taing	202	3	14		
	5	Short Hole	140	3	18				14	Ayre of Virda	342	4	8		
	6	Water Hotel	337	4	9				15	Longafield	346	4	13		
	7	Gardie	165	3	15				16	T. Montgomery	510	5	3		
	8	Outra Neap	482	5	2				17	Da Neabes	175	3	16		
	9	Leagart	355	4	11				18	Lochside	386	4	7		
		OUT	2740	34						IN	3269	36			
										OUT	2740	34			
										TOTAL	6009	70			

Marker's Signature . . . .

S.S.S		Handicap	
70		Net Score	

Player's Signature . . . .

I Walk the Line

I keep a close watch on this heart of mine
I keep my eyes wide open all the time
I keep the ends out for the tie that binds
Because you're mine
I walk the line

Johnny Cash, Copyright 1956, Carlin Music Corp (UK)

This is a Serious Business

Charlie Hutchison, secretary, Whalsay Golf Club

The clubhouse was actually designed as the waiting-room for the airstrip next door, so we share it with anyone waiting for a plane. Planes landing and taking off can be a problem for golfers but the airstrip isn't used very much.

Whalsay lies on the east side of the Shetland mainland, and this is the most northerly golf course in the United Kingdom, and possibly the most easterly as well. It was founded in 1976 by a few local fishermen who took an interest in the game, and who built it up by sheer hard work. When we started it was just the open hill. We started with absolutely nothing, and we just cut bits out of the hill to make greens. There was a hard core of about ten players. This year we're up to about 120, some from as far away as Sweden, and quite a few from the Shetland mainland. Maybe 60 local, and 60 from elsewhere.

Golf is taken seriously here. It's a serious business, and anyone who says they play just for a fun . . . well, get them out on the course and they become serious very, very quickly. We offer completely unlimited membership. It's £65 for full members, that's people living on the island, and for those outside it's £35. Bairns are £5, and we encourage all and sundry to join. Everyone is welcome. I would say we have excellent tees, very good greens in the summer and the fairways . . . are just the open hill. We do have problems with sheep and some rabbits. The occasional pony. You can come out in the morning and find a pony's galloped across a green, and there's 16 holes, not just the one. But it's an excellent test of golf – 6,009 yards, 18 holes, par 70 and we operate a system of preferred lies because the fairways can be a problem. We're hoping to improve that aspect of the course, planting grass. It's a hilly course, which is good for the health – and the wind is always a factor. Even a few knots can make a big difference, because there's no shelter. It comes straight in off the sea, and you get the full benefit of the North Sea and the North Atlantic.

We've had a lot of support financially from the local council and advice and support from the golf union, both ladies and gents, although no financial help.

On the first tee, we're looking out on the course, which is built on a headland at Skaw Taing. It's a spectacular location for any kind of golf course. That's the Shetland mainland to the left, and the islands called Out Skerries, A hundred people live out there, and then I suppose we're looking at Norway.

The ninth is probably one of the best holes on the course. If you make a mistake with your drive, you're into the sea, and if you don't get your second shot on to the green, you're in the sea as well. There's a geo just to catch your drive and a drop into the sea behind the green, with the coast right along the full length of the fairway.

We have quite a few visitors, but most visitors to Whalsay tend to have connections with the island. There's not a great deal of tourism as such. It's a self-contained place. The island lives by fishing.

No aeroplanes have been downed by golf balls yet. It's actually out of bounds, so it isn't a problem.

Thinking About Newmarket

A dangerous small boy was swinging a new driver at an invisible ball on the hotel mat. Three men, leaning on the visitors' book, were arguing about a certain mashie. A girl in the lounge was shrilly defending her conduct on the home green. At the next table to me in the dining-room sat a man in plus-fours who cheered his solitude by practising approach shots with his soup spoon. When the spoon, fresh from a bunker of oxtail, was no longer playable, he did a little gentle putting with a bread pill and a fork.

I sat there thinking about Newmarket.

H.V. Morton, *In Search of Scotland*

Afterword

ANYONE considering a journey similar to Arnold Evelyn MacLachlan's might care to browse through the following small selection of inspirational works.

I cannot recommend H.V. Morton's *In Search of Scotland* and its sequel, *In Scotland Again*, highly enough. Both were enormous bestsellers in the 1930s, published by Methuen, and are worth seeking out in second-hand shops. Morton (no relation) is a tireless, incredibly nosy traveller, erudite, very funny and very acute. His prose style is a joy. His comments on golf and golfers, and the historical figures who played it, are fascinating and pithy. If I had the money I'd republish all his stuff.

Michael Bamberger's *To the Linksland* (Mainstream, 1993) is a wonderful collision between an American *faux-naïf* golf nut, the European pro-golf circuit and Scotland. It owes a lot to Michael Murphy's completely bonkers and very, very Sixties *Golf in the Kingdom*, a sort of *Zen and the Art of Motorcycle Maintenance* for Pringle-sweater wearers. The only copy I know of personally is in Falmouth, England, although apparently Clint Eastwood is planning to film it. Hmmm . . .

Travellers in Arnold Evelyn's bike-tracks will find Peter Irvine's *Scotland the best!* (Mainstream) and *Scottish Island Hopping* – a *Guide For the Independent Traveller* (Polygon) indispensable, along with the current issue of *Scotland, Home of Golf* (published annually by Pastime, and listing all Scottish golf courses, or nearly). Watch for inevitable inaccuracies, though. Much more detailed but limited geographically is the excellent *North Golf* guide produced for the Highland tourist boards each year by the *Northern Times* in Golspie. Robert Price's topographical tome *Scotland's Golf Courses* (Mercat Press) is, despite appearances, completely absorbing and a mine of information on such essentials as glaciation and drumlins. Anyone finding a copy of the late-nineteenth-century Haddington publication *Scottish Life and Humour* by William Sinclair should snap it up. Some of the jokes are great, although his golf stories can creak a bit. Angus MacVicar's *Salt in my Porridge* and *Golf in My Galluses* are both fun (Hutchinson and Fontana paperback) but the most serious analysis of the thought processes and inner approach most useful to golf is not, in my opinion, in a book about golf at all. It is in Norman Maclean's stunning *A River Runs Through It*, in the context of fishing. But it was written by a Scot, so that's all right. Games and literature and life and alienation are scalpelled compulsively in Richard Ford's *The Sportswriter*, but for sportswriting of a more enjoyable kind, the good bits of Hunter S. Thompson's *The Curse of Lono* and of course, 'The Kentucky Derby is Decadent and Depraved' from *The Great White Shark Hunt*, are indispensable (Picador). Nearer home, the great Scots writer Clifford Hanley, under-appreciated these days, quite brilliantly pillories golf and its adherents while outlining the entire history of Scotland in his book *The Scots*; and he makes it all wonderfully entertaining. Robert Louis Stevenson's *Dr Jekyll and Mr Hyde* offers, to my mind, a real insight into golfing psychology.

The chapter headings in this tome come from a volume every would-be hacker should avoid like the plague: *The Rules of Golf, Including the Rules of Amateur Status, as Approved by the Royal and Ancient Golf Club of St Andrews*. Mine was inherited from my wife's Aunt Ruby, and stems from 1979. I must also pay tribute to the excellent work of Olive M. Geddes and her colleagues at the National Library of Scotland for *A Swing Through Time: Golf in Scotland, 1457 to 1743*, the sources for which I have raided unscrupulously. Buy the book, though (published by Her Majesty's Stationery Office), and help save the economy.

Apart from that, all I can say is avoid all golf books and keep your head still.

Tom Morton